THE END OF THE WORLD

Maria Manuel Lisboa is Professor of Portuguese Literature and Culture at the University of Cambridge, and a Fellow of St John's College, Cambridge. She specialises in nineteenth- and twentieth-century Portuguese and Brazilian literature, focusing on gender and national identity. She has written four monographs, including one on the renowned Portuguese artist Paula Rego. Maria Manuel Lisboa received the 2008 *Prémio do Grémio Literário*.

The End of the World:
Apocalypse and its Aftermath in Western Culture

Maria Manuel Lisboa

Open Book Publishers CIC Ltd.,
40 Devonshire Road, Cambridge, CB1 2BL, United Kingdom
http://www.openbookpublishers.com

© 2011 Maria Manuel Lisboa
Some rights are reserved. This book is made available under the Creative Commons Attribution-Non-Commercial-No Derivative Works 2.0 UK: England & Wales License. This license allows for copying any part of the work for personal and non-commercial use, providing author attribution is clearly stated. Details of allowances and restrictions are available at:

http://www.openbookpublishers.com

As with all Open Book Publishers titles, digital material and resources associated with this volume are available from our website:

http://www.openbookpublishers.com/product.php/106

ISBN Hardback: 978-1-906924-51-5
ISBN Paperback: 978-1-906924-50-8
ISBN Digital (pdf): 978-1-906924-52-2

Cover image: David Fox, New Zealand, flooded coastal forest (2010)
Typesetting by www.bookgenie.in

All paper used by Open Book Publishers is SFI (Sustainable Forestry Initiative), and PEFC (Programme for the Endorsement of Forest Certification Schemes) Certified.

Printed in the United Kingdom and United States by
Lightning Source for Open Book Publishers

This book is dedicated to our planet, with best wishes for many happy returns. In memory of my mother-in-law, Winifred Brick and my uncle, Ilídio Lisboa.

This World is not Conclusion.
A Species stands beyond—
Invisible, as Music—
But positive, as Sound—
It beckons, and it baffles—
Philosophy—don't know—
And through a Riddle, at the last—
Sagacity, must go—
To guess it, puzzles scholars—
To gain it, Men have borne
Contempt of Generations
And Crucifixion […].

Emily Dickinson

Where have all the flowers gone?
Long time passing
Where have all the flowers gone?
Long time ago
Where have all the flowers gone?
Girls have picked them every one
When will they ever learn?
When will they ever learn?
Where have all the young girls gone?
Long time passing
Where have all the young girls gone?
Long time ago
Where have all the young girls gone?
Taken husbands every one
When will they ever learn?
When will they ever learn?
Where have all the young men gone?
Long time passing
Where have all the young men gone?
Long time ago
Where have all the young men gone?
Gone for soldiers every one
When will they ever learn?
When will they ever learn?
Where have all the soldiers gone?
Long time passing
Where have all the soldiers gone?
Long time ago
Where have all the soldiers gone?
Gone to graveyards every one
When will they ever learn?
When will they ever learn?
Where have all the graveyards gone?
Long time passing
Where have all the graveyards gone?
Long time ago
Where have all the graveyards gone?
Covered with flowers every one
When will we ever learn?
When will we ever learn?

Pete Seeger

Contents

	Page
List of Illustrations	ix
Acknowledgements	xiii
Prologue	xv
1. Apocalypse Now and Again	1
2. The World Gone M.A.D.	17
3. And Then There Was Nothing: Is the End Ever Really the End?	49
4. Falling Out with Hal and Hester	103
5. Dying of Happiness: Utopia at the End of this World	131
Afterword: *Libera Me, Domine, De Vita Æterna*	171
Bibliography	177
Index	187

List of Illustrations

	Page
Figure 1. Hieronymus Bosch *The Last Judgement*, triptych fragment (1506-1508) Oil on panel Munich: Altepinakothek	xvi
Figure 2. William Blake *Death on a Pale Horse* (c. 1800) Drawing Cambridge: The Fitzwilliam Museum © Fitzwilliam Museum	xvii
Figure 3. René Magritte *L'invention collective* (*Collective Invention*) (1935) Oil on canvas Private collection © Photothèque R. Magritte – ADAGP, Paris 2011	4
Figure 4. William Blake *Nebuchadnezzar* (c. 1795) London: Tate Colour monotype print with additions in ink and watercolour	4
Figure 5. René Magritte *Les merveilles de la nature* (*The Wonders of Nature*) (1953) Oil on canvas Chicago: Museum of Contemporary art © Photothèque R. Magritte – ADAGP, Paris 2011	5

Figure 6. Peter Paul Rubens   6
Adam and Eve in Paradise (1599)
Oil on panel
Antwerp: Rubenshuis

Figure 7. John Guillermin   7
King Kong (1976).
Paramount Film Studios © mptvimages.com

Figure 8. John Guillermin   10
King Kong (1976).
Paramount Film Studios

Figure 9. John Martin   18
The Last Man (1849)
Oil on canvas
The Board of Trustees of National Museums and Galleries on Merseyside, the Walker Art Gallery, Liverpool
Liverpool: Walker Art Gallery

Figure 10. Gustave Doré   19
Adam and Eve Driven Out of Eden (1865)
Engraving
Public domain

Figure 11. Albrecht Dürer   29
The Four of Horsemen of the Apocalypse (1511)
Woodcut
The William M. Ladd Collection
Minneapolis: The Minneapolis Institute of Arts

Figure 12. Reuven Dafni   57
Corpses in a Mass Grave (29 April 1945)
Germany: Bergen Belsen
© Yad Vashem, Archival Signature: 2545

Figure 13. Marc Chagall,   59
Apocalypse in Lilac, Capriccio (1945)
London: The Ben Uri Jewish Museum of Art

List of Illustrations   xi

Figure 14. Anselm Kiefer (German, b. 1945)   62
Lot's Wife (1989)
Oil paint, ash, stucco, chalk, linseed oil, polymer emulsion, salt and applied elements (e.g., copper heating coil), on canvas, attached to lead foil, on plywood panels; 350 x 410 cm
Cleveland: The Cleveland Museum of Art. Leonard C. Hanna, Jr. Fund 1990.8.a

Figure 15. Caspar David Friedrich   72
Wanderer above the Sea of Fog (1818)
Oil on canvas
Hamburg: Kunsthalle

Figure 16. Peter Paul Rubens   78
The Virgin as the Woman of the Apocalypse (c. 1623-24)
Oil on panel
Los Angeles: The J. Paul Getty Museum

Figure 17. Ingmar Bergman   106
The Seventh Seal (1957)
AB Svensk Filmindustri. *Det sjunde inseglet/The Seventh Seal* (c)1957
Stockholm: AB Svensk Filmindustri
Still photographer: Louis Huch

Figure 18. Ingmar Bergman   107
The Seventh Seal (1957)
AB Svensk Filmindustri. *Det sjunde inseglet/The Seventh Seal* (c)1957
Stockholm: AB Svensk Filmindustri
Still photographer: Louis Huch

Figure 19. René Magritte   109
La condition humaine (The human condition) (1933)
Oil on canvas
Gift of the Collectors Committee
Washington: National Gallery of Art
© Photothèque R. Magritte – ADAGP, Paris 2011

Figure 20. Thomas More   131
A Map of Utopia (1516)
Woodcut
Cambridge: St. John's College

Figure 21. Michelangelo Buonarroti   156
Christ as Judge of the World (1475-1564)
Rome: Sistine Chapel, Vatican

Figure 22. El Greco (Doménikos Theotokópoulos)   158
(1541-1614)
The Opening of the Fifth Seal (or *The Fifth Seal of the
Apocalypse* or *The Vision of Saint John*) (1608-14)
Oil on canvas (top truncated)
New York: The Metropolitan Museum of Art, Rogers Fund, 1956
© The Metropolitan Museum of Art

Figure 23. John Martin   172
The Great Day of His Wrath (1851-53)
London: Tate
Oil on canvas

Figure 24. Michelangelo Buonarroti   173
The Flood, right-hand panel (1475-1564)
Rome: Sistine Chapel, Vatican

Acknowledgements

I am indebted to many people who helped, encouraged and supported me, did things for me, and said 'there, there...' at times when the end of the world appeared to be an attractive option, relatively speaking.

Bernard McGuirk, Máire Ní Mhaonaigh and Peter Evans generously agreed to offer a critical reading of this book.

Coral Neale provided me with valuable examples of apocalypse in films, books and the visual arts.

David Fox, the ideal companion on holidays I will never take, agreed to allow me to reproduce one of his remarkable photographs for the cover, provided the print, and, following a logic that escapes me, thanked me for it.

Susan Mansfield and Karen Weber saved me from unhelpful demons and from my own never-failing incompetence in all matters practical and commonsensical. Robert Hinde proofread the manuscript.

Chris Woodhouse and Alex Lucini, Computer Officers at St. John's College, miraculously never attempted to strangle me, not even once.

Sue O'Reilly and Hykel Hosni suggested some valuable reading which helped me consolidate my thoughts.

Rory O'Bryen let me benefit from his expertise on blondes, monkeys and digital images.

David Lowe and Sonia Morillo Garcia I thank for absolutely everything. I am also ever grateful to Colin Clarkson at Cambridge University Library, who goes where my legs cannot.

My students suggested I have a look at truly ghastly examples of end-of-the-world books they had read as teenagers. Margaret Clark did the same with regard to books with which she had traumatized her children over the years.

Helen Coutts and Helen Lima de Sousa helped me with tracking down the images.

Victoria Best and Robert Evans always tell me affectionately not to be silly whenever I need to hear it, and make me howl with laughter even when life gets dark.

Chris Dobson encourages me repeatedly to delve ever more deeply into my inner silliness (seeing as, according to him, I have no option anyway). Mary Dobson kindly urges me to ignore him.

Hilary Owen has stayed the course. Teresa Moreira Rato, my no-questions-asked friend of over forty years, knows that a friend is someone who is on your side, even if or particularly when you are in the wrong, once offered to punch two classmates' noses on my behalf, and would help me to hide a body if ever the need arose.

Ismene Lada-Richards offers me love and (in the unlikely event that I should ever prove too sweet to look after myself), her on-call services in exterminating anyone who might even slightly annoy me.

Last and first, Michael Brick and Laura Lisboa Brick.

I am grateful to St. John's College's Fellows' research grant which paid for the costs of obtaining visual materials for this book and to Alessandra Tosi for making this the most pain-free, pleasurable and efficient of all my experiences of bringing a book into being.

Prologue

This book began as one thing but has ended as something quite different, which arguably is what research in general ought to be (exploration, discovery), but is, nonetheless, perplexing for the secretly teleological author. Often, if not always, at least in the Humanities, when we begin we already think we know what we will find. In this case the original intent was exactly what its title still purports it to be now: an analysis of the theme of apocalypse in works of literature, film and the visual arts. In the doing, however, the thing done, as some might have predicted with a topic of this magnitude, ran away from its author, not unlike the rogue manufactured beasts (machines, computers, nanoparticles, manufactured biological organisms) discussed in chapter 4. It simply proved too big to fit within the framework that was envisaged. In any changing environment, needless to say, a creature with its eye on survival at its peril fails to mutate. Such a requirement has operated here. What set out to be an in-depth analysis of a set of ideas has metamorphosed into a panoramic illustration of them. This entailed, potentially, both problems and merits. The problem was the risk of an end product which turned out to be little more than an inventory of examples. The merit would be the achievement of a blueprint of ideas outlined persuasively and in sufficient depth to open up lines of enquiry by future scholars. It is to be hoped that the latter has been achieved.

In the Beginning Was the End: Get Them Young

> Give me a child until he is seven, and I will give you the man.
> St. Ignatius de Loyola

The world had ended, so why had the battle not ceased? (Rowling, 2007: 513). The narrator's perplexed lament in J.K. Rowling's *Harry Potter and the Deathly Hallows*, the last volume of the Harry Potter series, in many ways encapsulates the quandary at the heart of the argument that follows. After the end of the world, how can anything remain, continue, let alone begin

xvi   The End of the World

again? The fact that it almost always does, in narratives of apocalypse from foundation narratives such as Genesis in the Old Testament to science fiction in contemporary film and fiction, inscribes the Harry Potter phenomenon within what is possibly the oldest narrative motif in our culture. The theme of apocalypse in Rowling (the possibility that Voldemort *will* succeed in becoming master of death and of the world) links it to central motifs in children's and adolescents' literature but also to the earliest apocalyptic narrative of Western culture: the expulsion of Adam and Eve from Eden. Whether in the Bible or in *The Famous Five*, it is always the same story, the same recurrent tropes and themes: orphaned heroes (Adam and Eve after God abandons them); school stories (the acquisition of knowledge, forbidden or not); the struggle between good and evil (disobedience to parents and teachers); narratives of quest (to grow up or contrarily to return to childhood and paradise). Whatever the differences, there is a common thread: someone falls.

According to theorists such as Vladimir Propp (Propp, 1968), Julien Greimas (Greimas, 1983), Bruno Bettelheim (Bettelheim, 1991) and Jack Zipes (Zipes, 1994), whatever the age group of the target audience, with minor modifications all narratives, from children's fairy tales to X-rated horror movies (in some ways they are not unalike) are structured according to a limited number of plots.

It is perhaps for this reason that themes and archetypes more naturally to be expected in adult fiction and art are in fact pre-empted by reading experiences in childhood and adolescence. The struggle between good and evil, and the fearful possibilities opened up by the eventuality of the

Figure 1. Hyeronymus Bosch, *The Last Judgement*

latter's triumph, form the basis of the earliest narratives, from Greek myths, epics and tragedies to traditional fairy tales. In literature for children and adolescents the development of plot action from beginning to end can cover a wide range of problems also present in literature for adults, ranging from the process of maturity which defines the *bildungsroman*, to the radical change which occurs in narratives of apocalypse. And similarly, some of the most harrowing images in the canon of the visual arts would not be out of place either as publicity posters for chainsaw massacre-type horror movies or, alternatively, as book covers for children's fairy tales (although admittedly, by the likes of the Brothers Grimm).

Within any narrative canon, whether the upheaval depicted verbally or visually is small and confined to the sphere of domesticity (the archetypal Jane Austenian plot of the nineteenth-century domestic novel of manners), or more considerable, in plots of somewhat wider socio-moral import (Dickens, Tolstoy), or massively transformative (fictions of the end of the world), a common thread can be found that changes stasis to revolution and steady-state worlds into scenarios of significant difference.

Figure 2. William Blake, *Death on a Pale Horse*

Before moving on to a detailed contemplation of depictions of end-time in adult literature, film and the visual arts, therefore, it is interesting to consider briefly the ways in which the seeds of future cultural expectation are laid down in early narrative experiences in childhood and adolescence. In the chapters that follow it will be suggested that, in contemplating the possibility of an ending which refers not merely to our own individual deaths but to the end of the world that contains us, it is possible to identify stages not unlike those of the mourning process following a bereavement: overwhelming incomprehension, guilt and anger, attribution of blame, remembrance and preservation, and finally rebuilding. Beginning, however, with texts covering an age range from toddler to teenager, early literature covers a wide spectrum of disruption: from a minor disturbance in domestic routine, albeit with mild but significant long-term consequences within the emotional life of a traditional nuclear family (*The Tiger Who Came to Tea*, Kerr, 2006); to an unrecognizable new reality in post-nuclear worlds (*Henry's Quest,* Oakley, 1986; *Z for Zacchariah,* O'Brien, 1998; *Brother in the Land,* Swindells, 1999; and *The Village that Slept,* Peyrouton de Ladebat, 1963).

Signifying Apocalypse

In current parlance 'apocalypse' means upheaval and destruction but, as will be discussed in detail, originally it implied also discovery and epiphany (the revelation of something new and often better). Either way, however, the return of a Messiah, in any but its most restrained versions, tends to happen only after a considerable portion of humanity has died. Furthermore, whether in the Book of Revelation or in American evangelism's millenarian visions of the Rapture, salvation following global apocalypse is usually attained only by a happy few. Within most theo-cosmogonies, therefore, planetary cataclysm only ever has a positive net value from the point of view of the small minority who are saved. And salvation, moreover, always comes at a price, that price often involving terror and destruction.

In scenarios of apocalypse, at the heart of terror there lies always the explosive combination of the possible and the unknown: the possibility of transgression and the crossing of a line from what is familiar into unimagined, unimaginable territory. As Derrida (Derrida, 1974) very well knew, lines, and what they demarcate, map the territory of the status quo, and separate as well as safeguard it from all that it is not, all that differs from it. The abnormal, be it in the form of crime, transgression, incest, cannibalism, vampirism, body-snatching, possession, phantasmagoria, cataclysmic world-end or any other brand of horror/terror, usually involves, at its gestation, the dissolution of what was supposed to be an indelible line: namely, that which supposedly separated the known from the unknown, the taboo from the desired, the self from the other, the animate from the inanimate, the living from the dead, but now shows them to be akin. And it is because of what is *not* fantastic but instead disquietingly familiar (and therefore plausible) beneath the thin veneer of childishness or silliness, whether in children's literature, horror narratives or science fiction, that we ought to be at least as disturbed as entertained by the outcome of the outlandish events involved in all these genres.

The translation of radical upheaval into the realm of childhood and/ or of domestic concerns is not new. Few texts are as violent as a Perrault or Brothers Grimm fairy tale. In the gruesome universes of Stephen King or Thomas Harris's Hannibal Lecter, the majority of adult spectators witness violence and as a result exhibit shock and fear, rather than the unseemly composure presupposed in the average primary school-age reader of fairy tales arguably just as brutal. It is possible that the very abundance of children's and adolescent literature dealing with the concept of moral and physical apocalypse testifies to the perceived need to address in narratives for the young the reality and nature of our atavistic fears. And in that sense, adult narratives of horror and disaster become comprehensible as throwbacks to something experienced at an early stage (in individual childhood, in cultural history or in our biological/species memory) with an added dimension of primitivism and viscerality.

The Shape of Apocalypse

Scenarios of apocalypse (in the past sixty years often but not always taking the form of nuclear war), are recurrent themes in texts addressing themselves to different age groups, from young children (in the works mentioned above) and young adults (*Lord of the Flies*, Golding, [1954] 2002, *The Shadow on the Hearth*, Merrill, 1950) to adult literature and film (to be addressed in the chapters that follow). Following the parameters of traditional fairy tales, and in a mode reminiscent of Freud's assessment of early childhood as defined by pre-moral, anarchic, untamed savagery, it is not necessarily in adult narratives but in literature for the young that the most uncompromising forms of moral revisionism and unalloyed fear are to be found.

Henry's Quest (Oakley, 1986), a comic strip of life post-peak oil for six to nine year olds translates a very contemporary preoccupation into a combination of adventure story, romance of quest and fairy tale. Henry, a young shepherd, lives in a bucolic country setting reminiscent of the chivalric times of King Arthur. An unexpected anachronism discloses the fact that the country lacks one essential element: gasoline, necessary to run the shiny cars and limousines that currently decorate King Arthur II's throne room as historical heirlooms. The king charges Henry with the quest to find gasoline, a mission, which involves a variety of knightly adventures. He arrives safely on the other side of the forest, and finds what appears to be a large city, or what remains of it after a holocaust, now ruled by a corrupt government and a fearful emperor-dictator. In a predictable happy ending, Henry outwits the enemy, escapes with the sought-after gasoline, and returns home. In what is presumably intended as an ecological morality tale for our times, pre-empting a subsequent genre of post-peak oil apocalyptic film and fiction (for example Alex Scarrow's novel of 2008, *Last Light*), in *Henry's Quest*, themes central to the Western imagination, both old and modern, can be discerned and invite further comment. Most apparent is the phenomenon discussed in chapter 3, whereby, following apocalypse, in the process of rebuilding that follows, the seeds are sown for a future repetition of the present disaster. It is to be supposed, for example, that once in possession of oil, the bucolic kingdom of Henry's birth will evolve rapidly into the kind of industrialized, technological culture in which global cataclysm becomes possible once again.

Apocalypse and Back to Basics

Post-apocalyptic survival literature has provided some of the most enduring teenage classics, including narratives whose persistence in print and worldwide availability in translation attest to the importance of the theme. In *The Village that Slept*, Monique Peyrouton de Ladebat's classic Robinsonade of 1980, a boy and a girl who remember only that their names are Franz and Lydia, are the survivors of an unspecified accident. Each recovers consciousness to find they are lost on a mountain, with no memory of how they came to be there. They stumble upon one another and subsequently discover a baby strapped in his carrying sack. Having tried and failed to find a path down the mountain, they realize they will have to take care of themselves and the baby until such a time as they might be rescued. On the outskirts of a deserted village Lydia finds a small house and Franz discovers an Alpine hut stocked with provisions and a few books. The children settle in and by the time winter comes they have made themselves secure against the weather and the loneliness. The novel ends happily: the children (as it turns out the sole survivors of a plane crash) succeed in hoisting up an SOS flag which is eventually spotted by a search plane. They are duly rescued and returned to civilization and to their respective families. The choice of prepubertal characters (Lydia is ten, Franz is twelve and the baby is only just weaned) allows only speculation regarding a long-term scenario of sex leading to the continuation of the species. Nonetheless, all the ingredients are there, including that of genetic/racial diversity: a Caucasian girl and boy and a baby of Asian origin.

Better Alone? The Imperative of Continuity

Like de Ladebat's memorable last-man-(last child)-on-Earth narrative, Robert C. O'Brien's *Z for Zacchariah* (O'Brien, 1998), also targeted at young adolescents, features as its central protagonist a young girl. Ann Burden, whose very surname gestures to the weighty task allotted to her by fate (nothing less than guaranteeing the preservation of human life on Earth) has lived alone in a valley in the eastern United States for over a year following a nuclear war which appears to have rendered all land outside the valley contaminated and uninhabitable. The valley itself, described in remembered local folklore as having its own weather system, may have escaped contamination thanks to possessing its own microclimate deep in a valley between two steep mountains. Ann believes that she is the only human being left in the world but one day she sees a stranger climbing over a ridge into the valley, dressed in a plastic radiation protection suit and carrying a cart covered with the same material. Tellingly, obeying the same instinctive suspicion of strangers harboured by other fictional survivors of apocalypse (clearest in Cormac McCarthy's *The Road* of 2007, to be discussed) Ann watches him nervously from a hide-out in a cave. Using a Geiger counter, the man determines that the valley is uncontaminated and in his joy bathes in a stream (one of two running through the valley) which however, unbeknownst to him, and unlike the second stream, carries contaminated water from beyond the mountains. He becomes sick, and Ann comes out of hiding to help him. He introduces himself as John Loomis (throughout the book Ann calls him Mr. Loomis, in a clear indication, which proves justified, that right until the end he does not lose his status of stranger-danger). Mr. Loomis is a scientist who survived the nuclear attack in his underground lab and subsequently ventured out in a protective suit with the intention of finding other survivors. Albeit aware from his delirious disclosures that Loomis had murdered another man in order to keep the suit for himself, Ann continues to care for him. When he recovers they make plans for survival by cultivating the valley, but sexual tension grows and in due course he attempts to rape her. Ann escapes and for several months the two play a game of cat-and-mouse around the valley. In what is arguably the only indication of survivor ruthlessness in an otherwise exemplary demonstration of good samaritanism, Ann kills the family's dog, Faro, which had also survived and is now being used by Loomis to track her down. Ann tries another rapprochement with Loomis but he shoots her in the ankle. Realizing that she has no option but to leave the valley, Ann steals the protection suit and the cart. She talks to Loomis one last time and in a belated moment of remorse he points her in a direction beyond the valley where he had seen birds circling, suggesting the possibility that there is some life left in the world beyond the valley. The book's title is explained when Ann recalls that in one of her books, a Bible-themed children's alphabet book, Adam, whose name begins with the first letter of the alphabet, was the first man, and presumes that Zachariah, the last person named in the book, must therefore be the last man left somewhere on Earth. The evidence of the circling cloud of birds in the distance (they are not vultures) suggests that somewhere over the valley there may be at least one other human being left alive: ideally, another man with whom her now pubescent self (whose name also begins with an 'A') might eventually begin to reconstitute the species and the world.

Safety in Numbers: Communities of Pioneers

Children's Laureate Robert Swindells's *Brother in the Land* (Swindells, 1999) follows an analogous plot, and is also reminiscent of adult novels of post-apocalypse such as *The Road* (McCarthy, 2007) and Paul Auster's *In the Country of Last Things* (Auster, 2005), to be discussed. Danny Lodge, a teenager, is one of the survivors of nuclear war. Written in the first-person like *Z for Zacchariah*, Danny chronicles events in the year-and-a-half that follows a large nuclear conflagration which destroyed the world he knew. On the day war breaks out, his mother dies but his father and brother, Ben, survive. As the weeks pass and survivors begin fighting over food, Kim, a friend of Danny's, sums up the situation: 'Cavemen versus gentlemen is no contest' (Swindells, 1999, 41). She is proved right.

In chapter 5 the rise of dictatorships following apocalypse will be discussed, including the implementation of programmatic genocide as a means of speeding up the selection of the fittest in newly-formed worlds. In Swindells's novel, as social structures begin to disintegrate, a state of emergency is declared. The local Commissioner sets in motion the culling of the elderly, the burned, the sick and the injured, and imprisons the remaining survivors in a camp where they are used as slave labour. In the ensuing chaos Danny and Ben are left orphans and seek sanctuary at the home of Sam Branwell, a smallholder who, along with several other survivors, has formed a resistance group called Masada (Movement to Arm Skipley Against Dictatorial Authority), aiming to overthrow the Commissioner and prevent him from creating a feudal society. In due course the Commissioner is overthrown and Branwell is established as the new leader. Although a new community is built on the lines of a liberal co-operative, shortage of food supplies forces people into scavenging. Some turn to cannibalism. In the second winter after the war, Danny, Kim and Ben leave the camp and set off to Holy Island, in Northumbria, where Danny hopes to find refuge. Ben dies of radiation sickness on the way and Danny begins writing an account (A Book of Bad News?) which he plans to leave for future generations to read as a warning against future wars. In due course Danny and Kim arrive in Holy Island and join a community of survivors and Kim gives birth to their baby: a child whose place of birth carries all the hallmarks of a salvific new beginning.

Old News in New Clothes

'Give me a child before the age of seven and I will give you the man.' St. Ignatius de Loyola's (Loyola, [1522-24] 1964) well-known saying, albeit originally uttered with a different intent, condenses much of what is at stake in narratives of apocalypse targeting a young audience. In children's and teenage literature in the West, the trauma of apocalypse as radical change reappears with some insistence. Many of these narratives carry a strong streak of Christian allusiveness: the effect of early trauma and loss (Edenic or otherwise) representing the starting point for recovery (post-lapsarian rebirth) in the future. Whether merely with the intention of reflecting atavistic fears of apocalypse or with the pedagogical aim of alerting future generations to the dangerous path trodden by humanity in an age of weapons of mass destruction (nuclear or otherwise), in contemporary literature for young readers the nature of the trajectory from a familiar reality to unexpected nothingness and thence to a fresh start offers both a stark warning and the balsamic hope that, in the end, even the end may not really be *The* End. This conjecture also forms the basis of the observations to be developed in this book with regard to adult fiction, film and the visual arts. The project proposed here seeks to investigate various aspects of apocalyptic emplotment in literature and film, with some reference to examples from the visual arts.

Chapter 1, *Apocalypse Now and Again* outlines the parameters of the discussion to be developed.

Chapter 2, *The World Gone M.A.D.*, introduces the basic outlines of destruction underpinning the argument to be developed throughout the rest of the book. It will address what might be termed 'apocalypse neurosis': the fear of disruption on a macrocosmic scale. It identifies a representative range of texts, films and visual images that have depicted end of the world scenarios and outlines their limitations as well as their possible political and ideological implications in various contexts. This chapter also discusses possible period-specific motivations for these recurring preoccupations, and suggests parallels between previous epochs and what, in the twenty-first century climate of environmental and security concerns, are fast becoming very pressing and very generalized fears, reflected in the media and in changing priorities in political debate, legislature and policy-making. The ethical/punitive dimension of apocalypse triggered by human behaviour is shared by otherwise disparate texts from Biblical passages such as the Flood, the Cities of the Plain, Ecclesiastes, Isaiah and Revelations, to European Neo-Classicism and Romanticism (Marvell, Herculano, Tennyson) and modernism (T.S. Eliot, Fernando Pessoa), recent and contemporary literature (George Orwell, Isaac Asimov, Aldous Huxley, José Sara ago), popular fiction (Michael Crichton, Kate Aitkinson), children's and teenage literature (Robert O'Brien, Robert Swindells) and film (*Fail-Safe, The Day After Tomorrow, Threads, Planet of the Apes, The Children of Men*). Many of these will be analysed in detail in this chapter.

Chapter 3, *And Then There Was Nothing: Is the End Ever Really the End?* addresses a broad spectrum of fiction and nonfiction on the subject of planetary destruction and argues that ultimately only very rarely is total annihilation envisaged. Almost without exception, from biblical renditions to modern science fiction, what invariably structures narratives of apocalypse is the logic of the near-miss: near-universal annihilation with just enough life left intact (at least one human being of each sex, sufficient land, water and resources) to guarantee a reasonable likelihood of a new beginning. This chapter will consider the immediate plight of those left behind in the aftermath of planetary near-destruction, and elaborate on the notion that all scenarios of apocalypse are also morality tales leading to the medium-term effects of an opportune lesson well-learnt and a new ethic of non-repetition of past mistakes (including moral recklessness, social dissipation, ungodliness and the hubris of knowledge/power run-amok). A significant number of the texts and films considered, however, possibly for pedagogical reasons (the consciousness that old habits die hard and that even near-cataclysmic lessons may not always be thoroughly understood), warn against re-born statuses quo that in essential ways replicate the dogmas and problems that brought about their destruction in the first instance (John Wyndham, Ira Levin). The most sophisticated examples of this (Aldous Huxley, Margaret Atwood, Paul Auster), end at best inconclusively, with a variety of scenarios of fragile, post-historical survival with no guarantees.

Chapter 4, *Falling Out with Hal and Esther*, considers the question of a common denominator discernible in a large number of scripts of apocalypse in literature and film, in particular within the genre of science fiction. It focuses on the concept of apocalypse as retribution for flawed human agency: namely, its creation of artefacts capable of usurping the dominion of their creators, leading to nonhuman rule over the world (*2001: A Space Odyssey, Oryx and Crake,* 'Compassion Circuit,' *I, Robot, Blade Runner, Armageddon*).

Chapter 5, *Dying of Happiness: Utopia at the End of This World*, discusses literature of utopia: the ways in which science fiction, in conjunction with philosophical and political thought leads to the counter-intuitive possibility that the end of the world might be brought about not by global destruction but as a consequence of the establishment of utopia, in a variety of different formulations. Wider implications of the idea of utopia, the measures taken to establish it and the effects of its permanence in the long-term will be discussed in relation to authors from Plato and Thomas More to H.G. Wells, E.M. Forster, Aldous Huxley and Julian Barnes.

1. Apocalypse Now and Again

Since this partial answer to his prayer, Hannibal Lecter had not been bothered by any considerations of deity, other than to recognize how his own modest predations paled beside those of God, who is in irony matchless, and in wanton malice beyond measure.

Thomas Harris

Therefore, thus says the Lord God: […] Your covenant with death shall be cancelled and your pact with the nether world shall not stand. When the overwhelming scourge passes, you shall be trampled down by it. Whenever it passes, it shall take you; morning after morning it shall pass, By day and by night; terror alone shall convey the message. For the bed shall be too short to stretch out in, and the cover too narrow to wrap in. For the Lord shall rise up as on Mount Perazim, bestir himself as in the Valley of Gibeon, To carry out his work, his singular work, to perform his deed, his strange deed. Now, be arrogant no more lest your bonds be tightened, For I have heard from the Lord, the God of hosts, the destruction decreed for the whole earth.

Isaiah 28: 16-22

Now the number of the army of the horsemen was two hundred million; […] I heard the number of them. And thus I saw the horses in the vision: […] and out of their mouths came fire, smoke, and brimstone […] By these three plagues a third of mankind was killed by the fire and the smoke and the brimstone which came out of their mouths. For their power is in their mouth and in their tails; for their tails are like serpents, having heads; and with them they do harm.

Revelation 9: 16-19

In at least seven film and television re-makes, King Kong, the eponymous hero, is entrapped thanks to the frailty of elemental desire for the helpless blonde heroine, and is taken prisoner to America, the land of the free, which, being also the land of opportunity, makes the gigantic ape a profitable commodity in the capitalist market place. Any number of old and renewed preoccupations are played out here: nature versus civilization, innocence pitted against corruption, race/species confronted with its other, in the battle ground of assorted ideologies.

The story of King Kong is among other things an unedifying translation of the long-standing Western fear that nature's representatives of unbridled, elemental forces (apes, savages, black men) desire white flesh (a blonde woman) and, if allowed, will violate it to commit the ultimate desecration: forcible penetration of the white man's property, leading to miscegenation (the latter being translatable as the destruction of the principle of racial purity upon which rests a certain understanding of civilization-as-we-know-it). Kong's difference and proclaimed (in)(sub)-humanity, like that of any typical colonizable other, represents the thrill, the threat, the motivation and the pretext for that other's exploitability.

In the Beginning

Kong originates from far away Skull Island in the Indian Ocean, ie. as far from civilization (Europe, the United States) as it is possible to be – the skull, appropriately, being the brute, serviceable structure which anatomically encloses and protects but is not the real powerhouse of the human body (the brain). The other inhabitants of the island, with a fine disregard for prehistoric accuracy and evolutionary timelines, include plesiosaurs, pterosaurs and dinosaurs, as well as primitive humans. The nod to prehistoricity, nonsensical though it is, since it brings together dinosaurs and humans in chronological synchronicity, satisfies standard science fiction requirements: namely the blanket belief that although 'back then' in the mists of primeval time was where all that was wild and unformed was to be found, it was also from that mystical long-long-ago that innocence unblemished by the moral patina of civilization (the noble savage, the awe-ful, awe-inspiring ape) might be recoverable. If inside the skull lies the ultimate object of quest (the truth, enclosed in the knowing brain), that truth, it turns out, may lie not at the end of any road but in its primeval beginnings. In J.G. Ballard's haunting novel, *The Drowned World* (Ballard, 2008), astronomical phenomena are melting the polar ice and simultaneously warming and flooding the world to destruction. The effects are cosmic but also individual and neuropsychic. As the planet's climate warms up and moistens, a regressive trajectory back to polymorphous origins becomes apparent: from solid Earth to primeval soup, from contemporary animal life to Triassic fauna and flora, from civilized communal behaviour to primitive savagery, from human *compos mentis* consciousness to nonverbal, psychotic, infantile, uterine dependency. In this new old world, all notions of organized ethics make way for a return to instinctual rule, and the revelations that accompany this chronological reversal result, in the context of an un-nuanced world, in an amoral (uncivilized, un-evolved) behavioural palette in black and white. At another level, the implied corollary is of course the fear that inside modern human beings there lurks always the primitive ancestral precursor. In *The Drowned World*, the process of regression leads to a recapitulation of evolutionary history in reverse, at both an environmental and a psycho-individual level. Contemporary animal and plant forms die out and older ones re-appear in a planet itself now fast reverting to an earlier geological state. At the same time, the remnants of humanity left in habitats which are now both hot and watery, *en route* back to their primeval beginnings, undergo a form of psychosis which is described as a waking unconsciousness in some ways imaginable as the foetal experience in the womb:

> In response to the rises in temperature, humidity and radiation levels the flora and fauna of this planet are beginning to assume once again the forms they displayed the last time such conditions were present – roughly speaking the Triassic period. [...] Everywhere there's been the same avalanche backwards into the past. [...] Is it only the external landscape which is altering? How often, recently, most of us have had the feeling of déjà vu, of having seen all this before, in fact of remembering these swamps and lagoons all too well. [...] *These are the oldest memories on Earth, the time-codes carried in every chromosome and gene.* Every step we've taken in our evolution is a milestone inscribed with organic memories. [...] Just as psychoanalysis reconstructs the original traumatic situation in order to release the traumatic material, so we are now being plunged back into the archaeopsychic past [...]. As we move back through geophysical time so we re-enter the amniotic corridor and move back through spinal and archaeophysic time, recollecting in our minds the landscapes of each epoch. (Ballard, 2008: 42-44, italics added)

Similarly, in Kevin Reynolds's *Waterworld* (Reynolds, 1995), the central character, known only as the Mariner, a pilgrim-type nomad forever on the move along a flooded planet's ubiquitous waterways, apparently in search of an unspecified answer to an undisclosed question, is exposed as a regressive mutant, a mammal with webbed feet, presumably on a reverse evolutionary trajectory to the form of the amphibians that ventured onto dry land.

Figure 3. René Magritte, *Collective Invention*

Figure 4. William Blake, *Nebuchadnezzar*

Figure 5. René Magritte, *The Wonders of Nature*

In Philip K. Dick's *The Simulacra* (Dick, 2004), too, in the aftermath of widespread radioactive contamination, Neanderthal-like humans begin to be born in northern California, itself now returned to an immensity of primeval forests, while in William Blake's *Nebuchadnezzar*, the Biblical character from the Book of Daniel is punished by God for boasting of his achievements and erecting an idol. The punishment sees him losing his reason and reverting to animal status.

And in Magritte's enigmatic *The Wonders of Nature* (1953), life appears to regress to a pre-animate geological state, against the background image of a ship resembling those in which in the fifteenth and sixteenth centuries, the Portuguese and the Spanish began to de-mythify the mysteries of the unknown world.

What We Are Now

King Kong, the ape from a geographically, chronologically and evolutionarily remote island (which includes the standard period marker of dinosaurs), not only stands as the atavistic progenitor of civilized humanity's self-assuredness ('look how far we have come'), but, paradoxically, also casts an unexpected light on the ways in which contemporary, scientific and urban statuses quo compare unfavourably with the untarnished wholesomeness of the wild ('look how badly we have turned out'). It is Kong, the wild beast, for example, rather than his human

Figure 6. Peter Paul Rubens, *Adam and Eve in Paradise*

captors, who paradoxically offers an exemplary demonstration of all that, in civilized society, is least instinctual and most culturally refined: namely, the act of dying in the name of love.

The idea of King Kong's giant phallus penetrating the fairy tale princess's untouchable virginity – supposedly reserved for the seed of future patriarchal lineages – impugns the invincibility of all kinds of trusted demarcations: those which define and demarcate species and races but also deeds of territory, property and general ownership (including the ownership of female flesh and of its issue). In Western iconography, the blonde is both the reliquary of untarnished femininity and the bait to temptation. Gentlemen *and* beasts both prefer blondes: in Western Garden-of-Eden iconography Eve is definitely a svelte blonde, or she was so, at least, until she partook of the forbidden fruit, at which point her brunette roots started showing through and she became a dark temptress.

The blonde is the time-honoured trope of fantasy. She may be the theory, however, but she is not necessarily the praxis, and in this game of courtly love, the big ape is no exception to the masculine rule, with the added bonus that, species-difference notwithstanding, its/his love for the girl, evinced through an improbable semblance of flirtatiousness, is real. In a moving

Figure 7. John Guillermin *King Kong* (1976)

scene in John Guillermin's 1976 film, Kong snatches the girl; not only, however, does he not eat her but, as in the traditional, largely performative scenarios of courtship between man-girl down the ages, his scrutiny of his catch culminates in the tenderest and most reverent of caresses. Kong, it transpires, is just another Adam/Lancelot, led to perdition by a beloved female.

Where to from Here?

In scenarios such as the one outlined above, of course, beginning with Genesis, behind every usable female there lies a darker force and an annihilating project, namely the destruction of God's Eden, in the first book of the Pentateuch, leading to the Fall, in what must be one of the earliest narratives of apocalypse. In the aftermath of talking snakes bearing gifts of apples, things will never be the same again, although apocalypse (in the original meaning of the term), usually tends to be not an absolute wipe-out, merely a clearing of the decks in the anticipation of a new beginning.

In what follows it will be argued that in narratives of apocalypse, whether in text, film or image, the end of the world is never quite that. Almost without exception, from the Ancient Greeks and the Bible to contemporary science fiction, in the aftermath of Armageddon, following near-global destruction (whether brought about by divine wrath or by dangerous scientific advancement – eg. nuclear power), there is usually enough left over to permit a new beginning: as suggested before, at the very least one man, one woman, some representative animal and plant species and enough resources to sustain them and ensure continuity.

There is also, however, as we shall see, and that will be one of the central points to be developed, enough left of the old mind set to justify the fear that, once survival is consolidated, the factors which led to near-miss destruction in the first place will also be reinstated. Reinstated again and again and again, but seldom with any likelihood that (leaving aside God who in any case also never actually seems to mean what he threatens) one day the real thing might indeed happen and a point of no return be in fact crossed. Or at least that was the case until the dawn of the nuclear age, inaugurated on 6 August 1945 in Hiroshima.

Until then, historically, the idea of actual global wipe-out had been almost unimaginable, which might explain why it had been and still is so seldom *imagined*. With extreme rarity (Nevil Shute's popular, twice-filmed novel, *On the Beach* (1974) and Kevin Brockmeier's *The Brief History of the Dead* (2006) being exceptions), whether in fiction, film or art, the end usually is not really the end. This general principle applies in popular science fiction with happy endings and uplifting morals (in films such as *Deep Impact*, Leder, 1998; *The Day After Tomorrow*, Emmerich, 2004; *Independence Day*, Emmerich, 1996, all examples of modern techno-Westerns in which the cavalry, usually in the form of can-do American military science, ultimately saves the day); but it applies also even in the darkest, most uncompromising post-apocalyptic narratives (J.G. Ballard's *The Drowned World*, 2008, Cormack McCarthy's *The Road*, 2007, Philip K. Dick's *The Penultimate Truth*, 2005, Paul Auster's *In the Country of Last Things*, 2005).

Back to What?

Back in the jungle, meanwhile, or rather, snatched out of it and plunged into the glare of grim modernity in downtown Manhattan, King Kong escapes from the clutches of the profit-making free-market forces that had intended to exhibit him as a circus freak. In John Guillermin's 1976 re-make, Kong, on the loose in New York, and in possession of his hostage/princess (the latter now trapped in an emotional no-woman's land of fear of the monster mingled with pity bordering on complicity), finds refuge on top of the twin towers of the World Trade Centre which he straddles like a modern day colossus.

If the metaphor in 1976 was not particularly subtle (Kong is the booty of neocolonial trading rapaciousness, torn like the erstwhile black cargo of slavery out of his natural habitat, in the name of Western entrepreneurship), in real life, events have conspired to ensure that the problem he represented endures and continues to disturb. As is the case with many modern sci-fi narratives, at the heart of the moral conclusion urged upon the more or less knowing consumer are basic archetypal plots traceable back to Western foundation narratives beginning with the Old and New Testaments. In this twentieth-century film rendition, the elemental forces represented by King Kong are brought down (literally) on the roof of the World Trade Centre's twin towers, the phallic icons of capitalist greed. Twenty-five years later, on 11 September 2001 the same symbols were razed to the ground by the forces of an elemental religious fundamentalism which the West no longer commanded the vocabulary to understand. History is sometimes translated into art and then back again, tying a final loop to events. In the event now known as 9/11, the twin towers were reduced to ashes by agents of the would-be wrath of one particular God (Allah) unleashed against the symbols of another (Mammon). Whatever interpretation one gives to this event, one thing is certain: this particular small-scale apocalypse was not

Figure 8. John Guillermin, *King Kong*

the end of anything, merely the re-visiting of a not even-particularly new or original, although undeniably vicious circle. With any luck, in the long term, 9/11 will prove to be not the first stage of a definitive climax, not an actual Ground Zero following which there is nothing, but merely another bloody episode (not the final one) of a very old story.

In *King Kong* the eponymous hero, trapped on top of two buildings whose very name gestures to the forces (trade, profit, greed) that brought him to his present plight, chooses suicide. He releases the girl, who, while clutched in his gigantic hand, had acted as the human shield against the gunfire of circling aircraft. Willingly donning the mantle of sacrificial lamb to the slaughter, he is shot down, but leaves in his wake moral uncertainty (in the shape of himself, transfigured from representative of primitive savagery into martyr to sacrificial love) and loss (in the shape of his erstwhile hostage, herself now transfigured from sexual prey into a *mater dolorosa*/lover/daughter reluctant to embrace freedom by abandoning the giant ape).

The Unacceptability of Nothing

The symbiosis of advanced technological possibilities and divine wrath enacted by the events of 9/11 has precedents in popular culture, such as *The Terminator*, James Cameron's film of 1984, to be discussed. The dread of apocalypse (the end of the world, the end of civilization-as-we-know-it, our own individual deaths) is arguably the most universally shared phenomenon of the human psyche, and transposes boundaries of time and geography, to some extent erasing cultural difference. The idea of the cessation of being may be the only truly universal fear, and resistance to it explains a number of widely accepted prohibitions, such as for example murder or suicide.

> [T]he dread
> Of dying, and being dead,
> Flashes afresh to hold and horrify.
> The mind blanks at the glare. Not in remorse
> The good not done, the love not given, time
> Torn off unused – nor wretchedly because
> An only life can take so long to climb
> Clear of its wrong beginnings, and may never;
> But at the total emptiness for ever,

> The sure extinction that we travel to
> And shall be lost in always. Not to be here,
> Not to be anywhere,
> And soon; nothing more terrible, nothing more true. (Larkin, 1977)

Murder and suicide both prevail alongside other taboos (kin-slaying, incest) and share with them a fear of the end as well as concomitant imperatives regarding the preservation of life and the viability of the species against the threat of extinction. It is not surprising, therefore, that the dread of finitude, whether of the self (through death) or of the commonweal (through social anarchy, the collapse of the rule of law), or of the physical environment (through global destruction), should be a meta-narrative since our earliest cultural manifestations.

Palaeo-neurology has suggested that in mammals the integration of the five senses into a single anatomical structure (the neocortex) was an evolutionary occurrence of which language was an accidental off-shoot. Language's desirability in terms of survival resided in an enhanced ability to make sense of the world through sensory speculation ('if I fall off that cliff I might hurt myself and die') rather than through empirical verification ('I will jump off that cliff and see what happens') (Dunbar, 1993; Bradshaw, 1993; 1995). Through the acquisition of language, the polymorphous linguistic and imagistic ways in which human beings articulate (make sense of) the world led, beyond the requirements of physical survival and self-perpetuation, to literature, philosophy, art and science as tools for engaging with and managing our environment. In human beings instinct but also reason are the *sine qua non* of survival and continuity. Humans are the only species known to engage in the production of something (culture, as a by-product of reason) which is not only superfluous to the requirements of survival, but expensive as regards the energy-time expenditure necessary to produce it. It may be argued, however, that cultural artefacts, which deal with phenomena as diverse as emotion, ethics and cognition, are in fact powerful species-unique tools, massively advantageous to the animal desideratum of understanding in order to survive. And what could be more urgent than the imperative of understanding the possibility of an end?

Just Curious

The fear of irreversible destruction, that which both individual and group instinct must grasp in order to avoid, goes hand in hand with a curiosity for knowledge detectable in *homo sapiens* as far back as the hunting scenes of Paleolithic cave art, and as recently as current debates on the danger of planetary destruction through global warming, nuclear conflict or scientific experimentation. The CERN Large Hadron Collider had no obvious purpose other than the desire on the part of scientists to witness the original primal scene following which the universe began. The experiment of Wednesday 10 October 2008 aimed to reveal what happened in the first nanosecond after the Big Bang. It also carried a small possibility of unleashing destruction at an inter-galactic level: a rip in the fabric of the universe, orgasm no longer as *petit mort* but as all-encompassing death, the triumph of King Kong's elemental phallus originating not in Skull Island but inside the human skull, in brains arguably much too clever for the good of us all. 'Now I am become Death, the Destroyer of Worlds' (Oppenheimer, 1945). Or alternatively, 'My name is Ozymandias, King of Kings. Look upon my Works ye mighty and despair' (Shelley, 1818). It is an old story, much repeated.

The fact that the above passages were originally written on Tuesday 9 October 2008, the day before the launch of the Hadron Collider, on the assumption that they *would* be read, confirms that whatever revelations emerged from Hadron, neither did the experiment rip the fabric of the universe nor did the writer of this really believe it would. Nonetheless, the fact that cosmic annihilation might have occurred but the trial was even so attempted, represents the repetition of a phenomenon inscribed in all our cultural narratives. Despite prior warnings, Pandora's box *was* opened (in some versions of the story by her husband, not her, although she is usually blamed: *cherchez la femme*). In Greek mythology Pandora was the first woman, created by the Olympian Gods and given in marriage (together with the poisoned dowry of her dangerous box) to the leader of the Titans, in punishment for their theft of fire. Of course the treacherous deities knew the box would be opened. Who could resist it? But, more to the point, why had the Titans stolen fire in the first place? Because they could? Because they were curious? Because they wanted to know what it was?

As a species, we are inquisitive and sometimes greedy. Curiosity is desire, and we want our desires to be satisfied. The control of fire marks a key stage in human prehistory but hindsight being what it is, the first human to play with it did not know that if you play with fire you might get burnt. S/he simply did it for no reason, or perhaps only because it might be fun. Just like Hadron. In the myth of Pandora's box, once all evils had been released into the world the only thing left inside the box was hope, and even hope, like fire, turns out to be a mixed blessing. It is because of hope that we keep going when all seems lost, keep looking because something better might be just around the corner, keep attempting to fulfil desire because it might just be possible.

And it is also because we keep going, looking and trying, that things keep going wrong, cyclically, and with the perennial possibility that final satiation might coincide with final annihilation. Which of course by definition it would have to, because once you have attained all, only nothing can follow. Lot's wife looked back even though the interdiction came from on-high. So did Psyche and Orpheus, even though they stood to lose what they most valued, and in Genesis Eve's curiosity lost humanity paradise, thereby triggering the first apocalypse in the Judaeo-Christian imagination. On the other hand, Adam could have stopped her, or at least refrained from doing what she suggested, but did not. Why not? If he had, she could not really gainsay him: he was bigger and stronger and he did, after all, have free will. The truth is that like her and like all their descendants thereafter, he too was curious, and although even if we are curious we can stop ourselves if we wish, often we do not. We know it can be dangerous and we are afraid, but we go ahead even so. Owning fire and knowledge brings us closer to being Gods, and we are punished in the attempt. On the other hand, without fire we would sit in the dark, and if unpicked, the fruit of the Tree of Knowledge would presumably stay on the branch until it rotted. Curiosity is desire (for Knowledge, carnal or otherwise) and in the end desire overcomes fear and propels the practices and narratives of disciplines as diverse as theoretical physics, theology and the humanities. Curiosity sometimes kills cats (and worlds), but as the word apocalypse in its semantic ramifications indicates, it also opens up new possibilities.

Same Again, Please

> But the first verdict seemed the worst verdict
> When Adam and Eve were expelled from Eden,
> Yet when the bitter gates clanged to
> The sky beyond was just as blue.
> For the next ocean is the first ocean
> And the last ocean is the first ocean
> And, however often the sun may rise,
> A new thing dawns upon our eyes. (MacNeice, 2005: 36)

If history repeats itself and each ending leads to a new beginning, does the cycle mean that nothing new is ever possible? That all permutations of meaning have always already been exhausted and no new ones can occur? The Greek term *apokalupsus* or *apokalupsis* implies an unveiling either of future events or of the unseen realms of heaven and hell. It signifies laying bare, making naked; a disclosure of truth, instruction concerning things before unknown; events by means of which things or states or persons hitherto withdrawn from view are made visible to all manifestation; revelation; appearance. James Berger, identifies three meanings of the term apocalypse: first, *eschaton*, referring to the actual imagined end of the world as presented in the Book of Revelation, in millenarian movements and in visions of nuclear or environmental Armageddon; second, significant catastrophes or rupture points which mark the end of something within clear limits, such as for example the Holocaust, Hiroshima, 9/11; and third, apocalypse as an uncovering or revelation regarding both the nature of was put an end to and the nature of the alternatives (Berger, 1999: 5).

In all the senses identified by Berger apocalypse evokes not only what was obliterated but also the reason for its destruction, that which made cataclysm deemed to be necessary or even desirable. It gestures, furthermore, to what follows. If apocalypse represents a moment of extreme cultural trauma (Berger, 1999: xvi), the aftermath of it must be a return to equilibrium defined as a state that differs significantly and momentously from what was erased. If what prevailed prior to apocalypse was unacceptable and led to near-wipeout, what follows must be completely different, and the destruction of what was undesirable becomes construable as the *sine qua non* of a new order, built on the remains of what survived. Jehovah flooded the Earth but preserved enough for a new beginning. The establishment of utopia, as discussed in chapter 5, almost without exception demands a prior radical purge.

If, however, in imagining what follows apocalypse, some of what preceded it is preserved and re-visited, the effect of the new (for good or evil) is compromised by the unavoidable influence of this archeological palimpsest on any future development. The concept of reverse evolution already discussed with reference to *The Drowned World* (Ballard, 2008, *Waterworld* (Reynolds, 1995) and *The Simulacra* (Dick, 2004) carries multiple implications on a spectrum which ranges from the biological, to the philosophical, to the metaphysical. Western thought, whether explicitly or implicitly, is structured by a presupposed dialectic of development that preempts Hegel and dates back to Ancient Greece or possibly earlier. Darwin's paradigm of ever more adaptive change is only one of many possible formulations of the same principle, and, as a whole, these underpin the fundamental paradigm of Western logic: namely that things, with occasional interruptions, change for the better (evolve). If they either moved backwards or changed for the worse, the conclusion must be eventual annihilation, and that would be equivalent to what is in effect a philosophical impossibility: arrival at a vanishing point, which, like crossing over the line of the horizon, is something that can be articulated in words but has no real meaning.

The imperative of what one might call constructive change explains the difficulty, debated in chapter 3, of linking any understanding of apocalypse to absolute finitude. Structurally, the human intellect may lack the hardware to process the concept of an absolute ending, which would by definition involve constructing the hypothesis of something which is nothing, and which we could not witness because we would not be there. Although we imagine the fear of it (*horror vacui*) we are not really afraid of it because, as a matter of fact, we cannot imagine it. Therefore, we do not.

2. The World Gone M.A.D.

In order to improve your [chess] game you must study the endgame before anything else; for, whereas the endings can be studied and mastered by themselves, the middlegame and the opening must be studied in relation to the endgame.

José Raúl Capablanca

It's time it ended…[a]nd yet I hesitate, I hesitate to… to end.

Samuel Beckett

[The] problem is this: the next holocaust will leave this planet uninhabitable, and the moon is no Switzerland.

Kurt Vonnegut

mother the wardrobe is full of infantrymen
i did i asked them
but they snarled saying it was a man's life

mother there's a centurion tank in the parlour
i did i asked the officer
but he laughed saying Queen's regulations
(piano was out of tune anyway)

mother polish your identity bracelet
there is a mushroom cloud in the back garden
i did i tried to bring in the cat
but it simply came to pieces in my hand
i did i tried to whitewash the windows
but there weren't any
i did i tried to hide under the stairs
but I couldn't get in for the civil defence leaders
i did i tried ringing candid camera
but they crossed their hearts

i went for a policeman but they were looting the town
i went out for a fire engine but they were all upside down
i went out for a priest but they were all on their knees
mother don't just lie there, say something please
mother don't just lie there, say something please

Roger McGough

> Then the Lord saw that the wickedness of man was great in the land, and that every intent of the thoughts of his heart was only evil continually. And the Lord was sorry that He had made man in the land, and He was grieved in His heart. And the Lord said, I will blot out man whom I have created from the face of the land, from man to animals to creeping things and to birds of the sky; for I am sorry that I have made them. (Genesis 6: 5-7)

Even before it was actually practicable to destroy the entire planet, indeed since the dawn of earliest human consciousness, the fear of global catastrophe has informed the human psyche, resulting in persistent returns to cultural renditions of apocalypse. And while clearly the best way to calm fears is *not* to suggest soothingly that one should not worry too much about the axe murderer just spotted sneaking under the bed, in *The Imagination of Disaster* Susan Sontag (1979) argues that disaster films and narratives both reflect and deflect their epoch's anxieties regarding the possibility that what at any given moment is fiction may become (post-nuclearly or otherwise) reality.

In Ancient Greece the ruling deities, for all their capriciousness, confined their destructive rampages to individuals, or at most to selected groups (of which the Trojans are an example). In the Western consciousness, narratives of apocalypse began with the Flood in Genesis, or arguably as early as the

Figure 9. John Martin, *The Last Man*

Fall. When Adam and Eve were driven out of Eden in the opening chapters of Genesis, that particular world, albeit at that point admittedly restricted to a population of two, came to an abrupt end.

Figure 10. Gustave Doré, *Adam and Eve Driven Out of Eden*

But there was of course a follow up, leading to where we find ourselves now.

> For the last blossom is the first blossom
> And the first blossom is the last blossom
> And when from Eden we take our way
> The morning after is the first day. (MacNeice, 1982: 36)

Which is nice to know, and while the trauma and consequences of the Fall have haunted the Western imagination ever since, up to contemporary literature and film, the resulting narratives almost never hypothesize total destruction. In the common parlance usage of the term (widespread or global destruction), of course, relative apocalypse, apocalypse but only up to a point, appears to be a contradiction, since the term suggests a trajectory from all to nothing, from plenty to absence, from being to nothingness. Apocalypse is like God: if you really believe in it, there can only ever be one of it. We can understand apocalypse now, apocalypse whenever, but we may find it difficult to envisage apocalypse now and then, apocalypse now and again. Nonetheless, possibly because absolute nothingness, given the *horror vacui* we inherited from the Greeks, is an even more difficult concept to grasp than infinity, in our contemplation of the possibility, *nihilo interruptus* is usually as bad as it gets. Instead of zero, then, both in theological and cultural discourse, apocalypse may in fact mean a widespread wipe-out but, with rare exceptions, it is usually followed by a new beginning, something which (and this may not be a coincidence) dovetails nicely with our biological and cultural inbuilt reluctance to say goodbye forever and disappear. Within the spectrum of Western speculation in both high and popular culture, apocalypse now and again (and again and again and again), is in effect mostly (and at most) what you get, and, with remarkably few exceptions, in the end life on Earth never really ends. Instead, apocalypse invariably appears to imply also the certainty of a new beginning. There are many versions of being born again, although, as will be discussed in chapter 3, they do not necessarily involve a really thorough cleansing, a wholly holy re-birth.

Universal Death

In the Garden of Earthly Delights, the temptation offered by the serpent was twofold: gnosis, attainable from eating of the fruit of the Tree of Knowledge, and immortality, attainable from eating the fruit of the Tree of Life. The two combined would result in humanity becoming like God, something not to be countenanced because it would probably be followed by the end of the world. But why so? Admittedly, when Oppenheimer famously uttered his fear that he (a man) had 'become God, the destroyer of worlds,' global nuclear apocalypse became possible. The possibility of Adam and Eve becoming God, it now appeared, had been merely postponed, and its dangers were crystallized by the achievement of the Manhattan Project.

Even before that, however, the end of the world, if you believe in God, or even if you only believe in random bad luck in the form of natural disasters, as hypothesized by environmentalists and astrophysicists, has always been possible, even outside the sphere of human irresponsibility. If the steady-state world (the normal order of things, civilization as we know it) is a status quo in equilibrium, a scorched-Earth apocalypse (the end of the world), would be the epitome of extreme iconoclasm, for which Eve's actions and the meteor that wiped out the dinosaurs would have been merely a dress rehearsal (unless, of course you happened to be a dinosaur). The real thing would be not merely change or revolution but fully-achieved destruction, at the end of which process whatever had been there before became absolutely corroded and nothing else was possible.

In the matter of apocalypse, the possibility of life (or the end of it) imitating art has found its clearer manifestation in events surrounding the unfolding of the Cold War in the second half of the twentieth century, a period which saw a dangerous synchronicity of instability in international relations combined (in the new nuclear age) with the previously unprecedented know-how for planetary destruction. Writing about Hiroshima at the height of the Cold War, Susan Sontag wrote: 'It became clear that, from now on till the end of human history, every person would spend his individual life under the threat not only of individual death, which is certain, but of something almost insupportable psychologically – collective incineration and extinction which could come at any time, virtually without warning' (Sontag, 1979: 224).

In contemplating the possibility of large-scale or even global destruction, even some of the world's finest minds (as well as some not so fine) seem to have found the challenge too much. Let us consider William Poundstone's account:

> By 1950, a number of people in the United States and Western Europe had decided that the United States should contemplate an immediate, unprovoked nuclear attack on the Soviet Union. This idea, which went by the euphemistic name of 'preventive war,' held that America should seize the moment and establish a world government through nuclear blackmail

> or surprise attack. [...] The preventive war movement found support among many of undeniable intelligence, including two of the most brilliant mathematicians of the time: Bertrand Russell and John von Neumann. [...] Life magazine quoted von Neumann as saying, 'If you say why not bomb them tomorrow, I say why not today? If you say today at 5 o'clock, I say why not one o'clock?' [...] US Secretary of Navy Francis P. Matthews [...] in 1950 urged the nation to become 'aggressors for peace.' (Poundstone, 1993: 4-5)

In one of the many U-turns he underwent on the subject of nuclear war, in the early 1950s Russell reneged on the pacifism he had endorsed in both world wars and became known for numerous hawkish pronouncements in public lectures and letters to the military establishments in the US and UK:

> One must expect a war between USA and USSR which will begin with the total destruction of London. I think the war will last 30 years and leave a world without civilized people, from which everything will have to be built afresh – a process taking (say) 500 years. (Poundstone, 1993: 70)

> As I go about the street and see St. Paul's, the British Museum, the Houses of Parliament and the other monuments of our civilization, in my mind's eye I see a nightmare vision of those buildings as heaps of rubble with corpses all round them. (Poundstone, 1993: 71)

His extremism in this respect, a match for today's wildest Jihadist commands, is confirmed in a letter written in 1948 to Walter Marseille

> The Russians, even without atomic bombs, will be able to destroy all big towns in England [...]. I have no doubt that America would win in the end, but unless W. Europe can be preserved from invasion, it would be lost to civilization for centuries. *Even at such a price, I think war would be worthwhile. Communism must be wiped out, and world government must be established.* (Poundstone, 1993: 79, italics added)

With reference to the unleashing of planetary cataclysm, it is essential to consider, more recently, figures as influential as Ronald Reagan, president of what was soon to be the world's only superpower, in the aftermath of the collapse of the Soviet Union. Reagan, as will be discussed in detail in chapter 5, saw the Cold War as a cosmic struggle between good and evil and believed in the immanency and desirability of Armageddon as the preparation for the Kingdom of God on Earth (Berger, 1999: 135-37). More recently, following the epoch-changing events of 9/11, the Mayor of New York, Rudolph Giuliani addressed a population in a state of shock and warned that as the initial incomprehension gave way to a view of the raw facts, 'the number of casualties will be more than any of us can bear ultimately.' Sontag and Giuliani were dealing with both the real horror that already is with us, and with the unimaginable horror which might be: neither can be really understood because each is 'more than we can bear.' But if so, the inability or unwillingness either to confront or imagine what is unbearable may increase its likelihood, by undermining, apart from anything else, the safety net hoisted under the ideological infrastructure of nuclear power as the prime suspect in the potential unleashing of Armageddon. In order to be so afraid of it that we ensure it never happens, we first need to imagine it, to believe it really is possible. Nuclear deterrence, promoted as the best guarantee of peace, depends on a rationale that gambles on the preventive effects of actually envisaging the possibility of Mutually Assured Destruction (M.A.D.) and of truly grasping the likelihood that in a global thermonuclear conflict, everybody loses. The reasoning that informs the hypothesis of mutually assured destruction, therefore, rather than seeing nuclear weapons as a threat to peace, makes them its guarantor. Something, however, regarded by many, including Oppenheimer himself, as a flawed argument and an unacceptable risk.

The Russell-Einstein Manifesto was issued in London on 9 July 1955, at the height of the Cold War. It highlighted the dangers posed by nuclear weapons and called for world leaders to seek peaceful resolutions to international conflict. The signatories, eleven preeminent intellectuals and scientists, included Max Born, Linus Pauling, Joseph Rotblat, Bertrand Russell, and most notably, Albert Einstein, days before his death on 18 April 1955 (two days before Hitler's birthday):

> In the tragic situation which confronts humanity, we feel that scientists should assemble in conference to appraise the perils that have arisen as a result of the development of weapons of mass destruction, and to discuss a resolution. [...]
>
> We are speaking on this occasion, not as members of this or that nation, continent, or creed, but as human beings, members of the species Man, whose continued existence is in doubt. [...]
>
> We have to learn to think in a new way. We have to learn to ask ourselves, not what steps can be taken to give military victory to whatever group we prefer, for there no longer are such steps; the question we have to ask ourselves is: what steps can be taken to prevent a military contest of which the issue must be disastrous to all parties?
>
> The general public, and even many men in positions of authority, have not realized what would be involved in a war with nuclear bombs. The general public still thinks in terms of the obliteration of cities. [...]

> But this is one of the minor disasters that would have to be faced. If everybody in London, New York, and Moscow were exterminated, the world might, in the course of a few centuries, recover from the blow. But we now know [...] that nuclear bombs can gradually spread destruction over a very much wider area than had been supposed. [...]
>
> The best authorities are unanimous in saying that a war with H-bombs might possibly put an end to the human race. [...]
>
> Here, then, is the problem which we present to you, stark and dreadful and inescapable: Shall we put an end to the human race; or shall mankind renounce war? [...]
>
> We appeal as human beings to human beings: Remember your humanity, and forget the rest. If you can do so, the way lies open to a new Paradise; if you cannot, there lies before you the risk of universal death. (Einstein and Russell, 1955)

Or, as Marilynne Robinson put it more succinctly: 'This is an interesting planet. It deserves all the attention you can give it' (Robinson, 2006: 32).

At the opposite end of the tactical spectrum from the deterrent effect of M.A.D., the options are either forgetting the knowledge we already possess for achieving global destruction, which is not possible, or voluntary nonparticipation (unilateral, leading to universal, disarmament). To date, the voices of the signatories of the above manifesto remain untranslated into foreign policy, although their reasoning figures prominently in the cultural imagination.

Just a Terrible Accident: The Big Oops!

The *Bulletin of Atomic Studies* was founded after World War II by, among others, several of the physicists involved in the construction of the first atom bomb. Its cover always features a clock whose hands move closer to or further from midnight depending on the estimated likelihood of nuclear war starting somewhere in the world at the time of each issue going to press. They came closest to midnight in 1962, during the Cuban missile crisis, when President John F. Kennedy estimated the likelihood of nuclear war as being 'somewhere between one out of three and even' (Lebow and Stein, 1994, 5). War, however, was only ever one of several possible routes towards the end of life on the planet. 'The superpowers could have stumbled towards Armageddon through muddle and miscalculation' (Rees, 2003, 26). These words, from none other than Professor Sir Martin Rees, that most establishmentarian of figures (Astronomer Royal and sometime Master of Trinity College, Cambridge) introduce a long catalogue of possible pathways to global destruction, including a number *not* involving nuclear conflict (biohazards, unforeseen outcomes in robotics or nanotechnology, 'extreme risk' experimentation in the field of Physics or even accident) any of which could have and still might bring about the almost unimaginable. There are many ways to skin a cat. Or, as Robert Frost would have, albeit possibly with a somewhat different intent,

> Some say the world will end in fire,
> Some say in ice.
> From what I've tasted of desire
> I hold with those who favour fire.
> But if it had to perish twice,
> I think I know enough of hate
> To say that for destruction ice
> Is also great
> And would suffice. (Frost, 1920)

Either way, then, by fire or ice, intentionally or not, all too many roads lead to Nothing. What the notion of end of the world brought about by human error lacks in heroism (since it is not a case of honourable defeat by a mighty enemy) it makes up for in the scale of its uncontrollability (if we are our own worst enemies it is likely that we will not be able to keep ourselves in check or avoid making a mistake we cannot put right because we do not fully understand it). In John Badham's *WarGames* (1983) David Lightman is an intelligent, underachieving teenager (psycho-typically, although not in this film, the forerunner of the archetypal malcontent youth ripe for radicalization and for grooming in terrorism) who spends most of his free time playing arcade video games or surfing on his computer. During an automated modem search, he finds a program seemingly affiliated to a game company offering a list of games, the most exciting of which carries the title Global Thermonuclear War. Lightman begins to play, targeting his hometown of Seattle for missile strikes. In reality, Global Thermonuclear War is not a game but the War Operations Plan Response (W.O.P.R.) of the Pentagon, the computerized military system that selects and instigates the right response strategy in the event of a Soviet attack. The system had been previously set up to replace human initiative, which ironically, in a previous test situation, was seen to be fallible (due to hesitation on the part of commanding officers to press the button that would unleash war). As

Lightman begins to play the supposed game, in the situation room deep below Cheyenne Mountain, Colorado, the military believe a Soviet strike is underway. The source of the false command is traced, and Lightman is arrested and taken away for debriefing on the assumption that he is a Soviet agent. While under arrest, he realizes that the W.O.P.R. is still playing Global Thermonuclear War and unless stopped will unleash a full-scale counterattack. After much additional action involving Dr. Stephen Falken, the original creator of the program, and in a cliff-hanger ending, Lightman makes one last desperate attempt to stop the computer: he programs it to play an unwinnable game of noughts and crosses followed by successive permutations of all the possible nuclear scenarios, looking for a situation in which it can triumph. None being available, the computer decides on no action as the best option, and its voice system, addressing its creator, sums it up: 'A curious game, Professor Falken... The only winning move is not to play.' (Badham, 1983)

Not playing can mean not taking part in the game at all. An alternative scenario, however, might involve ending the game by check-mating the opponent. Within the framework of nuclear war, however, check-mate would mean that endgame really would be the *last* game. Or, in historical terms, the end of the world. In a real-world scenario not only are all the players – rather than just a single one – defeated but the game board itself is destroyed. Faced with this possibility, the only avoidance strategy (the lesson learnt after near-miss destruction) is that of nonparticipation, achievable either through the bilateral acceptance of the possibility of mutually assured destruction or by the logic that underlies the advocacy of nuclear disarmament.

Nonparticipation, however, just like the alternative, involves all sides knowingly *not* playing. In *WarGames* the missiles had originally been placed under computer control because an earlier blind trial had shown the likelihood that, in the event of a nuclear attack, a number of the officers in charge of launching them would in the end not do so. A similar scenario is presented in Russell Mulcahy's 2000 version of *On the Beach*, where Dwight Towers, the American nuclear submarine commander, disobeys (but in this case too late to avoid global catastrophe), the order to fire his missiles.

Even ultimate human unwillingness for destruction, therefore is not risk-free, but in any case, as discussed, even outside the sphere of terror, while the wherewithal of destruction exists, either unilaterally or bilaterally, the potential remains for human or machine error, as depicted not only in *WarGames*, but also in many other films, of which well-known examples are *Fail-Safe* (Lumet, 1964; Frears, 2000) and *By Dawn's Early Light* (Scholder, 1980).

Morality Is not Enough

In *Fail-Safe,* Stephen Frears's in many ways remarkable film of 2000 (a re-make of Sidney Lumet's earlier version released in 1964, shortly after the Cuban missile crisis), as in *WarGames*, error, not terror, sets in motion a chain of events which quickly go beyond the point of no return. Due to a computer failure, American nuclear bombers under the command of Colonel Jack Grady (George Clooney) are deployed against Moscow. Standard procedure means that in such a situation, once a predetermined fail-safe point has been passed, Grady, like all fighter bombers, is trained to ignore any order to abort the mission, even if the order appears to be issued by the voice of the President (which Soviet technology is known to be able to simulate). Interestingly, in this film the powers-that-be (the presidents of the USA and USSR) are both intelligent men, capable of reasoned persuasion and genuinely determined to work for the greater good, including, in a worst-case scenario, damage limitation in events that can no longer be controlled. Although the American President gives to his Soviet counterpart all the data necessary to destroy the US nuclear bombers before they reach Moscow, one plane, commandeered by Grady, gets through and will inevitably reach target. Faced with the inevitable, the two leaders come to a pragmatic, but even so (or perhaps because so) ghastly solution for avoiding the escalation of the conflict. An American nuclear bomber is ordered to assume attack position over the New York sky space and both the American Ambassador in Moscow and the American UN representative are asked to stand on the roofs of Ground Zero locations in each city with their mobile phones switched on. If the bomber heading for Moscow succeeds in getting through and dropping its bomb, the American President, as a demonstration of good faith will issue the order to his own chief bomber pilot (whose wife happens to be on a day-trip to Manhattan with the children) to drop his on New York. Ironically, in this film, there is no clear distinction between the good (Grady, charismatic widower, father of a young boy and ace bomber commander) and the bad/ugly (the militaristic dogs of war on both sides). The script sets up all the hallmarks of the in-the-nick-of-time, saved-by-the-seat-of-your-pants happy ending of standard Hollywood fare: the boy is orphaned of his mother and it is inconceivable he should also lose his heroic father; other charismatic characters stand to lose their nearest and dearest but only if sod's law prevails; valiant heroes (the American ambassador, the United Nations representative) are laid out as potential burnt offerings (in this case literally); the forces of good committed to a peaceful conclusion are actually the ones with their respective fingers on the nuclear buttons; and George Clooney is in charge. We also know that in the past, the widowed Grady and his son had shared a private code: to the question: 'Are you positive?' the answer: 'Only fools are positive' had been the means by which paradoxically, in situations of doubt, they assured one another that they really meant what they were saying. Now, as Grady is about to drop the bomb on Moscow, his hysterical son is put on the phone to his father, and assures him that the order he received was a mistake. They exchange their private code, but even so (and the reason for this is left unclear) Grady, unlike the bomber personnel in *WarGames*, follows established procedure and the bombs are dropped. The foreseen happy ending is not delivered, or at least not without a terrible price being paid.

By Dawn's Early Light (Scholder, released in 1990 and set in 1991) follows a very similar plot to *Fail-Safe*, and was the last film to depict the events of a fictional World War III, before the real-life collapse of the Soviet Union and the end of the Cold War. In this film, set in a Soviet Union undergoing turmoil and radical political change, a group of renegade Soviet military officers steal a nuclear missile and launch it towards Russia from Turkey. The Soviet city of Donetsk is destroyed by the stolen missile. When it hits, Soviet defense systems see that the weapon was launched from Turkey, and conclude that a NATO attack is in progress. In the aftermath of Soviet retaliation against the United States, and as required by a prior treaty between the US and China, the latter launches an attack against the Soviet border. Moments after the Soviet attack is launched, the Americans receive a teletype from their counterparts in the Soviet Union stating that they have now determined that the first missile was not launched by NATO. The Soviet Premier tells the US President that the Soviet Union will accept (without retaliating) a limited US counterstrike that will kill between six and nine million people. However, should the US counterstrike be any larger, the Soviets will have no choice but to retaliate in kind — meaning that an all-out nuclear exchange would almost certainly ensue. A convoluted plot develops, involving the mistaken belief in the death of the US President. Command of the Armed Forces is assumed by the Secretary of the Interior who orders a massive strike against the Soviet Union. In a nail-biting climax, the former President, discovered to be alive, orders the destruction of Air Force One, the Secretary of the Interior's command plane, with seconds to spare before the order is issued to escalate the nuclear conflict.

Figure 11. Albrecht Dürer, *Four Riders of the Apocalypse*

The disturbing scenarios of these two films, both featuring as their central protagonists the men with their fingers on the nuclear button, are the manifestation in popular culture of widely prevailing fears in an era which began with the detonation of the bombs in Hiroshima and Nagasaki. *Fail-Safe* (Frears, 2000) concludes idealistically, or at least with the safeguarding of a least-bad resolution: in a short dialogue between the two leaders, to the question of what to say to the survivors in their respective nations, the reply is 'We will tell them that it will never happen again.' An assurance which, however, is immediately belied by the scrolling on screen of a long list of countries which, at the time of the film's release, controlled nuclear weapons. The balance of the equation is not reassuring, relying, as it does, on the willingness of two conflicting nuclear powers to agree to acts of large-scale national self-sacrifice (one city each, in the case of *Fail-Safe*, millions of dead in the case of *By Dawn's Early Light*, in either case with the short-term result of almost certain political suicide for each leader). There are many ways of shooting oneself in the foot, and the likelihood that the foot would be sacrificed in order to save the leg is not necessarily the most likely choice. One would not wish to hedge one's bets on the possibility of the wicked stepmother suddenly coming to see Snow White's good points. Or vice-versa.

The trope of a global problem is maintained in many recent and not so recent narratives and films on the theme of the end of the world, an extreme example being Olaf Stapledon's *Last and First Men* (1999) which deals with the emergence and extinction of eighteen different human species over a period of two billion years, or his *Star Maker* (Stapledon, 1999), in which the eponymous demiurge serially creates and obliterates worlds in different cosmoses throughout infinite time, in the pursuit of aesthetic perfection. Stapledon's philosophical take on the hidden cause of random cataclysms is not, however, the standard fare of apocalyptic science fiction which overall tends to stay closer to home both intellectually and as regards cosmic geography. A very early text by Simon Newcomb, *The End of the World* [1903] (1976) sees a professor and a small group of his companions emerge from a subterranean chamber to discover that the surface of the Earth has been destroyed by a collision with another planet, a catastrophe they attribute to the agency of a higher power that directs the cyclical creation and annihilation of successive orders of Being.

Often, in narratives of apocalypse, from Genesis to the most recent science fiction, only hypothetical explanations are offered for the original disaster, broadly encompassed within what the entertainingly shared vocabulary of theology and insurance companies calls Acts of God (with no accepted liability in either case). As is also often the case with these narratives, an initial raindrop quickly builds up to a flood (a widespread catastrophe). In José Saramago's *Blindness* (1997), to be discussed, the affliction in question begins with one isolated case, subsequently spreads to a few people and rapidly becomes generalized. In John Wyndham's *The Day of the Triffids* ([1951], 1984), on the other hand, near-universal blindness is instantaneous, leading to the gradual revelation that a small minority has been spared. The significance of that minority will be the subject of chapter 3.

They're Behind You!

Science fiction, particularly but not only in its apocalyptic sub-genre, is almost always allegorical and political. 1950s American communist paranoia ghoulishly translated real life episodes (the execution of Julius and Ethel Rosenberg, the McCarthy witch hunts), into large-audience books and films. The urgency of political purging endured well beyond the 1950s, and in fiction and film it was only moderately exaggerated, then as now. The spirit as well as the intent remain the same, and urge action against the danger of the alien, the other. *Any* other. But in fact we all know whom we mean, of course, then and now. Or do we?

In science fiction, just like in standard blockbuster horror movies, the depiction of the unknown alien has benefited from the scariest achievements of special effects. Paradoxically, however, the more alien (ie. unbelievable) the alien, the less likely it is to achieve a lasting effect of fear. Thus, archetypal invaders from outer space (in *Alien*, Scott, 1979; *Armageddon*, Bay, 1998; *Independence Day*, Emmerich, 1996; *War of the Worlds*, Spielberg , 2005) in general cannot match the potential horror of a threat rendered in the vocabulary and within the realm of the familiar (*Rosemary's Baby*, Polanski, 1968; *To the Devil a Daughter*, Sykes, 1976; *The Omen*, Donner, 1976). And in any case sometimes, of course, though not often, the alien is amiable (*Close Encounters of the Third Kind*, Spielberg, 1977) or downright lovable (*E.T.*, Spielberg, 1982). The latter two cases, however, are uncommon. At best the alien, as will be discussed presently, is cruel in order to be kind (*The Day the Earth Stood Still*, Wise, 1951) but, more commonly, it is cruel because it wishes or needs to be, usually in order to make a political point.

The first version of the now cult film *Invasion of the Body Snatchers*, made in 1956 at the height of the McCarthy era, did not trouble to conceal (what, indeed, would have been its point otherwise?) an unsubtle gesture towards a perceived enemy close to home, namely the Red under the bed. Based on the novel *The Body Snatchers* by Jack Finney (originally serialized in *Colliers Magazine* in 1954 and published as a novel in 1955) the film has had three re-makes. It was selected for preservation in the United States National Registry by the Library of Congress as being culturally, historically, or aesthetically significant and in an American Film Institute poll of 1,500 people from the creative community in 2008, it was ranked among the top ten best films in the science fiction genre. In the first version, set in the fictional town of Santa Mira, California, the locals are gradually being replaced by perfect simulacra grown from plant-like pods that kill and dispose of their human victims. The Pod People, who are indistinguishable from normal people except by their lack of emotion, work together to spread more pods — grown originally from seeds that drifted into the Earth's atmosphere from outer space — with the aim of eventually replacing the entire human race. The film climaxes with a seemingly crazed hero, the local doctor, running onto the highway frantically screaming to the passing motorists about the alien force. In a moment that breaks the 'fourth wall' rule in film (a character revealing consciousness of the audience, abolishing its protective separateness and thus dragging it into the 'reality' of the film) he looks into the camera and shouts 'They're here already! You're next!'

In a subsequent version favoured by the studio because it left greater grounds for optimism, the story is told in flashback and begins with the hero about to be sent to a psychiatric hospital. He tells a doctor his story and, in the closing scene, pods are discovered at a highway accident, thus confirming his warning. The FBI is notified, but at the end of the film doubt remains as to whether they intervene in time to save the Earth.

In the more famous 1978 version starring Donald Sutherland, the central character watches a gathering which suggests that the aliens have succeeded in taking over. Matthew, the central character, watches dozens of children being led into a dark theatre to be transformed. Later he is spotted by Nancy, the sole other survivor of the take-over. Supposing, as indeed the audience still does, that he is human, she walks towards him. Matthew responds by pointing to her and emitting the piercing pod scream that will alert the other Pod people. Nancy is left alone and helpless. It is unclear whether she will survive or indeed whether that has any relevance in a world in which, even if she did, she might be the last human being left.

Invasion of the Body Snatchers is representative of a number of literary and film renditions of similar themes, two obvious examples being first, and already embedded in literary and cinematic tradition, the genre of possession or transformation of individual human beings by alien entities, whether demonic, vampiric, werewolfish or other; and second, the theme of alien usurpation of the dominance until that point claimed by humanity as a species. Given the vast bibliography already accumulated on the first category, what follows will concentrate on the second, of which *Invasion of the Body Snatchers* is a canonic example. It is worth pausing briefly, however, to consider three versions of the traditional vampire genre which, like plots of alien-invasion, puts forward the politicizing motif of the insurrection of erstwhile minorities against preexisting statuses quo.

Sickness and Health

First, the box office sensation *I Am Legend* of 2007, directed by Francis Lawrence from Richard Matheson's novel of 1954, in which, an epidemic of bacteria brought into existence in the aftermath of nuclear war turns everyone on Earth into vampires. The last remaining man, Robert Neville, like Nancy in *Invasion of the Body Snatchers*, lives life under a state of siege, which concludes with his realization at the end of the film, just prior to his barricades being overrun by invading hordes of vampires, that normality is always a relative concept, and, at any given moment definable merely as that which the majority (in this case vampires) agree it is. In this radically changed world, therefore, vampirism becomes the norm and Neville himself, the eponymous singularity, is destined for legend.

A similar logic operates in Walter M. Miller's short story, 'Dark Benediction' (2007) and in the series of young adult novels by Stephenie Meyer, the *Twilight* books, which have also been adapted for the cinema. 'Dark Benediction' is not strictly speaking a vampire story, but the concept that structures it is similar to that underpinning tales of vampirism. A mysterious condition which produces dark blemishes in the skin (epidermis) of its sufferers ('dermies') also induces in them urges of physical affection and a desire to caress the uncontaminated, thus transmitting the condition. In *Twilight*, a Romeo and Juliet plot with minor modifications, two teenagers from groups which habitually are mortal enemies (humans and vampires), fall in love. In these last examples (and possibly even in *I Am Legend*, Matheson, 1954) however, unlike in standard vampire plots, instead of the usual moral demarcations (vampires and the diseased are bad and best avoided for fear of contamination), ambiguity is allowed to prevail. In 'Dark Benediction' (Miller, 2007) Paul falls in love with the contagious Willie and after some internal struggle touches her so as to become like her. In *Twilight* (Meyer, 2007) non-vampire Bella wishes to become a vampire for the love of Edward who is one, while Edward wishes to prevent this happening, for love of her. And although no such suggestion is clearly made in *I Am Legend* (Matheson, 1954), it might reasonably be argued that ultimately, for the hero, being caught and bitten by the vampires would be a happier option than life behind barricades as the last non-vampire left on Earth.

Definitions of good and evil, right and wrong, desirable and undesirable (and by implication the validity of customary social definitions of self and other) are therefore left in question in these three narratives. And, by implication, although at the end it is clear that vampires and 'dermies' are still at best a persecuted oddity and at worst a danger to the commonweal as it had previously understood itself, neither of those definitions will necessarily or even probably endure. At any given point we may think we know what is right and wrong and we may even accept collateral damage as an inevitable price worth paying in order to preserve one and exclude the other. Persecution, following this principle, may lead to the elimination of some innocents but is seen to be ethical because it guarantees the good of the commonweal, even if it carries a dimension of silent disquiet: namely, that what we would normally consider unquestionable may not actually be so).

That disquiet, nonetheless, once articulated, persists: is it really better to shun (quarantine) or (if they resist it) cull the other? What about plague victims or lepers? Or sufferers of tuberculosis or AIDS? The logic that once underpinned assumptions we now regard as morally dubious also underpins much of what we still believe. If vampires or werewolves existed, we might hesitate to grant them equal rights, but who's to say we would be right?

Different Normalities

Returning to the genre of science fiction as the central concern here, similar ethical irresolutions (from all ends of the ideological spectrum) as well as a revisionist logic regarding what is both normal and good operate in some of the best works of science fiction/horror, including texts such as Brazilian writer Lygia Fagundes Telles's 'Rat Seminar' and 'The Ants' (1986), Michael Crichton's ferocious anti-Green movement diatribe, *State of Fear* (2005) and John Wyndham's masterpieces, *The Day of the Triffids*, *The Kraken Wakes* ([1953] 1980), *The Chrysalids* ([1955] 1984), *The Midwich Cuckoos* ([1957] 1984) and, less well known, *Web* ([1979] 1983), many of which were subsequently made into films. All share a common thread: the possibility that in the future, as the logic of evolution makes likely, the supremacy of the human species might be lost either to another species or to a variant, more advanced form of *homo sapiens*.

In Fagundes Telles's two short stories, following orthodox Darwinian reasoning, the outcome of varying conditions results in the possibility of two species previously treated by humans as vermin (rats and ants) taking over the world. 'Rat Seminar,' first published in Portuguese in Brazil in 1977 tells of a conference (the seventh to date) convened by the Brazilian government (but including representatives of the USA and other nations) to discuss the problem of rats which are rapidly taking over the country, and possibly the planet. In a nation under a state of emergency in which rats number one hundred per capita of the population, the political profile is revealed as that of a right-wing regime which, as had been the case in real life in the past in a Latin American context, welcomes American intervention in its affairs. As the population struggles against a rodent take-over which is already threatening food and utilities supplies, the representatives of the various governments meet in an isolated luxury mansion, refurbished at vast expense for that purpose. Criticism from the press is dismissed as a conspiracy between left-wing interests and the rats. The story opens with a young Public Relations officer reporting to his boss, the Secretary of State for Public and Private Well Being (revealed, as a by-the-way, as having been involved in two real-life right-wing coups in the past) on details pertaining to the luxurious arrangements available to the delegates (choice foods and wines, including an expensive *Pinochet* vintage, a heated swimming pool filled with coconut milk, private jets for use of the participants). The Secretary of State, who fittingly suffers from gout (an affliction culturally associated with life-long self-indulgence) is installed in accommodation whose expensive décor includes a statue representing Justice, blind-folded and holding the conventional sword and scales. In the course of the conversation a number of facts transpire: first, that the rat problem is not confined to Brazil and is now prevalent the world over, even in environments as inhospitable as the North Pole, where rats have mutated and now have long fur; second, that information is released to the Press and the public on a strictly censored and revised basis, presenting the situation as fully under governmental and military control; and third, that in reality, rats are now in control of large parts of the country, where hunger has led people (somewhat counter-productively) to eat the cat population. As the conversation continues, an unidentified rumbling noise increases in volume. Further investigation reveals that the rats have infiltrated the mansion, chewed up the telephone wires, devoured all the food and are now beginning to threaten the residents. As the situation reaches cataclysmic proportions, all the lights go out and those who can, escape. The young PR officer, in an attempt to avoid becoming rat fodder, seeks refuge, ironically, in a fridge. After sometime he succeeds in escaping. A subsequent de-briefing discloses the situation he left behind:

> He walked through the empty house, hollowed out, no furniture, no curtains, no carpets. Just the walls. And the darkness. Then a mysterious noise began, scratchy, seemingly from the Conference Room and he realized that [the rats] were there, meeting behind closed doors. He couldn't even remember how he got outside, he would never fully recall how he ran, he ran for miles. When he looked back, the mansion was all lit up. (Telles, 1986: 86)

'The Ants' (Telles, 1986) involves two young women – a medical student and a lawyer – who are driven out of their accommodation by fear of ants which, in the dark of night, emerge from their nest and are gradually reassembling the skeleton of a dwarf whose bones had been left by a previous occupant in a box under one of their beds. As in 'Rat Seminar,' the suggestion of a power take-over carries similar ideological implications: the representatives-in-the-making of the status quo (in this case not of political power but of medicine and the law) are displaced by those previously deemed to be lesser beings, literally as regards size (in the case of both ants and dwarves) and status (vermin, medical anomalies). The implications are not necessarily lacking in ambiguity. As the disempowered replace the powerful, the ethos, nevertheless, remains unchanged: power is claimed by force and is exercised through violence by those previously ostracized by the outgoing status quo. In the new world coming into shape following the ousting of the powers-that-were, and in line with most narratives of apocalypse, as discussed in chapter 3, the cast may change but the script does not.

The Winning Gene

The thread that links Fagundes Telles's onslaught on representations of the political and decision-making strata (the educated, professional middle classes) to some of John Wyndham's most successful works is the concept not just or not principally of strength in size and/or numbers but also intellect (the capacity for reasoned methodology) as the weapon of choice in the battle for the survival of the fittest. If what granted supremacy to humans as a species was intelligence, it stands to reason that that, too, will be the factor that in due course will most likely lead to its overthrow. In *The Midwich Cuckoos*, *The Day of the Triffids*, *The Kraken Wakes* and *The Chrysalids*, the battle lines are drawn according to the criterion not of physical but of intellectual supremacy (and may include the concept of collective intelligence). In all these novels, the power of organized groups to overcome unusual odds invites any number of interpretations. Central to them all, however, lies the presupposition that the weak chain in humanity's dominance is individualism, an inbuilt trait which may in the long term limit communication and the transfer of knowledge, thus obstructing collective species interests. Whether articulated through the discourse of politics, science or ethics, the message, in much science fiction, appears to be that divided we cannot rule. Or at least not for long.

The Midwich Cuckoos is set within the eponymous Midwich, a typical small English rural village. Some months after an unexplained forty-eight hour period during which the entire village falls into a deep sleep and remains isolated from outside contact, a follow-up study reveals that every woman of child-bearing age in the village is pregnant, with all indications that the pregnancies were initiated during the 'Dayout.'

When the children, half of each sex, are born they are all identical, and, although somewhat unusual in appearance, seemingly normal. As they grow, however (at more than twice the normal rate of human children), it becomes apparent that they are in some respects not normal. They possess telepathic capacities which include the ability to force their will on others and to control their actions and body functions. They share two distinct composite or group minds, male and female. When one child of either sex learns something, all the others of the same sex share that knowledge without needing to acquire it individually. As a group, therefore, their learning capacity far exceeds even exceptional human capability. A number of small incidents show that if threatened or even if mistakenly perceiving a threat, the children (now generally referred to as the Children, with a capital 'C') will defend themselves, usually with disproportionate strength. In any conflict situation their unusual control over the minds and actions of others means they always win. In due course it transpires that the 'Midwich Dayout' was not an isolated incident, others having occurred elsewhere in the world. It quickly becomes apparent that the survival of humanity as the dominant species can only be maintained by means of the extermination of the Children (something carried out without qualms in other places, including one group in an Inuit settlement north of Canada and two behind the Iron Curtain, but deemed unacceptable in civilized England). The problem is articulated by the Children themselves in simple Darwinian terms:

> Sooner or later you will try to kill us. However we behave you will want to wipe us out. [...] It is a biological obligation. You cannot afford *not* to kill us, for if you don't, you are finished. [...] If we exist, we shall dominate you – that is clear and inevitable. Will you agree to be superseded and start on the way to extinction without a struggle? (Wyndham, [1957] 1984: 196-99)

In *The Day of the Triffids* a similar confrontation with group force threatens the wipeout of humanity. A meteorological phenomenon never fully explained, and therefore conceivably originating either in human error or in natural cataclysm, results in widespread blindness, not only in London, where the novel is initially set, but, as it will transpire, worldwide. One of Wyndham's great strengths as a writer of science fiction is that he resists the urge to explain the bizarre, thus avoiding the silly or cockeyed endings that characterize much of the genre. In *The Day of the Triffids* the possibility is vented, although never offered as more than that, that the shower of 'comets' whose light emissions led to blindness was not a meteorological phenomenon but the result of scientific enterprise gone wrong (radiation accidentally released by one of the many satellites of various nationalities known to be circling the Earth for military, scientific and commercial purposes). Whatever the reason, near-universal blindness in humans offers the opportunity for the triffids – a recently recorded species of largely harmless plants of unknown origin and farmed worldwide for their valuable oils – to embark upon a global take-over of the planet. The fact that their preferred mode of attack is to blind by striking out at the eyes of its victims with poison-laden tentacles suggests at the very least an affinity between a seemingly natural phenomenon (the shower of comets) and a natural phenomenon put to unnatural use (the mass cultivation of a plant species of unknown – possibly extra-terrestrial – origin for commercial gain). The fact that the 'comet' might have had human origin but triffids may be aliens with some anthropomorphic qualities (they walk, they seemingly talk or at least communicate with one another) but not others (unlike humans, in the pursuit of vital resources they operate as a group rather than in competition with one another) offers a comment on the long-term viability of humanity as a species. As a group the triffids force an understanding of human characteristics such as the gift for scientific endeavour (the use of satellites) and the urge towards commercial endeavour (the cultivation of profitable species) which, unless harnessed, will ultimately act against humanity, effectively propelling it along a reverse trajectory down a path from advanced civilization to Stone Age barbarity.

> Up there […] there were – and maybe there still are – unknown numbers of satellite weapons circling round and round the Earth. […] Now suppose that one type happened to have been constructed to emit radiations [..] that would […] damage the optic nerve […] Then suppose there were a mistake, or perhaps an accident […]. But – that somehow or other one thing I'm quite certain of – that somehow or other we brought this lot down on ourselves. (Wyndham, [1951] 1984: 247)

Whatever the case may be, the contest between humans and triffids is played out according to the script of atavistic jungle warfare in which the outcome will be the subjection of either to the other. In the course of this, even victory for humankind will come at the price of a backslide in prior evolutionary achievement ('the first generation labourers; the next, savages,' Wyndham, 1984: 260), back to an earlier stage of existence defined by the struggle for survival:

> Where *everybody* has to work hard just to get a living and there is no leisure to think, knowledge stagnates, and people with it.[…] A [small] community cannot hope to do more than exist and decline. […] If there are children we shall be able to spare only enough time from our labour to give them just a rudimentary education; one generation further, and we shall have savages or clods. (Wyndham, [1951] 1984: 204)

Wyndham's gloomy prophecy for life post-apocalypse has been echoed repeatedly in survival literature in film and fiction (for example the cult BBC series *Survivors*, Nation, 1975-77; Hodges, 2008-10) and nonfiction writing, an example of the latter being James Lovelock's (of 'Gaia theory' fame) urgent support for 'the compilation of a 'start up manual for civilization,' copies of which should be dispersed widely enough to ensure that some would survive almost any eventuality' (Rees, 2003: 24). In *The Day of the Triffids* the point is driven home succinctly:

> [...] we'll have to plough, still later we'll have to learn how to make plough-shares, later than that we'll have to learn how to smelt iron to make the shares. What we are on now is a road that will take us back and back and back until we can – *if* we can – make good all that we wear out. Not until then shall we be able to stop ourselves on the trail that's leading down to savagery. But once we can do that, then maybe we'll begin to crawl slowly up again. (Wyndham, [1951] 1984: 203-04)

The same rationale determines the final outcome in *The Kraken Wakes* and *The Chrysalids*. The former describes escalating phases of what appears to be an alien invasion. In the first phase, objects from outer space land in the ocean. Journalists Mike and Phyllis Watson, while on honeymoon, happen to witness the event. For a while the phenomenon is not recognized as an alien arrival, and even when it is, conflict initially does not appear inevitable. The alien visitors appear to require conditions of extreme pressure to be found only in the deepest parts of the ocean, an area of the planet of no interest to human beings, which indicates that the two species might coexist indefinitely. An early investigation of the phenomenon by means of a bathysphere, however, results in the latter's destruction by the deep-sea visitors, using unknown technology. Escalating hostilities provoked by the sinking of several ships and the retaliatory explosion of nuclear devices in the oceanic deeps initiate Phase Two, with massive attacks on ships, blockades on world shipping routes, and invasions of coastal communities by unknown sea tanks, followed by Phase Three which sees the aliens melting the ice caps, causing sea levels to rise and worldwide flooding, ultimately leading to social and political collapse. By the time an ultrasonic device capable of destroying the enemy is developed, most of the Earth's surface is under water and the world population has been reduced to less than a fifth of its previous size. Although in the end victorious, humanity is forced to the conclusion that it had been forced to engage in a primeval struggle in which only one side could triumph.

> [...] the situation I had hoped we could avoid now exists – and is in the process of being resolved. Two intelligent life forms are finding one another's existence intolerable. [...] any intelligent form dominates by, and therefore survives by, its intelligence: a rival form of intelligence must, by its very existence, threaten to dominate, and therefore threaten extinction. [...] The same urge drives them as drives us – the necessity to exterminate or be exterminated. (Wyndham, [1953] 1980: 180-81)

The Chrysalids echoes the problem outlined in *The Midwich Cuckoos*. A new form of intelligence, this time originating not in alien invasion but in mutation, can only survive in clandestinity. In a world in which, centuries after what appears to have been a large-scale nuclear war (something which, in the absence of surviving historical records, is remembered only as the myth of tribulation, a possible reference to Biblical annihilation in Daniel 9: 27) human society struggles to suppress deviancy (mutation) or even difference. Any human, animal or plant life deemed not to conform to purity standards is destroyed. The central characters, a group of children in possession of telepathic gifts which in some ways resemble the composite mind of the Midwich children, understand the danger they would face should their deviancy be uncovered.

> Still our whole consideration if we were to survive must be to keep our true selves hidden. To walk, talk and live indistinguishably from other people. (Wyndham, [1955] 1984: 86)

In both these novels, as in *The Day of the Triffids*, the perceived danger to the status quo lies in the superior power of group effort in the face of a habitually fragmented, divided, individualistic status quo. What is recognized as the adversary's strength (superior abilities in group communication) in fact defines the nature of the wider social group's weaknesses: a tendency for competition rather than collaboration, divisiveness rather than cooperation, and, paradoxically, the determination to survive as a rigidly defined group rather than a willingness to permit the dissolution of the barriers that divide self from other. The implications, when translated into the pragmatic interactions between nation-states, political groups and definitions of social ethics, need no further elaboration. It has been evidenced, most recently, in the Middle East (Egypt, Syria, Iran), by the power of mobile phones, e-mail and twitter for the purposes of enabling resistance and revolution.

The Light at the End of the Tunnel…

… as per Robert Lowell's cynical suggestion, may be that of an on-coming train. In Kurt Vonnegut's classic, *God Bless You, Mr. Rosewater* (Vonnegut, 1992), the end of the galaxy is envisaged in a novel-within-a-novel authored by Kilgore Trout, a failed science fiction writer encountered by the central protagonist, Eliot Rosewater. In Trout's novel, the Earthling protagonist who has travelled to the end of the universe is offered short-leave to go back to Earth because there has been a death at home. The chilling answer to the enquiry as to who has died is 'It isn't *who* has died. It's *what* has died. What's died, my boy, is the Milky Way' (Vonnegut, 1992: 173-74). But not really, of course. Not even in Vonnegut is the ultimate fear of galactic destruction seriously entertained, other than within safe limits, namely in a fictional work at twice-remove, by a fictional failed writer destined never to be taken seriously.

Instead, in science fiction, the end of the world, or its near-miss, as a rule are either dealt with ironically or not at all. Within the genre of lampoon, Douglas Adams's novels in the series *The Hitchhiker's Guide to the Galaxy* (Adams, 1979) also satirize the prospect of apocalypse without even the vestige of unease that prevails at the end of Kubrick's *Dr. Strangelove or: How I Learned to Stop Worrying and Love the Bomb* (Kubrick, 1964). In *So Long, and Thanks for All the Fish* (Adams, 1984), Ford Prefect claims to have saved the universe from destruction just in time. Accompanied by him, Arthur Dent, the Earthling anti-hero, takes a friend to the planet where God's Final Message to His Creation is written. With the help of Marvin, the paranoid android, he finally deciphers it and reads the following: 'We apologize for the inconvenience' (Adams, 1984: 201-02). In this eccentric scenario of the end of the world, the pity of it all is that, faced with global extinction, the prevailing emotion on the part of a polite computer is mild embarrassment. Things could not get much worse.

The end of the world as spectacle, and again as a tale within a tale, removes all possibility of fear from other plots whose intention, like Adams's, is ostentatiously to provoke laughter: in Catherine L. Moore's 'Vintage Season' (Moore, 1989) and Robert Silverberg's 'When We Went to See the End of the World' (Silverberg, 1989), for example, time-travelers take holidays to the past to witness the Earth's final moments and the aftermath of nuclear war.

Panic Laughter

Resorting to irony, satire and lampoon does not of course exclude (and may indeed reinforce) the possibility that these satirical examples, like other more deadpan fictions of apocalypse, maybe be direct responses to the anxieties of a given epoch. In Margaret Atwood's *The Handmaid's Tale* (Atwood, 1991) the postscript to the novel is set at an academic conference of historians whose area of expertise is the historical period described in the diegetic occurrences of the novel. Academic discourse regarding the events documented in the Handmaid's account of life in the Republic of Gilead is both caricatured and caricatures or at least distances itself from the emotional intensity of the narrative's events, through a combination of documentary objectivity academic pedantry and paternalistic humour regarding a chronologically-remote historical period now regarded with professional detachment. Scholarly superciliousness reduces the Handmaid's harrowing account to an archeological tableau documenting the aftermath of a seismic shift in human society following an unspecified nuclear conflict in the distant past. And even in novels of apocalypse on a grand scale, such as James Blish's *A Clash of Cymbals* (Blish, 1974) or Poul Anderson's *Tau Zero* (Anderson, 2006), which envisage not just the destruction of the planet but of the entire universe, a get-out clause opens the doors to new cosmoses. In all these authors, as will be discussed in more detail in chapter 3, the implication of the aftermath of large-scale cataclysm is that of an eventual new beginning. The notion that perhaps in the gap between each cycle of being and nothingness 'all that will be left is two worlds, one dead and the other powerless to be born' (Seed, 2000, 5) almost always appears remote, a philosophical hypothesis rather than anything with conceivable empirical manifestations.

Really Meaning It

Rare exceptions to this rule of vestigial hope are Mordecai Roshwald's 1959 novel, *Level 7*, adapted for television by J.B. Priestley in 1966, Nevil Shute's *On the Beach* of 1957, twice made into a film, and Kevin Brockmeier's *The Brief History of the Dead* (2006). In *Level 7* the unnamed protagonist lives underground, on level 7 (the deepest) of a bunker-style military complex, where he is expected to reside permanently, fulfilling the role of commanding his nation's nuclear weapons. During his forced residence, a technical error results in the order to deliver the bomb that unleashes World War III. All surviving civilian life moves from the surface of a now radioactive Earth to a collection of underground shelter complexes (levels 1-5). Military personnel occupy levels 6 and 7. At the end of the novel, due to another mechanical malfunction, all remaining life, including that at level 7 is destroyed, the result being an absolute wipe-out.

Similarly, in Nevil Shute's *On the Beach* (Shute, 1974), set in Australia in the aftermath of a radioactive (cobalt as well as nuclear) conflict which has already destroyed the entire northern hemisphere, the remnants of animal (including human) and plant life live out the time that is left while they wait for the inevitable end, as radiation works its way down to the southern hemisphere on the planet's wind systems. In Shute's uncompromising scenario (made the crueller because conveyed through the point of view of characters almost uniformly characterized by painfully limited imaginations) a new beginning is not conceivable. The constraints of radioactivity with a half-life of thousands of years, together with the improbability that the necessary environmental and biological contingencies might ever again coincide, means that ultimately the possibility of new life on Earth is nonexistent.

And in Brockmeier's elegiac universe, the dead move into a state of limbo ('the City') which in all respects resembles everyday life: people live in houses, shop, work, make friends. They remain there while there is anyone left on Earth who remembers them. When the last person that does so dies, the dead finally move on to a not very clearly defined final destination. The plot focuses both on life in 'the City' and on Laura Byrd, a wildlife specialist employed by Coca Cola in a near future, at a time when the polar ice caps have begun to melt and many species have already become extinct. Following a global viral epidemic which rapidly kills all human life on Earth, Laura survives because she is the last of an expedition to the Antarctic, where, due to the low temperatures, the virus is ineffective. Laura's struggle against the elements and her eventual death will consign all the remaining inhabitants of 'the City' (whose varying links to her had ensured their enduring presence in the afterlife) to final oblivion. It is unclear whether, in a planet previously threatened by ecological disaster and terrorism (including environmental attacks), life in any form will be preserved on the planet.

The Magnitude of the Imagined End

In depicting the end of the world in film, marked cultural differences are to be found between Great Britain and the United States, partly driven, in the case of the former, by budgetary constraints on large-scale cinematic special effects. Thus, while the vast resources of the Hollywood film industry can afford to meet the demands of *grand-récit* production, in the former, the actual unfolding of apocalypse often remains a backdrop to individual tragedy. As Charles E. Gannon observes, in global disaster narratives made in the UK, unlike those made in the US,

> there is an unwillingness to step back to acquire a macroscopic view of the calamity. Accordingly, in *Threads* – and also in *The War Game* (1965) and in *The Bed-Sitting Room* (1969) – the audience is never provided with a bird's

eye look at the end of the world. The scale on which we witness the effects of the bomb never exceeds the devastation of individual buildings; the scope never expands to show a larger landscape. [...] Each view is intimate. (Gannon, 2000: 104)

In *On the Beach* (Shute, 1954), set in Australia but penned by an author with cultural roots still firmly planted in England's green and pleasant land, the wait for unavoidable annihilation is a simulacrum of normality (giving and attending dinner parties, home decoration, the planting of gardens that will never grow in a future that will never come). The last American nuclear submarine left on Earth, on a mission to Australia at the time of the conflict's outbreak, is left stranded in the southern hemisphere. In due course the exiled sailors make an exploratory journey back north to confirm what is already known: the death of the planet, through radioactive contamination. Back in Australia, the submarine commander, representative of a humanity soon to be entirely obliterated, buys presents to 'take back' to a wife and children whom he knows, but in thought and deed does not acknowledge to be dead. As the radiation drift approaches, he enacts the definitive representation of silent denial: he takes his submarine off shore, sinks it and goes down with it, refusing all non-Navy company (including his close friend Moira) because 'Uncle Sam wouldn't like it' (Shute, 1974: 276).

Although some American renditions of the end of the world (*The Day After*, Meyer, 1983, *The Day After Tomorrow*, Emmerich, 2004, *Armageddon*, Bay, 1998, *Independence Day*, Emmerich, 1996), just like smaller-scale disaster movies, preserve an initial attempt at audience identification by providing subplots that present certain characters as individuals ('people like us') going about their daily lives, the scale is quickly broadened to a panoptic view of mass destruction. In *Level 7* (Roshwald, 1959), for example, while global destruction is narrated from the intimate perspective (the diary) of the last man on Earth, his deindividuation (he is a soldier who, while being the first person narrator is known only as X-127) makes him also an archetype in a wide-span narrative.

Would You Believe It?

This section addresses the question of incredulity in the face of the unimaginable. In José Saramago's fiction of apocalypse, *Blindness*, also made into a film (Meirelles, 2008), and discussed at greater length in chapter 3, disbelief is the ruling emotion in the face of the moral consequences of disaster. Incredulity, and failed attempts at explaining the origins of the event are also central to *The Stone Raft*, an earlier novel by the same author (Saramago, 1996), in which the Iberian Peninsula breaks away from the rest of Europe and floats away into the Atlantic. Ensuing events are conveyed from a multiplicity of viewpoints: those of the characters experiencing them, a narrator reporting upon them to an unidentified audience and a third voice, possibly that of the author, which addresses itself directly to the reader but sometimes appears sceptical about the truth of its own narrative. The discovery of something which under moonlight looks like a stone ship but in the light of day is just a pile of stones is given a variety of explanations by different people, ranging from the geological to the fantastic, the effect being the ultimate dismissal of the possibility of ascertaining reality or truth in a world which in the past had taken both for granted. They, however, like the erstwhile peninsula's geographical status (it is now an island of sorts) and location (it is not fixed to the seabed but floats) have now become uncertain. The world, at the most comically literal of levels, has become a moveable feast and what in the past was reality no longer makes sense.

Uncertainty, regarding not necessarily specific events or their immediate causes but, to some extent, their remote origins and longer-term consequences are also central issues in Mimi Leder's film of 1998, *Deep Impact*. The world is threatened by an extinction-level event (E.L.E.): a seven-mile wide comet, named 'Wolf-Biederman' after the two people who discovered it, is on a collision course with Earth and is large enough for the impact to destroy all life on the planet. A joint American and Russian endeavour (the political message is unsubtle) dispatches a crew of astronauts on a spaceship portentously named Messiah to destroy the comet, using nuclear weapons. After some mishaps and loss of life among the crew of the *Messiah*, the bombs are detonated but the comet, albeit split into two chunks, is not destroyed. President Beck, a black man whose race, at the time of the film's release (exactly ten years before the election of Barack Obama) was by no means the least outlandish aspect of the film, acknowledges *Messiah*'s failure and announces that the government will conduct a lottery to select 800,000 ordinary Americans to join 200,000 preselected doctors, nurses, scientists, engineers, teachers, lawyers, writers, artists, soldiers, officials and representatives of key occupations. Together, they will be conveyed to underground shelters previously built in limestone caves in Missouri (back then with a possible nuclear attack in mind). These people will be part of a worldwide effort to save life on Earth from extinction. As the smaller of the two comet chunks ('Biederman') hits the Atlantic Ocean near Virginia Beach, creating a giant global tsunami, the world braces itself for the impact of the remaining portion of the comet, predicted to strike western Canada and create a cloud of dust that will block out the sun for two years, killing all remaining plant, animal, and human life forms other than those evacuated to the caves. The crew members of *Messiah* decide to destroy the larger fragment by flying into a fissure that has formed on its surface and exploding the remaining bombs on board. They die in the process, but succeed in breaking up the comet into small pieces thus preventing planetary extinction. In the face of the devastation, which however spares enough of the planet to guarantee continuity, the President makes an inspirational speech to the effect that the world will be rebuilt but in a different mould, with old errors put right and greater justice prevailing: 'Now we begin again' (Leder, 1998).

The film's political and religious symbolism is not nuanced and echoes that of Roland Emmerich's *The Day After Tomorrow* (Emmerich, 2004), in which another rudderless President leads a chastened community driven by a wrathful God into a revised pursuit of happiness, in a world in which the distribution of power has been radically altered: an exodus of US citizens seeks not just a better life but survival across the Rio Grande in Mexico, and is taught a lesson in true charity, receiving a welcome in the past not granted to Mexican emigrants in search of the 'Land of Opportunity'.

Moving from fictional speculation to documented reality, in terms of death rates the greatest cataclysm to date in human history was the Black Death that swept across the world in the 1340's and is estimated to have killed at least 75 million people between 1345 and 1348.[1]

In England the death rate was estimated at between 45-60% (Hatcher, 2008: 180). This extraordinary global wipe out is estimated to have produced social, economic and political effects discernible for at least one hundred and fifty years thereafter, and to have produced

---

[1] Wellcome Trust, http://web.archive.org/web/20080505153316/http://www.wellcome.ac.uk/Professional-resources/Education-resources/Big-Picture/Epidemics/Articles/WTD028089.htm

changes that radically altered established communities on a large scale, including in many cases for the better. In England, for example, according to Hatcher, in the aftermath of the catastrophe, the position of rural tenants and landless labourers was vastly improved, resulting in new definitions of social class in the long term:

> Such momentous mortality naturally had the potential to create confusion and disorder, but equally striking is the speed and power with which forces within society and economy moved to restore stability. [...] Whereas the historian is struck by the continuities, contemporaries would have been overwhelmed by the scale of the changes. [...] The sheer scale of deaths had resulted in a surplus of land and a shortage of labour, and set in train powerful forces that threatened to alter permanently the balance of social and economic power between lords and peasants. [... O]rdinary people were [...] enjoying their new freedom to make choices about whether to take possession of a relatively unattractive piece of land or when and for what wages they would work. (Hatcher, 2008: 224-25)

After the End

Whether the outcome is overall positive (survival, social democratization) or only partially so (old problems might rear their heads again, as will be discussed in chapter 3), in narratives of apocalypse the question always remains as to whether lessons have been learned which will safeguard against repetition in the future eventually leading to irremediable wipe-out. In the end, however, and as proposed in films such as *Solaris* (Tarkovsky, 1972; Soderbergh, 2002), to be discussed, we can only imagine what we already know. Whether in foundation texts such as Genesis or Revelation, in genre-defining narratives of science fiction such as H.G. Wells's *The War of the Worlds* (Wells, [1898] 2005), *The War in the Air* (Wells, [1907] 2005) and *The World Set Free* (Wells, [1914] 2007), or in the most extreme recent speculations on this theme, such as Margaret Atwood's *Oryx and Crake* (Atwood, 2003) and *The Year of the Flood* (Atwood, 2009), the world may undergo narrow escapes, but, echoing Ecclesiastes (and the title drawn from it of one of the central contemporary novels of apocalypse), even if we make the same mistakes again and our second chance only confirms our unavoidable species propensity to self-destruction, ultimately, Earth abides.

3. And Then There Was Nothing: Is the End Ever Really the End?

But Noah found favour in the eyes of the Lord. […] God said to Noah, The end of all flesh has come before Me; for the earth is filled with violence because of them; and behold, I am about to destroy them with the land. Make for yourself an ark of gopher wood […] And behold, I, even I am bringing the flood of water upon the land, to destroy all flesh in which is the breath of life, from under the sky; everything that is in the land shall perish. But I will establish My covenant with you; and you shall enter the ark—you and your sons and your wife, and your sons wives with you. And of every living thing of all flesh, you shall bring two of every *kind* into the ark, to keep *them* alive with you; they shall be male and female. Of the birds after their kind, and of the animals after their kind, of every creeping thing of the ground after its kind, two of every *kind* shall come to you to keep *them* alive. (Genesis 6: 5-20)

Vanity of vanities, saith the Preacher, vanity of vanities; all is vanity. What profit hath a man of all his labour which he taketh under the sun? One generation passeth away, and another generation cometh: but the earth abideth for ever. […] The thing that hath been, it is that which shall be; and that which is done is that which shall be done: and there is no new thing under the sun. Is there any thing whereof it may be said, See, this is new? it hath been already of old time, which was before us. There is no remembrance of former things; neither shall there be any remembrance of things that are to come with those that shall come after. […] That which is crooked cannot be made straight: and that which is wanting cannot be numbered. […] And I gave my heart to know wisdom, and to know madness and folly: I perceived that this also is vexation of spirit. For in much wisdom is much grief: and he that increaseth knowledge increaseth sorrow. (Ecclesiastes 1: 2-18)

The term palingenesis, also known as recapitulation theory or embryological parallelism, refers to that phase in the development of an individual plant or animal which theoretically repeats the evolutionary history of the taxonomic group to which it belongs. Sometimes expressed as Haeckl's law that ontogeny (the growth or size change and the development or shape change of an individual organism) recapitulates phylogeny (the evolutionary history of a species), this theory has been extensively refuted by science but remains attractive to writers of science fiction, who have variously drawn on the idea that the development of advanced species passed through stages represented by adult organisms of more primitive species. Birds, for example, would carry phylogenetic markers of their ontogenetical descent from reptiles (their feet resemble those of some lizards). In the sense of recapitulation, the word palingenesis or rather palingenesia can be traced back to the Stoics, who used the term to refer to the continual re-creation of the universe by a demiurge (creator) after its absorption into himself. In certain schools of philosophy the related concept of metempsychosis in its broadest sense denotes the theory that the human soul does not die with the body but is born again in new individuals or incarnations. Schopenhauer articulated a similar idea invoking not the soul but the will. Repetition, or recapitulation is at the heart of the analysis of apocalypse to be developed in this chapter, which discusses the representation in film and fiction of the term's dual meaning as destruction and renewal.

Failures of the Imagination

In Jack Arnold's film of 1957, *The Incredible Shrinking Man*, whose re-make is due out in 2012, it is not the world that faces extinction, only the hero, Scott, who through accidental exposure to radiation steadily decreases in size, until, it is to be assumed, he reaches vanishing point. *The Shrinking Man*, the original 1956 novel by Richard Matheson (of *I Am Legend* fame), a metaphor for human disappearance by reason of science gone wrong, perfectly illustrates Susan Sontag's view that science fiction on the theme of apocalypse addresses atavistic fears in the human psyche, namely the amorphous feeling that something terrible is about to happen (Sontag, 1979): a process arguably akin to that involved in the cultural constructions of myths.

Shrinking, of course, can also be read as a metaphor, writ both large and small, for the fear of a return from Being to Nothing: humanity *vis à vis the cosmos* or the embryonic self at a state of existence in which individuation from the body of the mother is not yet a possibility. The omnipotence of the all-encompassing watery womb within readings of apocalypse lends itself to many none-too-subtle interpretations. In psychoanalytic thought, the return to the womb has been brilliantly explored by object-relations theory (Chodorow, 1979; Dinnerstein, 1987) as the dreaded and desired loss of the self in a (m)other who was there was before that self existed. Not a paternal but rather a maternal deity, disturbingly imagined as a reality before Adam and Eve, the self, we ourselves, were a glimmer in the procreative eye of a powerful (pre)(pro)genitress whose being, we now find, is our *ex nihilo*: an entity preexisting and independent of that which it might or might not conceive (namely, us).

Water, Water Everywhere, and Not a Drop to Drink

It is no coincidence, therefore, that ultimately, and revealingly, in the Western imagination – from the old Norse *Ragnarök* (Sturluson, 1916) to Wagner's *Twilight of the Gods* (1876) which the former inspired, to Jehovah's Flood – a father's preferred mode of inflicting apocalypse on his unruly children involves the reinstatement of the primeval oceans of the womb. If you don't behave, I'll tell mother. In the *Ragnarök* ('final destiny of the Gods'), cataclysmic events which include a great battle foretold to result in the deaths of the Gods Odin, Thor, Freyr and the giant Loki, end in the submersion of the world in water, from which it later resurfaces newly cleansed. The surviving Gods meet and the world is re-populated by two human survivors. In Wagner's *Twilight of the Gods*, Odin attempts to by-pass his own daughter Brunhilde and gives the magic ring capable of granting world power to its owner (and itself made of gold stolen from the Rhine, which is the dominion of maidens) to her lover Siegried. In Wagner, the homosocial collusion between father- and son-in-law is undone by the mutual loyalty of an early 'monstrous regiment' of women. Brunhilde returns the ring to the Rhine maidens (Eve's sisters in seduction and temptation), and these destroy Valhalah, the dominion of the Gods. They do so, furthermore, and adding insult to injury, using the latter's weapon of choice: fire, which extinguishes the males although it is itself extinguishable by the watery element from which they originally sprang.

And in Genesis, in one of his moments of most blatant pique, God punishes the world with a flood, Noah builds his Ark, and the rest is history (or at least myth). The small print in the narrative of the Flood, however, includes the caveat that, albeit having allowed the world the benefit of the doubt and a fresh start, the grudging deity suspects that the second attempt will almost certainly fail, just like the first:

> Then Noah built an altar to the Lord and, taking some of all the clean animals and clean birds, he sacrificed burnt offerings on it. The Lord smelled the pleasing aroma and said in his heart: 'Never again will I curse the ground because of man, *even though every inclination of his heart is evil from childhood*' (Genesis 8: 20-21, italics added)

Plus ça change... In Miguel Torga's short story, 'Vicente' (Torga, 1987), the narrative of the Flood is replayed with a modification, namely that this time disobedience wins the day immediately, rather than being postponed a few generations. In the Ark, humanity and all the species cower in the face of the wrath of God. One creature alone, the raven Vicente (dark counterpart to the white dove which replaced the original black raven in Genesis 8: 7-9), defies confinement in the floating prison and takes flight, extending defiance rather than an olive branch. Just the tip of one tree on what used to be a hill remains above the water line and the waters continue to rise. As Vicente persists in not returning to the Ark, God apostrophizes the raven's disobedience and desire to explore alternatives (curiosity, of course, namely that of Eve, being that which had already once before led to the loss of paradise). Each antagonist faces a choice: for Vicente, either drowning or defeat, a return to the Ark and the abdication of the free will which had first driven him to fly off; and for God, either the abdication of supreme authority or the destruction of his finest creation: that self-same free will embodied in Vicente's audacity.

> Noah and the rest of the animals looked on at the duel between Vicente and God. And in the clear or confused mind of each, just one dilemma: either the waters did not submerge the branch on which Vicente had landed, the Lord preserved the greatness of the moment of Genesis – the absolute autonomy of the creature with regard to his creator – or, the branch once submerged, Vicente would die, his annihilation rendering meaningless that supreme event. The very meaning of life itself was inextricably linked to the act of insubordination [and to...] that black raven, drenched from head to foot, who, tranquil and obstinate, resting on the last possibility of survival, defied omnipotence. (Torga, 1987: 133-34)

In the end, the raven wins the battle of wills and the waters stop rising, leaving the bird perched on top the only tree branch left on Earth, which for him, too, as for Adam and Eve, but here with no strings attached, is yet another tree representing disobedient, stubborn life. Vicente, like Milton's Satan, is a charismatic villain, but unlike the latter he is also a triumphant one, and the reader's secret sympathies are satisfied.

In Western Europe the Fall in Genesis was arguably the first real apocalypse, in the course of which not just life, but eternal life was lost and a disobedient animal (not a raven but a reptile, the former's evolutionary forbear, whose scaly feet it shares) won the first skirmish. In 'Vicente,' God is temporarily defeated, although, as was the case with the events that took place in the original Ark (given that 'every inclination of [man's] heart is evil from childhood' Genesis 8: 21), the seeds may already be planted for a new cataclysmic repetition. And another, and another (although not necessarily *ad infinitum*, since, difficult though it may be to imagine, one day the end could really be the end).

Barring that, however, in a curious game in which the only options available to a thwarted Creator are either to concede defeat or to annihilate his own work, and as understood in *WarGames* (Badham, 1983), following the near-miss of global planetary destruction, the lesson learned by God is that the only winning move is not to play.

Not Quite the End

The broad spectrum of fiction and nonfiction on the subject of planetary destruction ultimately only very rarely envisages total annihilation. God almost invariably opts not to play and instead, almost without exception, from ancient Norse myth and Biblical renditions to modern sci-fi, what structures these narratives is the logic of the close escape: near-universal annihilation but with just enough life left intact to guarantee a reasonable likelihood of a new beginning. If the belief in a second chance underpins most apocalyptic thinking, however, the certainty that old habits die hard and old mistakes get repeated is equally fundamental to narratives of catastrophe. This chapter will address the plight of those left behind in the aftermath of planetary near-destruction. It elaborates on the notion that all scenarios of apocalypse are also morality tales that conclude with the medium-term effects of an opportune lesson well learned, and a new ethic of intended non-repetition in the future of past mistakes: moral recklessness, social dissipation, ungodliness and the hubris of knowledge/power run-amok.

As M. Keith Booker (2001), James Berger (1999), Joyce A. Evans (1998) and other writers on apocalypse observe, therefore, in general, either global destruction is narrowly averted or near-global cataclysm does actually take place, but in its aftermath previous mistakes are set right and a new (although, not very different or necessarily better) world is built. Or at least, that is the intention. In reality, and that is the basis of the argument that follows, the deep structures of the new world often have inbuilt in them the prototypes of old errors repeatable indefinitely.

Götterdämmerung (*The Twilight of the Gods*) is the title of the last of Wagner's cycle of four operas, *Der Ring des Nibelungen* (*The Ring of the Nibelung*). In the final moments, the Gods and their home, Valhalla, are destroyed. In Wagner the Gods are undone but the world is not. In the Norse mythology which he largely used as his source, however, the world itself is destroyed. *Ragnarök*, in old Norse 'Final destiny of the Gods' or 'Doom of the Gods,' is an event also referred in one poem in the *Poetic Edda*, compiled in the 13th century from earlier traditional sources, and in *Gylfaginning*, the first part of the *Prose Edda*, written in the 13th century and generally attributed to the Icelandic poet and historian, Snorri Sturluson.

Ragnarök narrates a great battle between the Gods, in which several, including the major figures of Odin, Thor and Loki are destroyed. The world is consumed by fire, but subsequently, reappears, new and fertile. The surviving Gods meet, and the world is re-populated by two human survivors, Lif and Lifbrasir. Their offspring will inherit the Earth, and the sun, personified as Sól (interestingly also – minus the accent – the Latin root for 'sun'), bears a daughter 'at least as beautiful as she,' (Sturluson, 87) who will follow the same path as her mother. Appropriately resonant with contemporary fears of a nuclear winter following global thermonuclear war (for example the world of Cormac McCarthy's *The Road*), in the Edda the world is plunged into prolonged winter, 'that winter which is called the Awful Winter:'

> In that time snow shall drive from all quarters; frosts shall be great then, and winds sharp; there shall be no virtue in the sun. Those winters shall proceed three in succession, and no summer between; but first shall come three other winters, such that over all the world there shall be mighty battles. In that time brothers shall slay each other for greed's sake, and none shall spare father or son in manslaughter and in incest; so it says in *Völuspá* (Sturluson, 1916: 78):

> Brothers shall strive
> and slaughter each other;
> Own sisters' children

> shall sin together;
> Ill days among men

> many a whoredom:
> An axe-age, a sword-age, shields shall be cloven;
> A wind-age, a wolf-age,

> ere the world totters. (Sturluson, 1916: 79)

The fabric of the community begins to fray in a way that supplants even the worst excesses of contemporary sci-fi, including Margaret Atwood's panorama of genetically molested creatures in *Oryx and Crake* (Atwood, 2003) and *The Year of the Flood* (Atwood, 2009):

> Then shall happen what seems great tidings: the Wolf shall swallow the sun; and this shall seem to men a great harm. Then the other wolf shall seize the moon, and he also shall work great ruin; the stars shall vanish from the heavens. Then shall come to pass these tidings also: all the earth shall tremble so, and the crags, that trees shall be torn up from the earth, and the crags fall to ruin; and all fetters and bonds shall be broken and rent. (Sturluson, 1916: 79)

In a continuation of the imaginings that have subsequently fed Gothic literature, horror fiction and canonic adolescent texts (notably the Harry Potter phenomenon, where a werewolf of the same name figures second only in malevolence to Voldemort himself, in a battle that might have triggered the end of that particular world),

> Fenris-Wolf shall advance with gaping mouth, and his lower jaw shall be against the earth, but the upper against heaven, — he would gape yet more if there were room for it; fires blaze from his eyes and nostrils. The Midgard Serpent shall blow venom so that he shall sprinkle all the air and water; and he is very terrible, and shall be on one side of the Wolf. In this din shall the heaven be cloven. (Sturluson, 1916: 79)

> And nothing then shall be without fear in heaven or in earth. (Sturluson, 1916: 80)

> "Afterward, when all the world is burned, and dead are all the Gods and all the champions and all mankind? [...] Shall any of the Gods live then, or shall there be then any earth or heaven?" (Sturluson, 1916: 83-84)

Fortunately, mindful of audiences' good will, and as is almost invariably the case in narratives from the most venerable early myth to Hollywood, the answer is yes.

> Hárr answered: "In that time the earth shall emerge out of the sea, and shall then be green and fair; then shall the fruits of it be brought forth unsown. [...]" (Sturluson, 1916: 84)

But not, however, without a caveat: namely, that just as previously it all came to an end, when it all begins again, the seed is already planted for the cycle to begin all over again. Perhaps.

> Now, if thou art able to ask yet further, then indeed I know not whence answer shall come to thee, for I never heard any man tell forth at greater

length the course of the world; and now avail thyself of that which thou hast heard. (Sturluson, 1916: 85)

At the end, then, counter-intuitively, Armageddon runs a full cycle, and perhaps, but only perhaps, permits a new beginning, albeit possibly only to strike again in an unspecified future. Which might explain why, in Wagner's *Götterdämmerung*, in the aftermath of four days and fifteen hours of operatic *sturm und drang*, the last bars unfold in a quietude in some respects even more menacing than the musical battering that went before.

The end of the world, *this* world, *that* world, prior to the coming of a new era features both in the Old Testament (the Book of Daniel) and in the New (Revelation). In *The Sense of an Ending*, Frank Kermode (1968) discusses visions of the end both as a theme and as a trajectory of narrative itself, but, as observed by James Berger, 'such visions have increasingly given way to visions of what happens after the end. The apocalyptic sensibilities both of religion and of modernism have shifted toward a sense of post-apocalypse' (Berger, 1999, xiii). Berger discerns a common thread of radical critique of the existing political and social order linking apocalyptic visions as chronologically disparate as the Book of Revelation, the work of Michel Foucault (Foucault, 2001; 2009) and the preaching of millenarian evangelical fundamentalists such as Hal Lindsey (Lindsey, 1973).

Apocalypse in Our Time

In contemporary analyses of apocalypse, the Jewish Holocaust during World War II figures large, the rivers of ink spilt on the subject of this particular cataclysm and its aftermath contradicting Adorno's famous summing up of humanity's moral cataclysm, to the effect that, after Auschwitz, nothing remains but silence. Adorno argued that the Holocaust had 'demonstrated irrefutably that culture had failed' (Adorno, 1992, 366). While agreeing that the Shoah represented an existential and ethical paradigm shift, 'a reality which, by [its] very nature, obliterate[d] thought and the human program of thinking,' Arthur Cohen questions Adorno's statement that when contemplating the Holocaust, 'absolute negativity is in plain sight,' and argues instead that the Holocaust was a transformative event whose effect was to show that the path to change lay through culture. It described 'a new beginning for the human race that knew not of what it was capable.' In Cohen's view, faced with the moral paradigm shift that was the Holocaust, a new beginning was

Figure 12. Reuven Dafni, *Corpses in a Mass Grave*, Bergen Belsen

possible, requiring the process of witness testimony acting as both haunting memory of loss and affirmation of survival: 'We must create a new language in which to speak of this in order to destroy the old language which, in its decrepitude and decline, made facile and easy the demonic descent' (Cohen, quoted in Berger, 1999, 60). For Cohen, post-apocalypse, the destruction of an advanced civilization offers the opportunity for a return to what truly matters.

Never Again?

Berger's statement that 'apocalyptic desire is a longing also for the aftermath' (Berger, 1999, 34) mirrors Cohen's belief (and in this context the term 'belief,' in the sense of 'faith without proof,' may be the operative word) in the possibility of a new beginning (that which Berger denominates 'the triumph of apocalypse over trauma […], of the utterly new beginning over the repetition of history,' Berger, 1999, 53). Each finds support in the abundance of fiction and film based on that principle.

The Boy in the Striped Pyjamas (Herman, 2008) is a film aimed at a young adolescent audience who often also read the original novel (Boynes, 2008) as a set text in secondary school. The theme of an uncomprehending

German child faced with the reality of the Jewish Holocaust presents him as vulnerable *because* he fails to understand what he is witnessing, something which in turn leads to his own death. At the end of the film the boy, the son of the concentration camp commander, sneaks into the camp to join the Jewish child whom he has befriended across the barbed wire, in order to search for the latter's father who has inexplicably disappeared. The two boys are caught in a crowd of men being herded into the 'shower rooms' where they are all gassed. What had seemed to be a narrative of one boy helping another escape from his deadly fate turns into the tragedy of random death for the two children. In the novel, the shock is partly transformed into catharsis by the final lines, according to which some retrievable hope remains, namely that in dealing with human evil, beyond a certain point, the sheer scale of it will ensure that nothing similar can ever happen again. The danger of such a belief, of course, weakening, as it does, the awareness that history can and often does in fact repeat itself, is that it might permit that very repetition. Or, if it does not, that that might be only because the point has been reached at which absolute obliteration means that there is nothing left to be repeated.

The idea of a tipping point which, if crossed, would trigger extreme consequences, which is also the rationale behind the safeguard of M.A.D. and also some of the films already discussed (*Fail-Safe*, Lumet, 1964; Frears, 2000; *By Dawn's Early Light*, Scholder, 1980), means that in *The Boy in the Striped Pyjamas*, error, rather than terror (or error within a larger scenario of terror), suffices to set in motion a chain of events at the end of which, for different reasons in each narrative but to similar emotional and rhetorical effect, a point of no return is crossed. Interestingly, *Fail-Safe* and *The Boy in the Striped Pyjamas* both conclude with epilogues that almost exactly echo one another: in the former, a short dialogue between the two nation's leaders in which one, in the aftermath of the Oppenheimer-style realization that he has become Death, asks despairingly what they can say to the survivors. The reply is 'we will tell them that it will never happen again' (Frears, 2000). In *The Boy in the Striped Pyjamas* a similarly-worded statement is made: 'Of course all this happened a long time ago and nothing like that could ever happen again. Not in our day and age' (Boynes, 2008, 216). They are both wrong, as is made clear at the end of *Fail-Safe* (Frears, 2000), by a slow scrolling of a list of countries which, at the time of the film's release, controlled nuclear weapons. Things, be they small or massive (on the scale of World War II or the Holocaust), can always happen again.

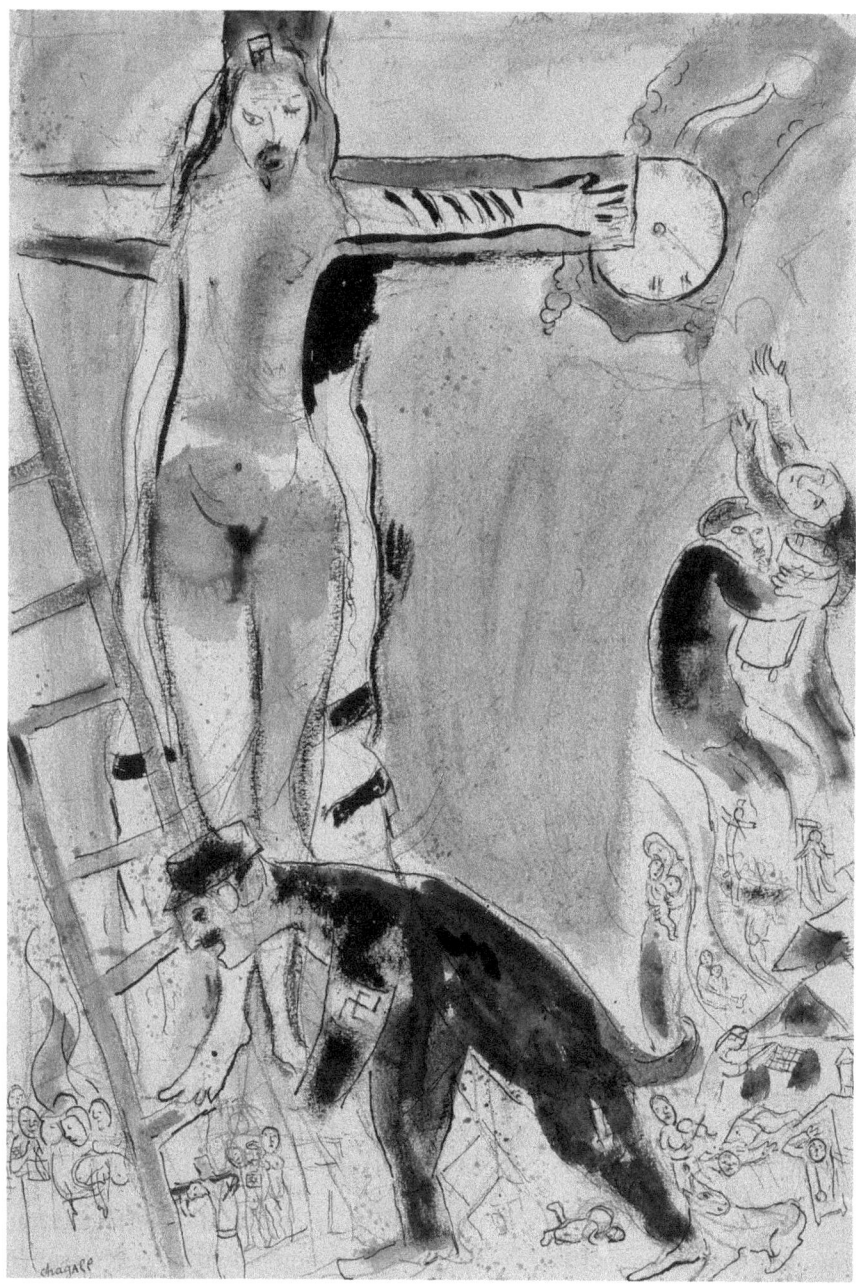

Figure 13. Marc Chagall, *Apocalypse in Lilac, Capriccio*
If anti-Semitism involves the assertion that the Jews killed Jesus Christ, in this image a vulture-like figure of Hitler, identifiable by the moustache and swastika, appears to pick at miniature figures of people sheltering under the ladder that leans against the cross where Christ hangs crucified.

60   The End of the World

In the case of the two films discussed, prior to the brutal endings, the sheer magnitude of the potential horror had led savvy audiences to believe that nothing other than a last-minute reprieve should be expected (the cavalry always arrives on time). Instead, the shocking climaxes move both films outside all reasonable genre expectations, locating them instead in the same league as classics such as Stanley Kubrick's laugh-hard-but-only-if-you're-stupid film, *Dr. Strangelove* (Kubrick, 1964) and Ray Bradbury's novel, *Fahrenheit 451* (Bradbury, 1976), the latter also made into a film, and all of which hopefully encourage the pedagogical realization that the worst really *can* and sometimes does happen. In Berger's sobering words, 'after the end, there will be something else – unimaginable.' (Berger, 1999: 34).

In Shute's *On the Beach*, the difficulty of comprehending the idea of an absolute end is articulated by the scientists and submarine crew that visited for the last time regions of the world where the radiation that eventually will spread to the entire planet has already put an end to all life:

> 'Did it ever strike you that nobody will ever – *ever* – see Cairns again? Or Moresby, or Darwin?'
>
> They stared at him while they turned over the new idea.
>
> [...]
>
> 'That's so,' Dwight said thoughtfully. [...] We're the last living people that will ever see those places.'
>
> [...]
>
> Peter stirred uneasily. 'That's historical,' he said. It ought to go on record somewhere, oughtn't it? Is anybody writing any kind of history about these times?'
>
> John Osborne said, 'I haven't heard of one. I'll find out about that. After all, there doesn't seem to be much point in writing stuff that nobody will read.'
> (Shute, 1974: 73)

And in Russell Mulcahy's unforgiving film of the same novel, Dwight Towers, having toured the northern hemisphere and ascertained the absolute eradication of life, including in his hometown and in his own home, where he finds his family dead in bed, returns to an Australia itself now in the last stages of demise. In one of the most effective and cruel scenes in the film, Towers seeks refuge in a café from what appears to be a lynch mob. This, however, turns out to be a group of two men and a woman in search of food. All four sit down, share a tin of baked beans, and part, without having exchanged a single word (Mulcahy, 2000). At the end of the world, clearly, polite meal-time conversation is no longer necessary.

Same Again

The supposition that a limit to horror can be reached beyond which it is determined that nothing similar will ever be permitted to happen again (Berger's 'utterly new beginning') is at the opposite end of the spectrum to Adorno's unforgiving nihilism. As an alternative to both, and in some ways even darker than either, other writers have argued that the Nazi death camps were neither an end point in human history nor a point beyond which any alternative, however bad, must necessarily be better. Instead, according to this line of thinking, the Shoah was simply a more efficient version of other historical genocides. In preceding and subsequent exterminations, the trains may not have run quite as impressively on time as under the Nazi genocidal machine, and the targets outlined in the original mission statement may not have been quite as near-as-dammit fulfilled; but even so, this line of reasoning would have it, it is dangerous to work on the principle that an event like the Holocaust was unique and unrepeatable either because in its aftermath we will forever guard against it or because after it there can only be silence. The danger, unpalatable but not inconceivable, that it could in fact happen again, makes any rhetoric that comfortingly or nihilistically suggests otherwise unwittingly complicit in the likelihood that what was in fact just a larger-scale version of an old story, might in fact be repeated.

'It is startling to realize how little is said in Kant's ethics about the more violent forms of immoral action. There are discussions of lying, deception, self-neglect, non-beneficence – but apart from suicide, a great silence about the darker actions' (Herman, 1993: 113). According to Berger, until the end, there will be narrative and after the end too: contrary to Kant's 'great silence' and Wittgenstein's certainty that if one cannot think it/speak it, 'thereof one must be silent,' Berger argues that the supposedly unthinkable is in fact always thinkable, because if we call something unthinkable, by definition we are already thinking it, and, we would now argue here, even the inescapable consciousness of our own laboured silence brings into being that which we seek to leave unacknowledged.

Very few apocalyptic representations end with the End. There is always some remainder, some post-apocalyptic debris, or the transformation into paradise. The apocalyptic desire *is* a longing for the end [...]. But apocalyptic desire is a longing also for the aftermath [...]. This combination of violent hatred for the world as it is and violent desire for the world as it should be has characterized apocalyptic representations and apocalyptic social movements since their first recorded instances. (Berger, 1999: 34)

The fact that imagining the world as it should be is almost as tricky as imagining no world at all is discussed in chapter 5 with regard to visions of utopia. In either case, ultimately, if the unimaginable – whether unimaginably bad or unimaginably good – is just that, ie. unimaginable, it stands to reason that in attempting to imagine it we fall back upon

Figure 14. Anselm Kiefer, *Lot's Wife*
Kiefer's work engages with the problems of history and memory, and often returns to the Holocaust. In Genesis 19: 26 Lot's wife, escaping from the destruction of the Cities of the Plain, disobeys God, looks back and is punished by being turned into a pillar of salt. In Kiefer the past both forgotten and re-visited at a peril is that of the concentration camps of the Holocaust, to which the rail tracks had led, and where humanity's potential for destruction was reaffirmed in a new language.

familiar scenarios. In Milton, even in Hell there is something: the infernal flames may issue no light but darkness is visible (Milton, [1667] 1990: 160), and hence perhaps his rather approachable Satan, who is in many ways someone we can understand. Someone like us. Thus, even if, as Berger supposes, the apocalyptic event divides history into before and after, the narration of what comes after must, by definition, be constructed by those who were present in the time before, and the narrative of what comes afterwards must therefore not only pre-suppose that there *is* something (and someone) left after apocalypse, but also that it and they are, even if only by antithesis, partly defined by what preceded them.

When we imagine apocalypse – the end of the world as we know it – what is imagined is never nothingness. At most it may be something completely different, but, whatever that may turn out to be, at that given point it is still something (some thing), even if it is ultimately destined to end in nothing (no thing), because at that point, at least in our imagination, there is always something to be experienced and someone experiencing it. In effect, as confirmed by most post-apocalyptic narratives, what tends to follow imagined apocalypse is essentially the past repeated. We can only imagine something that can be articulated in the vocabulary of what we already know. Adam and Eve lose everything but find a new world in its place. In Milton paradise is lost, but even as the first parents are expelled,

> Some natural tears they dropped, but wiped them soon;
> The world was all before them, where to choose,
> Their place of rest, and Providence their guide:
> They hand in hand with wandering steps and slow,
> Through Eden took their solitary way. (Milton, [1667] 1990: 388)

Moreover, in the admittedly less effective sequel that is *Paradise Regained*, they are promised a post-dated return:

> A fairer Paradise is founded now
> For Adam and his chosen Sons, whom thou
> A Saviour art come down to re-install,
> Where they shall dwell secure, when time shall be. (Milton, [1671] 1990: 435)

And tellingly, in the Book of Revelation, following the general apocalypse due to afflict humanity's remaining descendants at the end of the world, an angel will sketch out the New Jerusalem using earthly measurements:

> And he that talked with me had a golden reed to measure the city, and the gates thereof, and the wall thereof. And the city lieth foursquare, and the length is as large as the breadth: and he measured the city with the reed,

twelve thousand furlongs. The length and the breadth and the height of it are equal. And he measured the wall thereof, an hundred and forty and four cubits, *according to the measure of a man, that is, of the angel*. (Revelation, 21: 15-17, italics added)

Faced with the unimaginable, what we are able to articulate as its aftermath must by definition be just another version of what we already know, in measurements we understand: 'Humanity in its essence [...] is what these apocalypses unveil' (Berger, 1999: 10).

Imagine This

Curiously then, or perhaps not so curiously after all (given the philosophical impossibility of imagining something we have never witnessed and which, by definition, were we to witness it, we would not survive to relate), in the nuclear age the number of narratives that experiment with scenarios of absolute destruction is almost nil. Whether dealing with the possibility of natural disaster in film or fiction (*The Drowned World*, Ballard, 2008; *The Andromeda Strain*, Crichton, 1995), alien invasion (*Independence Day*, Emmerich, 1996; *The Blob*, Yeasworth, 1958) or man-made cataclysm of various forms (nuclear conflict: *Fail-Safe*, Lumet, 1964; Frears, 2000; *Armageddon*, Bay, 1998; *War of the Worlds*, Spielberg, 2005; biological war: Atwood's *Oryx and Crake*; *Virus*, Bruno, 1999; 'The Stolen Bacillus,' Wells, [1894] 1982; global warming: *The Day After*, Meyer, 1983), the end is never really the end, and, as films with indicative titles suggest, there is usually not only a day after, but even a *Day After Tomorrow* (Emmerich, 2004).

Exceptions are Thomas Hood's 'The Last Man' (Hood, 1826), Helen Clarkson's *The Last Day* (Clarkson, 1959), François-Xavier Cousin de Grainville's 'Le dernier homme' (de Grainville, 1992), Edgar Allan Poe's 'Conversation of Eiros and Charmian' (Poe, 1839), Camille Flammarion's *La Fin du Monde* (Flammarion, 1999), Nevil Shute's *On the Beach* (Shute, 1974), Robert Hugh Benson's *The Lord of the World* (Benson, 2005), Mordecai Roshwald's *Level 7* (Roshwald, 2004), Thomas M. Disch's *The Genocides* (Disch, 2000) and Stanley Kubrick's deadly serious lampoon, *Dr. Strangelove* (Kubrick, 1964).

In Poe, unexpectedly, the annihilation of life is brought about through the unleashing of an excess of the stuff out of which life is born: oxygen:

It had been long known that the air which encircled us was a compound of oxygen and nitrogen gases, in the proportion of twenty-one measures of oxygen, and seventy-nine of nitrogen, in every one hundred of the atmosphere. Oxygen, which was the principle of combustion, and the vehicle of heat, was absolutely necessary to the support of animal life, and was the most powerful and energetic agent in nature. Nitrogen, on the contrary, was incapable of supporting either animal life or flame. An unnatural excess of oxygen would result, it had been ascertained, in just such an elevation of the animal spirits as we had latterly experienced. It was the pursuit, the extension of the idea, which had engendered awe. What would be the result of a total extraction of the nitrogen? A combustion irresistible, all-devouring, omni-prevalent, immediate; the entire fulfilment, in all their minute and terrible details, of the fiery and horror-inspiring denunciations of the prophecies of the Holy Book.

Why need I paint, Charmion, the now disenchained frenzy of mankind? That tenuity in the comet which had previously inspired us with hope, was now the source of the bitterness of despair. In its impalpable gaseous character we clearly perceived the consummation of Fate. [...] Then, let us bow down, Charmion, before the excessive majesty of the great God!; then, there came a shouting and pervading sound, as if from the mouth itself of HIM; while the whole incumbent mass of ether in which we existed, burst at once into a species of intense flame, for whose surpassing brilliancy and all-fervid heat even the angels in the high Heaven of pure knowledge have no name. Thus ended all. (Poe, 1839)

Poe's tale of apocalypse foreshadows the scenarios of annihilation of a number of science fiction plots over one century later, including some already discussed. In general, however, the general rule stands that only rarely do such scripts end with the equivalent of a blank page or screen. Absolute destruction, leaving the Earth reduced to fire, stone and sand, has proved to be generally unthinkable, unimaginable in the sense of that which cannot be said or imagined. And after all, even in Poe, there is an afterwards, albeit only in the form of the narration made by Eiros to Charmion in the aftermath of the end of the world.

We have never seen nothingness, we cannot imagine it or describe it, in fiction, film or image, and at best (or worst), for Derrida, in customary gnomic style, 'the future can only be anticipated in the form of an absolute danger' (Derrida, 1974: 5). In *On the Beach* we anticipate an absolute end, but we do not give it words or images. 'In order to draw a limit to thinking we should have to be able to think both sides of this limit (we should therefore have to be able to think what cannot be thought)' (Wittgenstein, 1981, 27). On the other hand, whether because we like to scare ourselves with horror stories or because we sense that in order to avoid something we must first be able to imagine it, the possibility of apocalypse as the prequel to utter obliteration remains a fundamental part of our cultural imagination, acting among other things as a mechanism of self-defence, even if ultimately, as predicted by Wittgenstinian logic, since we have not been there we cannot articulate it. Instead, that 'whereof we can speak' are reparation scenarios after the events that led to the Scorched Earth outcome in the first place.

New Beginnings

Science (Rees, *Our Final Century*, 2003; *Our Final Hour*, 2003), science fiction (Wyndham, *The Chrysalids*, [1955] 1984; Miller, *A Canticle for Leibowitz*, 2007; Stewart, *Earth Abides*, [1949] 1973; Dick, *The World Jones Made*, [1956] 2003; *Dr. Bloodmoney*, [1965] 2007) and millenarian evangelical Christianity (the Book of Revelation; Lindsey, *The Late, Great Planet Earth*, 1973) have all envisaged apocalypse, whether satirically or with a proselytizing agenda, as a critique of existing societies, and usually, as a cleansing process, but always involving the possibility of the resumption of life: either on Earth or extra-terrestrially, in variations of space-stations or other-planet scenarios, or in a religious, metaphysical here-after.

Playing Safe

If one takes apocalypse to mean absolute wipe-out, logically, there can be no post-apocalypse within reality as we know it. Nonetheless, post-millenarian unorthodoxies, for example, while offering (threatening) radical difference in the aftermath of apocalypse, and maintaining that escalating sin will inevitably trigger the advent of global cataclysm, also believe in an ensuing Rapture following which the New Jerusalem will be established on Earth and the Kingdom of God will become the property of the righteous (who are of course, and without exception, their coreligionists). Membership of the Rapture club requires, of course, a preceding life of virtue.

While differing in some essential aspects from Millenarian convictions, ancient philosophies such as stoicism, Eastern beliefs such as Buddhism, and orthodox Christian thought, to give but three examples, also maintain that although perfection is only to be found in a variously defined eternity, it is the duty of human beings, notwithstanding, to work towards the betterment of *this* life. (To this effect, medieval Christianity, for example, punished with death those – Manicheans, *Alumbrados* and other assorted heretics – who preached that life and conduct on Earth mattered not at all, since salvation and damnation were individually predestined). For most established creeds, even on Earth, rules are rules. Could this be just in case there is nothing else? Or because whatever there might be in a possible Hereafter is thought to be organized along the same parameters as prevail here and now? Whatever the reasoning, in the end most schools of thought in one way or another make provision for an afterlife that in essence amounts to much the same as what was there before, namely a universe divided into self and other.

Just the Same Old Story?

Whether what comes after end-time is life in space stations, extra-terrestrial colonies or a transformed planet following divine obliteration and reconstruction by the enraptured happy few, the term 'post-apocalypse' turns out to be both a misnomer and a conceptual error. What follows apocalypse ought to be either nothing or something epistemologically different but in effect almost always turns out to be merely a not-very-revised version of prior realities.

Nowhere is this point upheld more literally, but also more effectively, than in Judith Merrill's novel of 1950, *The Shadow on the Hearth,* in various ways one of the most direct fictional statements of the fact that, for good or evil, things seldom change. A wide-ranging, surprise nuclear attack on the US in the late 1940s (memories of World War II and Hiroshima at that point still fresh on the mind) is narrated entirely from the point of view of a woman, Gladys, her two young daughters, and their maid, confined at home while the men are absent in the field of action. The brief glimpses Gladys gets of events in the outside world remind her of her memories of both world wars. Men do not feature significantly, other than those marginalized (feminized or at least female-identified) by circumstances: a school teacher on the run because, having previously played the role of Cassandra, opposed nuclear armament by the West and warned of the possibility of a nuclear attack on the US, he is now an undesirable; a young doctor too junior to have fully absorbed the lesson of unquestioning obedience to the authorities; and, at the end, the returned husband, wounded, incapacitated and in need of nursing. Although their outsider status lends these three men a certain amount of charisma, overall the women and girls are left to cope by themselves.

In the face of a changed reality of food shortages, looting gangs and radiation sickness (brought into this particular home by, of all unlikely enemies, a cuddly toy inadvertently left out in the radioactive rain), women respond with homely remedies: nourishing food, plenty of rest, a home visit from the doctor. These, improbably, in the end succeed where the emergency measures put in place (semi-authoritarian, vigilante-style policing, high-tech medicine) did not. As the men go and subsequently come back, the only sustainable reality is that of a domesticity maintained by stubbornly clinging to a familiar routine. If, as James Berger maintains, 'the moment of cataclysm is only part of the point of apocalyptic writing [...], the vehicle for clearing away the world as it is and making possible the post-apocalyptic paradise, the study of what disappears and [...] of how the remainder has been transformed,' (Berger, 1999: 6-7), in Merrill, it appears, the answer to the latter is that what remains has only changed through a temporary feminization of the status quo, in the absence of viable males. When the men return, it is to be supposed, so will the old order.

Like or unlike Merrill's in some ways soothing rendition of domestic routine enduring in the face of Armageddon, novels which intriguingly both deny and re-affirm this are M.P. Shiel's early, iconic novel *The Purple Cloud* published in 1901, Margaret Atwood's twin novels, *Oryx and Crake* and *The Year of the Flood*, and Mike Jackson's and Barry Hines's devastating hypothetical docudrama, *Threads* (Jackson and Hines, 1984). The latter was first broadcast on BBC 2 on 1 August 1985 as part of a week of programmes marking the fortieth anniversary of the atomic bombings of Hiroshima and Nagasaki.

All offer kaleidoscopic views of the planet in the aftermath of near-annihilation. In *The Purple Cloud* (Shiel, 1901), Adam Jefferson, the last man on Earth, a hero whose name counter-intuitively resonates with the possibility of new beginnings (Adam in Genesis named the world, Thomas Jefferson in the newly born USA laid down the outlines of the new nation), travels around the planet setting fire to cities already partly destroyed by poison gas from a volcano which had extinguished life on Earth. He acts therefore both as witness to the disaster and as participant in the thorough implementation of its final stages. In his travels, however, he meets a second Eve – not a first but a last woman – who may however (although this is never confirmed) offer the possibility of a new beginning. Shiel's novel, published at the beginning of the twentieth century, finds an eery echo in Margaret Atwood's *Oryx and Crake*, published in 2003 just after that century and millennium had drawn to a close. Narrated in flashback, in a plot which begins/ends with a last-man-on-Earth scenario and right until the very last pages defies full understanding, Atwood unfolds the nightmare of a Cities of the Plain-style world of dehumanization, engineered genetic modification, and social and moral fragmentation. The novel culminates with the revelation that the entire world's population has been extinguished by a deadly bacterium created and unleashed by Crake, a decadent adolescent turned-scientist, turned-vengeful God.

In preparation for the big wipe-out, Crake had created in his research unit, Paradice, a new species of child-like humans, the Crakers, made very much *not* in his own image. The Crakers, also known as the Children, are renditions of the Noble Savage and do not understand the dangers of the world. They also do not understand technology even in its simplest of forms. In his futuristic republic, Crake, somewhat like Plato before him, sought to eliminate the disruptions of emotion: love, lust and jealousy. He designed the Crakers to mate every three years, a frequency calculated to be sufficient to sustain population size. As in Plato's Republic, all forms of imagination, desire and need are abolished, in a community driven by the sole objective of perpetuation of the species. In a tradition that echoes the Platonic sociopolitical ideal but also Aldous Huxley's *Brave New World* (Huxley, [1932] 1977) and Ira Levin's *This Perfect Day* (Levin, 1994), weakness and illness are not tolerated and the Crakers automatically die at the age of thirty, 'suddenly without getting sick. No old age, none of those anxieties. They'll just keel over' (Atwood, 2004: 356). The novel is narrated from the point of view of the last man on Earth, Jimmy, now referred to as Snowman, an unlikely holy son chosen by Crake as guardian of the new species following the extinction of himself and the rest of the human race. At the end of the novel, Snowman, abandoned on the beach like a reluctant St. John the Baptist with no forthcoming Saviour to announce, learns from the Children that while he was away from them for a brief period, people 'like him' (two men and a woman) visited the Crakers. Jimmy delays an encounter with what may be the only other surviving humans on the planet. The following morning he seeks out the unfathomable trinity. The novel ends inconclusively: Jimmy looks at his blank watch which to him reads 'zero hour': 'time to go' (Atwood 2004, 433). This conclusion, both cryptic and unsettling, leaves open the possibility of a new beginning, albeit one already containing the potential for renewed internecine destruction in a variety of possible scenarios: three Adams fighting for one Eve; the visitors turning against Snowman; or Snowman left alone again with the children (nonviable simulacra of humanity), after destroying the last three members of his species, in a microcosmic replay of Crake's holocaust.

In Atwood's *The Year of the Flood*, which follows the same story line from the point of view of different characters, with references throughout to Crake as the creator of the virus ('the waterless flood'), we find that in the aftermath of almost global annihilation there are of course more survivors than was at first apparent, covering the spectrum from new gangsters, new dictators, new missionaries intent on reconstruction in the name of God (or of good), and new bemused bystanders: in short, all the components for a new start to a world which, albeit on a smaller scale population-wise, promises to be not very different from the one recently annihilated.

Merrill's, Shiel's and Atwood's tales of post-apocalypse explore radically different scenarios but, like some of the works yet to be discussed, share a common rationale of re-built communal life following almost universal destruction. The same is true even in works as extreme in their depiction of end-of-the-world plots as for example Cormac McCarthy's *The Road*, recently adapted to the cinema (Hillcoat, 2009). Here, too, as in Atwood's grim, no-future futuristic nightmares, survival at best and extinction at worst remain equally weighted at the end. McCarthy's novel, a macabre and elegiac combination of buddy movie, road narrative and adventure of quest, follows a father and son as they journey together for an indeterminate period of time across a desolate, post-apocalyptic landscape, in the aftermath of a nuclear cataclysm dating back some ten years, to a time shortly after the boy's birth. Civilization has been destroyed, and most animal and plant species have become extinct:

> He thought the month was October but he wasn't sure. He hadn't kept a calendar for years. They were moving south. There'd be no surviving another winter here. [...] He studied what he could see. The segments of road down there among the dead trees. Looking for anything of color. Any movement. Any trace of standing smoke. [...] He just sat there holding the binoculars and watching the ashen daylight congeal over the land. He knew only that the child was his warrant. He said: If he is not the word of God, God never spoke. [...] An hour later they were on the road [...] shuffling through the ash, each the other's world entire. (McCarthy, 2007: 2-4)

Amidst 'the ashes of the late world' (McCarthy, 2007: 10) the only living organisms the father and son encounter on their journey are a dog, some edible mushrooms, moss, and some shrivelled apples in an orchard. There is no sun, the atmosphere is suffused with ash, the climate has been radically altered and plants no longer grow. In a mockery of earlier consumerist societies, the remnants of humankind now consist mostly of cannibals, who, in a world where there is nothing left and no means of production, capture and eat their own species, in the form of refugees and travellers, themselves driven to scavenging for food.

As the narrative progresses it transpires that the boy's mother, pregnant with him at the time of the cataclysm, committed suicide some time before the story begins, as the only alternative to either a violent death or a slow one through starvation. She walks out without saying goodbye, armed with a sharp shard with which to slash her wrists (possibly her last gesture of love, since they had just two bullets left for three of them, McCarthy, 2007: 57), leaving her husband with one last question: 'Can you do it? When the time comes? Can you?' (McCarthy, 2007: 28). Following her departure, the man and the boy set off on their journey in search of the sea in warmer southern climates. In a world of extreme danger in which what is left of humanity has given way to the law of the jungle, they learn that survival may require that they too abdicate their humanity. In a narrative of survival *in extremis* in which the mother's suicide is open to interpretation either as self-sacrifice or as a betrayal of the duty of endurance for the sake of one's species, father and son, each 'the other's world entire,' try to keep faith and survive, while aware that, in a radically altered environment, suicide may after all be their only option. In due course the father dies, but after a symbolic three days awaiting almost certain death, the boy encounters not the feared stranger-danger but a family of four including one son and one daughter. They live in a relatively undamaged environment and invite the boy to join them, thus setting up the beginnings of a community at least as promising (or even more so) than that of the first family in Genesis. In this instance, and circumventing the unanswered Biblical quandary as to whom, other than their own siblings, were the mates available to the children of Adam and Eve, the boy in *The Road* will at least be able to reproduce with a girl who is not his blood relative. Life goes on.

> When Spring comes,
> If I am already dead,
> Flowers will bloom as usual
> And the trees will be no less green than last Spring.
> Reality does not need me.
> I feel extremely happy
> When I think that my death doesn't matter at all
> If I knew that tomorrow I would die
> And that Spring was the day after tomorrow,
> I would die happy, because it would be here the day after tomorrow.
> If that is the right time for it, when else would it come, other than at the right time?

I like everything to be real and right;
And I like it because it would be so even if I didn't like it.
Therefore, if I die now, I will die happy,
Because everything is real and everything is right.
They can pray in Latin over my coffin, if they like.
If they like they can dance and sing around it.
I have no preferences regarding a time when I will no longer be able to have preferences.
Whatever will be, when it is, is the thing that will be. (Caeiro, 1914: 137-38)

Figure 15. Caspar David Friedrich, *Wanderer above the Sea of Fog*

All is as it should be, then, as long as something still is. The unforgiving way in which a world portrayed as empty of almost everything is depicted in McCarthy's *tour de force* may get as close as any narrative has come to imagining the impossible, and to preserving an unresolved dialectic between probable defeat and vestigial hope. Something also expressed with no need for further words by the Germanic nineteenth-century Romantic imagination in search of new worlds of Caspar David Friedrich.

When Will We Ever Learn?

Sometimes, even with the benefit of advance warning (H.G. Wells's *The Time Machine*, [1895] 1982; John Wyndham's 'Consider Her Ways,' [1956] 1983), disaster cannot be avoided. In *The Time Machine* the protagonist, a scientist identified simply as the Time Traveller, sets off on a journey into the future. His experience of time travel and the spectacle he witnesses of the evolution of the planet are told in the first-person in a narrative within a narrative. During his time-travel adventures, the first-person narrator tells of how he observed the sun and the moon traversing the sky and the changes to buildings and landscape around him as he travels through time to the year AD 802,701, when most of the story takes place, and briefly even further in time. In AD 802,701 he finds an apparently peaceful, pastoral community of humans who call themselves the Eloi. Like Margaret Atwood's Crakers (Atwood, 2003), the Eloi, who are small, delicate and seemingly happy, appear to be unintelligent and child-like. The surface perfection of their playful, carefree existence is however shadowed by an inexplicable fear of the night-time hours of darkness. This, it is revealed, is caused by regular nocturnal attacks by the Morlocks, dwellers in underground caves, who occasionally turn against their masters and literally devour them. As he explores this landscape, the Time Traveller comments on the factors that have resulted in the Eloi's physical condition and social arrangements. He supposes that their lack of intelligence and vitality are the logical result of humankind's past struggle to transform and subjugate nature through technology, politics, art and creativity. The eventual achievement of this goal had led to a state of stagnation characterized by unimaginative and incurious contentment. With no work to do, humans also become physically weak and small in stature and intellectually disabled.

> It seemed to me that I had happened upon humanity upon the wane. I thought of the physical slightness of the [Eloi], their lack of intelligence, [...] and it strengthened my belief in a perfect conquest of Nature. For after the battle comes Quiet. Humanity had been strong, energetic and intelligent, and had used all its abundant vitality to alter the conditions under which it lived. [... N]o doubt the exquisite beauty of the buildings I saw was the outcome of the last surgings of the now purposeless energy of mankind before it settled down into perfect harmony with the conditions under which it lived [...]. This has ever been the fate of energy in security; it takes to art and eroticism, and then come languor and decay. (Wells, [1895] 1982: 31-33)

After many adventures among the Eloi and Morlocks, the Traveller returns to his machine and travels into the far future, thirty million years from his own time, where he witnesses the final moments of a dying Earth whose very rotation has ceased under the dimming light of a fading sun. As the world begins to grow dark, life on Earth comes to an end.

> I looked about me to see if traces of animal life remained. [...] From the edge of the sea came a ripple and whisper. Beyond these lifeless sounds the world was silent. [...] All the sounds of man, the bleating of sheep, the cries of birds, the hum of insects, the stir that makes the background of our lives – all that was over. [...] The sky was absolutely black. (Wells, [1895] 1982: 77-78)

Traumatized by the knowledge he has gained, he puts the machine into reverse, arriving back in his laboratory just three hours after he had left. He recounts his experiences to his disbelieving friends, one of whom returns the following day to find that the Time Traveller had left again, this time taking a camera, presumably with the intention of collecting evidence for his claims. Having witnessed the end of the Earth on his first trip but having omitted to check on the date of his own death, however, he does not return from his second foray into time.

Even with the advantage of both foresight and hindsight, the Time Traveller is faced with the classic philosophical impasse of all time travel fiction, namely that the future, even if knowable, is always unchangeable. This quandary forms the basis of one of the philosophical underpinnings of Western culture: from the Ancient Greeks' formulation of the unavoidability of fate to some of the most accomplished science fiction to date. Important examples of the latter are Connie Willis's *The Doomsday Book* (Willis, 1993) and 'Firewatch' (Willis, 2005), as well as John Wyndham's thought-provoking 'Consider Her Ways,' to be discussed.

If I Knew then What I Know Now

In *The Doomsday Book* (Willis, 1993) Kivrin Engle, a young historian specializing in medieval history in 2054 Oxford, uses available time-travel technology to carry out field work in her research period, fourteenth-century England. An equipment malfunction results in her arrival twenty years later than planned. As twenty-first century Oxford succumbs to a deadly influenza epidemic, Kivrin finds herself in 1348 England, the year of the arrival of the Black Death. While in the twenty-first century medical resources are eventually able to gain control over the flu bacterium, back in the fourteenth century Kivrin is powerless to do anything other than watch as an entire community succumbs to a disease which she knows in the future will be curable.

In Wyndham's 'Consider Her Ways,' a novella narrated in the first person, Dr. Jane Waterleigh wakes up in what appears to be a hospital, trapped in a gigantic body she knows is not her own, but with no memory of her past. As her memory gradually returns she recalls taking part in a scientific experiment using a drug thought to trigger alternative states of consciousness. As she gathers more information, she realizes that she has been propelled into the future, to a society consisting entirely of women, most of whom have never heard of men. In due course she meets a historian who gives her enough information to allow her to deduce that she is now living approximately one and a half centuries after her own time. She learns that shortly after the time of the experiment that led her to where she is now, a scientist, Dr. Perrigan, unintentionally created a virus that killed all the men in the world, leaving only women. After a period of chaos, famine and widespread social breakdown, the small number of women who at that point had attained an advanced level of education (found mainly in the medical profession), had assumed control.

In Wyndham's novella, a forerunner of Poul Anderson's *Virgin Planet* (Anderson, 1959) and Margaret Atwood's *The Handmaid's Tale* (Atwood, 1985), and with theological allusions which also echo the ones in *The Terminator*, to be discussed, the task of social reconstruction in the aftermath of the cataclysmic event follows a blueprint conceived according to a Biblical model: 'Go to the ant thou sluggard, consider her ways' (*Proverbs* 6: 6). Global social reconstruction leads to the formation of a Christian, four-tiered caste-based society: doctors, mothers, servitors and workers. Within this model, based on the hierarchical arrangement of an ants' nest, each class has a specified function. The mothers' role is that of a factory-style production line in childbearing, reproduction without men being now possible thanks to emergency research undertaken following the catastrophe. Upon returning to her own time the narrator seeks out Dr. Perrigan, just then embarking on the experimental work that in the future will lead to the accidental creation of the virus. Failing to persuade him of the disastrous consequences that his research will have in the future, she resorts to murder and burns his research papers. The story concludes with a conversation between two of her colleagues who having succeeded as expert witnesses at her trial in sparing her a charge of murder, saw her placed in a psychiatric hospital on a lesser charge of diminished responsibility. While lamenting the insanity triggered by the experimental drug and commenting in wonder at the intensity of the hallucinations it induced, one of them ponders as an afterthought that Dr. Waterleigh had never discovered that Dr. Perrigan had left a son, also a biologist (and also called Dr. Perrigan), at that point engaged in completing his father's unfinished work.

'Consider Her Ways' is more than just a standard science fiction story. Particularly notable is a lengthy argument between the first-person narrator and the historian as to whether the new all-female society is better than the old one. In 1956, Wyndham's speculation on the nature of an single-sex society and his references to genetic manipulation and drug-related experiences are eerily prophetic of contemporary concerns (the dangers of GM crops, ideological debates around the battle of the sexes, but, above all, the problem, now real, of decreasing fertility rates in the West, particularly among men).[2]

In 1959, three years after the first release of 'Consider Her Ways,' Poul Anderson took up the same preoccupations from a different angle, in the novel *Virgin Planet* (Anderson, 1959), whose title also carries Biblical associations. The same preoccupation with human extinction originating either in the disappearance or in the infertility of either sex, is also revived in Paul Auster's *In the Country of Last Things* (Auster, 2005), P.D. James's *The Children of Men* (James, 2000, made into a film directed by Alfonso Cuarón in 2006) and in Atwood's *The Handmaid's Tale*.

The Children of Men, first published in 1992, is set in England in the early twenty-first century and, like the other works mentioned, it centres on

---

2 http://male-subfertility.tripod.com/id7.html
http://news.bbc.co.uk/1/hi/health/4118976.stm

the consequences of mass infertility. The title of the book is derived from the Old Testament: 'Thou turnest man to destruction; and sayest, "Return, ye children of men"' (*Psalms* 90(89): 3). The narrative voice in the novel alternates between the third and first persons, the latter in the form of the diary kept by Dr. Theodore Faron, whose name is normally shortened to Theo. Theo is an Oxford don (a profession that bears some relevance to his future role as teacher/leader/conduit of enlightenment. The novel opens with the first entry in Theo's diary. The date is 2021, the year when the last human being to be born on Earth was killed in a pub brawl in Buenos Aires. The novel's events, however, have their origin in 1995, which is referred to as Year Omega. The year before, in 1994, for reasons unknown, the sperm count of men had plummeted to zero worldwide. The last generation of children are called Omegas, after the last letter in the Greek alphabet. In 2006 Xan Lyppiatt, Theo's rich and charismatic cousin, appoints himself Warden of England and one last general election is held. Thereafter, as discussed in chapter 5, and as is often the case in end-of-the-world narratives, democracy is abolished in response to global cataclysm, and dictatorship is established. Although, unlike the scenarios depicted in Atwood's *The Handmaid's Tale* and Wyndham's 'Consider Her Ways,' the main rationale for autocratic rule in *The Children of Men* is the fact that, faced with the end of the species, most people no longer have any interest in politics, Xan is nonetheless regarded as a despot by his opponents. The plot unfolds around Theo's encounter with a woman called Julian, a member of the Five Fishes, a group of dissidents that includes their leader Rolf (Julian's husband), Miriam (a midwife) and Luke (a former priest). An eventful plot unfolds with the revelation that Julian is pregnant not by her husband but by the now deceased Luke. Following the deaths of both Xan and Rolf the demiurgically named Theo takes control of Council. Theo(dore) – 'God's gift,' who, like God, in the long-distant past had lost/sacrificed a child (in Theo's case the daughter he accidentally ran over) – now presents to the three remaining Council members (three Wise Men) the baby, begotten by a man who, in his capacity as priest, was God's representative on Earth, and whom he now baptizes. Julian, like Em in *Earth Abides* (Stewart, 1973) and Molly, Mark's mother in *Where Late the Sweet Birds Sang* (Wilhelm, 2006, to be discussed), all stand as equivalent representative figures of the Woman of the Apocalypse in the Book of Revelation, herself variously interpreted as representing the Church, the Mother of Nations, Mary or Eve.

78   The End of the World

Figure 16. Peter Paul Rubens, *The Virgin as the Woman of the Apocalypse*.
The Woman of the Apocalypse appears in Revelation 12: 1-18. 'And a great sign appeared in heaven: A woman clothed with the sun, and the moon under her feet [...] And being with child, she cried travailing in birth [...]. And there was seen another sign in heaven [...] a great red dragon, having seven heads and ten horns [...]. And his tail drew the third part of the stars of heaven and cast them to the earth. And the dragon stood before the woman who was ready to be delivered: that, when she should be delivered, he might devour her son. And she brought forth a man child, who was to rule all nations with an iron rod. And her son was taken up to God and to his throne. [...] And there was a great battle in heaven. [...] And that great dragon [...] who is called the devil and Satan [...] was cast unto the earth: and his angels were thrown down with him.

The film version of *The Children of Men* (Cuarón, 2006) differs from the novel's plot in some respects but maintains the basic tenets of a race on its way to extinction, a world in retreat from human influence and on a return path back to nature, and a reprieve couched, as was the case in other works mentioned above, in the vocabulary of a recognizable Christian cosmogony. Aspects of James's novel (gender power imbalances, threatened fertility, species continuity, restoration of divine authority and the nature of authoritarian rule), central also to popular works such as Philip Pullman's trilogy, *His Dark Materials* (Pullman, 2007), will be discussed further in chapter 5.

Not Mending Our Ways

From the Book of Genesis to Hollywood, in the aftermath of apocalypse, whether in a chastened Earth struggling to rebuild itself, or, as is sometimes the case, in outer space's colonial new beginnings, narratives of reconstruction almost always present us at best with ambiguity. Mistakes, also the lynchpin of historical narratives, tend to repeat themselves, hubris still defines humanity, and, as Joyce Evans observes, post-holocaust narratives act as 'the extension of the [...] belief in [humanity's] invulnerable omnipotence' (Evans, 1998, 136). Thus, as M. Keith Booker remarks with regard to Philip K. Dick's *Dr. Bloodmoney* (Dick, 2007), unlike standard romanticized versions of a new and better world after holocaust, 'the negative aspects of a post-holocaust world are the ones that most resemble the characteristics of [contemporary reality]' (Booker, 2001, 94). On the other hand, even when post-holocaust narratives do not end hopefully (for example, if they fail to suggest the rebirth of human civilization), they 'tend to present the death of the old civilization in a highly romantic way' (Booker, 2001, 95).

In *The Blob* (Yeasworth, 1958), a town otherwise torn by conflict (rebellious teenagers on the one hand, the representatives of authority – parents, the police – on the other), becomes united in the joint battle to defeat the eponymous gelatinous monster from outer space. Although victory at the end does not come with an absolute guarantee (in 1958 the monster is frozen by being sprayed with fire extinguishers and transported to the North Pole, but there is always a vestigial possibility that in the future it may defrost and come back to life – another twist to our current fears of global warming), within the diegetic time span of the film, harmony reigns at the end, even where none had prevailed before. What is established in the aftermath of the Blob's visitation, therefore, is an exaggerated version of a nineteen fifties, socially harmonious idyll. Paradoxically, however, this is the very status quo in which dissent had prevailed and that in some way had initially invited the visitation of Nemesis in the form of the arrival of the Blob. And what is not addressed is the question of what it might have been about the nature of that particular society that brought about the punishment in the first place. Whatever it might have been, in any case, the possibility of the return of a defrosted Blob seems much more likely in a reinstated order largely unchanged and defined by business as usual. Another day, another Blob.

Similar irresolution prevails at the end of Bernard Wolfe's *Limbo* (Wolfe, 1952). Having fled from America to a remote island in the Indian Ocean during World War III, the protagonist, a brain surgeon called Dr. Martine has lived there for eighteen years studying the islanders' traditional technique of Mandunga, a kind of lobotomy used to control aggression. When he travels back to America after his long absence, Martine is horrified to discover that what remains of the world after widespread nuclear destruction is now ruled by the culture of Immob (immobilization), which involves voluntary amputation as a somatic form of disarmament, aiming to control human aggression. In anticipation of works such as Huxley's *Brave New World*, *This Perfect Day* (Levin, [1970] 1994), *The Penultimate Truth* (Dick, [1964] 2005) and *The Simulacra* (Dick, [1964] 2004), worldwide crowd control by an occult elite (achieved, in these four novels by the rule of fear and/or by the administration of docility-inducing drugs) is achieved, in *Limbo*, either by lobotomy, for the savages in the island or by bodily mutilation in the rest of the world, while at the same time a secret agenda promotes the escalation by both sides of nuclear weapons, in preparation for one final war. Martine ultimately understands that voluntary amputation, while presented as a radical strategy for preventing war is in reality a betrayal of that objective (since it itself involves violence). Furthermore, it conceals a fundamental power structure (the controlling forces running the two opposing regimes) that operates on the basis of individual alienation (lobotomized diminishment; the disadvantages of the amputee; the loner/misfit nature of Martine, similar to that of Ish in *Earth Abides*, Stewart, [1949] 1973, to be discussed). And finally it encapsulates the failure of human communal existence, ultimately leading back to war.

Really *New* New Beginnings

The cases in which the possibility of human continuity seems most hopeful are precisely those in which, following apocalypse, a radical difference is introduced in the re-constructed world. In Kate Wilhelm's *Where Late the Sweet Birds Sang* (Wilhelm, [1976] 2006), both the dangers of repetition (here represented in the most literal way by the motif of a world perpetuated by cloning) and the need for difference (taken to the point of extreme individual alienation) are central to the unfolding of the plot. Global human infertility and environmental death are brought about by the deadly coalescing of the twin off-shoots of scientific advancement: pollution and war. The answer is initially deemed to be found in the search for more of the same, namely the science-driven perpetuation of species, including humans, through cloning, as a device for replicating things literally as they were. Cloning, however, as an exaggerated version of inbreeding, in due course is found to carry the same problems (genetic degeneration, increasing species non-viability), only more so. In the end, the solution, although still fragile and susceptible to ultimate failure at the conclusion of the novel, is a two-fold return to past practices: sexual reproduction in the rare cases where fertility still endures, and a parallel retracing of history away from scientific solutions to the rural, agricultural, community existence of the Noble Savage. Mark, brought up in clandestinity by his biological mother in a period when such family arrangements were already part of prehistory and children (clones) were raised in state-run communities, escapes and returns to an atavistic social arrangement – now almost completely extinct – of family, group loyalty and genetic diversity achieved through sexual reproduction.

In George R. Stewart's *Earth Abides*, similarly, following near-extinction as the result of an unnamed epidemic, the remnants of humanity (the fittest in this new status quo), set about a new beginning under the leadership of Ish (whose name echoes that of Ishie, a real-life Native American who in the twentieth century was the last surviving member of his tribe). As is often the case in post-apocalypse novels, the central characters are better able to survive the changed circumstances because in the world that's now gone they had never fitted in, had formed no strong bonds and therefore had nothing much to lose by its disappearance: in *The Day of the Triffids*, too, Bill Masen describes not only his but the general situation of the group of survivors from the comet as being generally one of more or less rootless alienation:

> Curiously I realized that in all this I had met no other person who was searching for someone else. Every one of them had been [...] snapped clean away from friends or relatives to link him with the past, and was beginning a new life with people who were strangers. (Wyndham, 1954: 202)

Similarly, in *The Kraken Wakes* (Wyndham, [1953] 1980), Mike and Phyllis Watson, who some years before the events that lead to the world-ending disaster, had lost their only child, have no one left to worry about but themselves. And in *Earth Abides* (Stewart, 1973), Ish, the post-apocalyptic new Adam, who, prior to the epidemic had been one of society's alienated misfits (he 'always was solitary' with no 'need to talk to other people') realizes that 'in some ways, very curiously, he felt a new security and even satisfaction at the contemplation of a solitary life' (Stewart, 1973: 42).

Something Old in Something New

Throughout *Earth Abides*, a *sui generis bildungsroman* that takes Ish from youth to old age and death, the revelation granted to him (in the common usage but also apocalyptic sense of the term) is that retracing the path back to what was in place immediately prior to the epidemic is not an option. As is often the case in post-apocalyptic narratives, however, that being one of the central points developed here, finding a new form of existence proves to be more difficult than would at first appear, even in circumstances in which the old way had been destroyed. Instead of a radical new world, almost always, the chosen path to survival involves retracing and recreating human history: in the case of *Earth Abides*, by retracing humanity's footsteps far back to a rudimentary society structured along lines which possibly reproduce the earliest human communities:

> He had been in the Library hundreds of times before [...] But now under the new conditions, he felt a strange new sense of awe. Here rested in storage the wisdom by which civilization had been built, and could be rebuilt. Now that he knew himself soon to be a father, he had suddenly a new attitude, a feeling for the future. The child should not grow up to be a parasite, scavenging forever. And it would not need to. Everything was here. All the knowledge. (Stewart, 1973: 118)

Recreating what had been in place before, inevitably involves the recognition and perpetuation of old power structures and role allocations, privileging from the very beginning Ish's own position as male, demiurge and first comer in the processes of both the writing of history and the moulding of the future:

> That was the difference between woman and man. She felt only in terms of the immediate, and was more interested in being able to spot her child's birthday than in all the future of civilization. Again he felt superior to her. [...] But yet, as so often, her instinct was right – a great pity if the historical record should be broken at some point! Doubtless in the long run, archaeologists could restore the continuity [...] but it would save a lot of work if someone merely kept the tradition. (Stewart, 1973: 119-21)

> There must be others that he could find also to join with them – good people who would help in the new world. He would start looking for people again. He would look craftily, trying to keep away from all those who had suffered too much from the shock, whose minds and bodies were not what one wanted to build up the new society. (Stewart, 1973: 122)

In short, 'people like us,' suitable to join Em (Emma) as the 'mother of nations' and himself as the founding patriarch, in building a new 'world without end.' (Stewart, 1973: 123)

In a more metaphysically speculative way, in *Solaris*, Stanislaw Lem's novel of 1961, adapted to television by B. Nirnburgs in 1968, into a feature film by Andrei Tarkovsky in 1972, again by Steven Soderbergh in 2002, and into an opera by the German composer Michael Obst in 1995, there are no new worlds that the human mind can experience and the imperative of repetition is made both literal and ontological. Solaris is a planet covered by a malleable substance able to imitate human experience exactly. Its nature, which is that of a mirror, means that Solaris's own reality, if it indeed exists, is forever unavailable: wherever one looks, one sees only what one already knows. In this way, Solaris imposes upon those who experience it the realization of the limits of their perception. We can never grasp anything new or different, only that within which we already find ourselves. Just as in the nightmare scenarios of John Carpenter's *Escape from New York* (Carpenter, 1981) or Paul Auster's *In the Country of Last Things* (Auster, 2005), it is possible that an alternative reality exists, but we can neither imagine it, comprehend it nor gain possession of it. In Auster's novel, for example, Anna Blume travels to the unnamed city of the title where, after an unspecified large-scale event, reality has given way to a nightmarish self-enclosed world of violence, famine and shadowy dictatorial rule. In Auster, however, while like in *Solaris* repetition is the default mode, it is also that which must at all costs be avoided, lest one should lose oneself:

> Bit by bit, the city robs you of uncertainty. There can never be any fixed path, and you can survive only if nothing is necessary to you. Without warning, you must be able to change, to drop what you are doing, to reverse. In the end, there is nothing that is not the case. [...] The essential thing is not to become inured. For habits are deadly. Even if it is for the hundredth time, you must encounter each thing as if you have never known it before. No matter how many times, it must always be the first time. (Auster, 2005: 6-7)

With the cyclical relentlessness that commonly characterizes these fictional infernos, the world may have ended, but, as J.K. Rowling would have it, the battle nevertheless continues:

> You would think that sooner or later it would all come to an end. Things fall apart and vanish, and nothing new is made. People die, and babies refuse to be born. In all the years I have been here, I can't remember seeing a single newborn child. And yet, there are always new people to replace the ones who have vanished. (Auster, 2005: 7)

At the heart of Anna's quest in the city are two young men: her brother William, whom she had originally come to the city to rescue from a never-specified disaster; and Sam, the lover by whom she conceives a child which she later miscarries, from whom she is separated and with whom she is later reunited. In the meaningless void of a city in which slaughterhouses sustain a black market in human flesh, Anna escapes being killed but, prior to their reunion, Sam loses his mind:

> I gave up trying to be anyone [...]. The object of my life was to remove myself from my surrounding, to live in a place where nothing could hurt me anymore. [...] The idea was to achieve indifference, an indifference so powerful and sublime that it would protect me from further assault. I said goodbye to you, Anna; [...] I said goodbye to the thought of going home. I even tried to say goodbye to myself. [...] To want nothing, I kept saying to myself, to have nothing, to be nothing. I could imagine no more perfect solution than that. In the end I came close to living the life of a stone. (Auster, 2005: 162-63)

Sam's catatonia echoes that of Edmond in Meg Rosoff's heart-rending and hilarious *How I Live Now* (Rosoff, 2005). Written in the first person by yet another female narrator, in this instance fifteen-year old Daisy, it narrates with adolescent matter-of-factness what might possibly have been the end of the world. While on holiday in England with until-then unknown relatives, following her widowed father's second marriage to an unpleasant stepmother (Davina 'the Diabolical'), and in an Enid Blyton-ish absence of any grown-ups, Daisy and her cousins live through world-shattering events and their aftermath:

> The first thing that happened wasn't our fault. That was a bomb that went off in the middle of a big train station in London [...] and something like seven or seventy thousand people were killed.
>
> That obviously went down very badly with the population at large and was pretty scary etc., but to be honest it didn't seem to have much to do with us way off in the country. [...G]iven that we were about four million miles from the epicentre I'd say we stood a pretty good chance of surviving. [...]
>
> We went [...] and bought as much bottled water and canned things as we could carry home [...]. That still left a whole afternoon with the end of the world about to happen [...]. (Rosoff, 2005: 27-30)

Following separation from Edmond, her cousin (and lover, even though they were 'too young and too related,' Rosoff, 2005: 51), Daisy survives the war, is forced to return to a USA wrecked by global conflict and after some years succeeds in returning to England where she finds Edmond, now a post-traumatic mute who spends his days tending a garden that bears testimony to the unspeakable violence he had witnessed during the war:

> I've never had my own garden but I suddenly recognized something in the tangle of this one that wasn't beauty. Passion, maybe. And something else. Rage. [...]
>
> After that day, I could barely enter the garden without a huge effort of will. The air was suffocating, charged, the hungry plants sucking at the earth with their ferocious appetites. You could almost watch them grow, pressing their fat green tongues up through the black earth. They emerged selfish and starving, gasping for air. (Rosoff, 2005: 196-67)

Like Sam in Auster's novel, Edmond survives but only just, both physically and mentally, and like Sam, only with the help of the girl who narrates his tale to us. In Rosoff, too, the ending is inconclusive, leaving at best the possibility of a new beginning of sorts, but never free from the remnants of the past:

> I have no idea how damaged Edmond is [... S]o now I'm here with him and [...] all the hard work of running a farm and staying alive in a country deformed and misshapen by war. [...] And that's how I live now. (Rosoff, 2005: 210-11)

Within these altered realities, no further alteration is possible. In a manner akin to the reversal and repetition of a möbius strip, so, too, in *Solaris* (Tarkovsky, 1972; Soderbergh, 2002), *Escape from New York* (Carpenter, 1981), *In the Country of Last Things* (Auster, 2005) and *How I live Now* (Rosoff, 2005), a process of brutal de-familiarization of the familiar (the real) creates discomfort and unease in two mutually contradictory ways that, in coexistence, annul the possibility of meaning: by making what used to be familiar strange, and by emphasizing its fundamental immutability.

In *Solaris*, Lem's central epistemological position [...] is that we can never know the *noumen* of things; that we are forever imprisoned by the structure of our minds and bodies. (Franz Rottensteiner, quoted in Ketterer, 1974, 185).

> In other words, man's understanding of the external universe is fundamentally anthropocentric. [...] For Lem there are no new worlds that men can experience. Wherever man goes there are only extensions of himself. (Ketterer, 1974: 185)

In the infinitely malleable planet of Solaris there is no such thing as a new reality. Less intuitively obvious, but with the same effect in what has been argued above, is the hypothesis that even after cataclysmic (apocalyptic) change, we can only ever imagine more of what we already know.

There are of course exceptions, for example *I Am Legend* (Matheson, 1954) or 'Dark Benediction' (Miller, 2007), in which, as discussed previously, normality (non-vampirism, un-diseased existence) is a relative concept, always susceptible to change, and defined, at any given moment, merely as what a majority deems it to be. Mostly, however – including extreme cases such as for example Kurt Vonnegut's *Cat's Cradle* (Vonnegut, 1981) or J.G. Ballard's *The Crystal World* (Ballard, 1985), in which respectively the planet and time itself freeze – the end wrought by apocalyptic upheaval may after all take the shape of stagnant continuity (permanent immobilization) of what was already there. A tendency for business as usual may be both humanity's greatest strength and its greatest weakness.

Outlandish Hope

At the outer reaches of fictional survival, albeit with the support of some of science's most august minds, we find the kind of narrative that does accept the possibility of global annihilation but relocates left-over humanity on another planet, or at least in the search for one. Writing about the possibility of absolute planetary destruction, Martin Rees, Astronomer Royal, argues as follows:

> 'The thought of cutting off life's flow, of amputating this future, is so shocking, so alien to nature, and so contradictory to life's impulse that we can scarcely entertain it before turning away in revulsion and disbelief.' [...]

> It would be absurd to claim that emigration into space is the answer [... If] some disaster reduced humanity to a far lower population, living in primitive conditions in a devastated wasteland, the survivors would still find Earth's environment more hospitable than that of any other planet. Nevertheless, even a few pioneering groups, living independently of Earth, would offer a safeguard against the worst possible disaster – the foreclosure of intelligent life's future through the extinction of all humankind. (Rees, 2003: 169-70)

Walter Miller's defining novel, *A Canticle for Leibowitz* (Miller, 2007), is a rendition of this scenario in fiction. The story is structured in three parts: *Fiat Homo*, *Fiat Lux*, and *Fiat Voluntas Tua* (Let there be Man, Let there be Light and Let Thy Will be done). The parts are separated by periods of six centuries each. The first part begins 600 years after 20th century civilization has been destroyed by a nuclear war, known as the Flame Deluge. The war had led to a violent backlash (known as the Simplification) against the culture of advanced knowledge and technology out of which had sprung nuclear weapons. During Simplification, anyone of any learning and eventually anyone who could simply read becomes the target of lynch mobs. Illiteracy, as in the autocratic utopias of *This Perfect Day* (Levin, 1994), *Fahrenheit 451* (Bradbury, 1976), and to a limited extent Huxley's *Brave New World*, becomes the guarantor of social stability, and books are destroyed *en masse*. Isaac Edward Leibowitz, a Jewish electrical engineer working for the United States military, who survives the war and converts to Roman Catholicism, founds a monastic order, the Albertian Order of Leibowitz, dedicated to preserving knowledge by hiding books (*Memorabilia*), smuggling them to safety (*booklegging*) and, as in *Fahrenheit 451*, memorizing, and copying them. Leibowitz is eventually betrayed, martyred and later beatified as a candidate to sainthood.

The last segment, *Fiat Voluntas Tua* (*Thy Will Be Done*) is set in the year 3781, following catastrophic wars of various natures over a period of centuries. The world's two remaining superpowers, the Asian Coalition and the Atlantic Confederacy, have been embroiled in a cold war for 50 years, and it is rumoured that both sides are now assembling nuclear capabilities in space. The Leibowitzan Order's mission of preserving the *Memorabilia* has expanded to the preservation of all knowledge. The abbot, Dom Jethras Zerchi, recommends to New Rome that the Church reactivate long agreed contingency plans, code name *Quo Peregrinatur Grex* (Wither Wanders the Flock), involving unspecified vehicles in the Church's possession since 3756. Following a nuclear incident between the two superpowers and its rapid escalation, *Quo Peregrinatur* is launched, carrying a crew and the Order's *Memorabilia*, with the objective of perpetuating the Church on colony planets. In a valedictory passage at the end of the novel Brother Joshua, the last crew member to board the starship, shakes Earth's dirt from his sandals, murmuring '*sic transit mundus*' ('thus passes the world'). A final vignette depicts the devastation left on Earth: as seabirds and fish succumb to the poisonous fallout, a shark, the oldest living species on the planet, escapes contamination by moving down into deep water, although even there, it is noted, there is nothing left for it to eat. The knowledge preserved by the escaping flock, we suppose, would include the awareness of the nuclear possibilities that had necessitated this new exodus in the first place. Paradoxically, then, the mechanism now activated to ensure that even if the entire Earth is destroyed, its intellectual achievements are not, transplants to the new reality that which led to the destruction of the old one: at the end, what we witness is the beginning of a new but identical cycle, merely in a different place.

Escape into outer space, oceanic depths or, as in Poul Anderson's *Tau Zero* (Anderson, 2006), into another universe in a different time dimension, stretches science fiction to the limits of philosophical intelligibility but worryingly ultimately results in all-too-familiar scenarios. In the latter novel, for example, due to an engine malfunction a space ship is propelled through cycles of billions of light-years, beyond the end of the universe, and through to the early stages of a new one. There, the crew homes in on a newly-created planet where, paradoxically they find that the only vocabulary that can articulate the new reality is a risibly arcane one. Arcane and therefore also limited by all the hallmarks of the old reality, now dead: competitiveness, hierarchy, species entitlement:

> 'The important thing is that we be about the first intelligent life in those parts.'
> They stared at him.
> He smiled in a way they had not seen before. 'I'd like us to have our pick of worlds, when our descendants get around to interstellar colonization,' he said. 'And I'd like us to become – oh, the elders. Not imperialists; that's ridiculous; but people who were there from the beginning and know their way around, and are worth learning from. [...L]et's make this, as nearly as possible, a human galaxy, in the widest sense of the word "human." Maybe even a human universe. I think we've earned that right.' (Anderson, 2006: 186)

The law of the jungle, whether articulated in terms of a supremacy of intellect, territory, age, species, or, as will be discussed shortly, gender, would appear to remain a constant, whatever the universe may be.

Plus Ça Change: Needs-Must Dictatorship

In *Tau Zero*'s brand new universe, in a cosmologically different time dimension, a super-educated heroine who was formerly in charge of the space mission's personnel, now shows aspirations that are conservative in both political and gender terms, and dreams of becoming the traditional little woman behind a very macho throne occupied by her former subaltern:

> 'Kings get no holidays. [...] They look to you, the man who saved them, the man who dared survive, they look to you for – '
> He interrupted her in the most enjoyable way.
> 'Carl!' she protested.
> 'Do you mind?'
> 'No. Certainly not. On the contrary. But – I mean, your work – ' (Anderson, 2006: 189)

Ingrid Lindgren, now no longer top-notch cosmonaut but coy princess prettily diffident before her man, embodies the immediate reinstatement of old norms, even in what is most literally a different time and place. If cataclysm is the starting point for a new beginning, it is also often the opportunity for the rise of new forms of leadership redolent of all that was most familiar (and often most reactionary) in the time before. As in George R. Stewart's inexplicably well-regarded *Earth Abides*, in Anderson, too, even in a different universe, male fantasies of alpha-male superiority remain an immutable phenomenon.

And in Will Self's *The Book of Dave*, post-flood London society 500 AD (After Dave, which is approximately 2500 CE), is governed according to the embittered diary rantings of a London cabbie (short-hand for xenophobia, misogyny and general reactionarism) unearthed five centuries later, and adopted as the gospel of a new religion.

In this new world, an extreme backlash against the custodial lack of rights of divorced fathers in the twentieth and twenty-first centuries has resulted in a society in which men and women live apart because the men so choose: 'It'd be better` if we never 'ad to shack up wiv 'em in the first place – don't chew agree? Knock 'em up – then fuck off!' (Self, 2006: 348). In this new world, divorce courts now see 'mummies' (women) burnt at the stake as the normal outcome of disagreements over custody (the hated changeover of children from one parent to the other, after each allotted period of access).

> That you, Sharún Lees, on three separate occasions, did willfully retain your three kiddies and keep them concealed from their lawful dad; for this

heinous malefaction [...] you have been sentenced [...] to be burned and the noxious exhaust of your chellish body piped into your kiddies. Let it be marked, no Changeover – (Self, 2006: 387)

Similarly, in Atwood's *The Handmaid's Tale*, following nuclear, chemical and biological war, the Republic of Gilead (the name comes from Genesis 31:25 and Numbers 32:1 meaning 'hill of testimony' or 'mount of witness'), a country formed within the borders of what was originally the United States of America, comes under the control of a new theocratic government sustained by the rule of a military dictatorship. As in *The Children of Men* (James, 2000), a large portion of the population has become sterile. The underpinnings of the Republic of Gilead are derived from the Biblical story of Rachel, wife of Jacob. Rachel was barren. After many years, she finally achieves her desire for motherhood by persuading Jacob to impregnate her maid, Bilhah, who subsequently gives birth while reclining between her legs.

> And when Rachel saw that she bare Jacob no children, Rachel envied her sister; and said unto Jacob, Give me children, or else I die. And Jacob's anger was kindled against Rachel: and he said, *Am* I in God's stead, who hath withheld from thee the fruit of the womb? And she said, Behold my maid Bilhah, go in unto her; and she shall bear upon my knees, that I may also have children by her. And she gave him Bilhah her handmaid to wife: and Jacob went in unto her. And Bilhah conceived, and bare Jacob a son. (Genesis 30: 1-5)

In Atwood, the story is told from the point of view of the Bilhah figure, Offred, the latter a patronymic which describes her function: she is the property 'of Fred,' of her Commander, to whom she belongs as his concubine or tithed reproductive commodity. In a profane rendition of Mary's *fiat* in the Annunciation ('behold the handmaid of the Lord'), and like all women who are still fertile, Offred is the chattel of an (omni)potent male ruler, and is enslaved as Handmaid for the purpose of impregnation. She is part of the first wave of Gilead's women who still remember pre-Gilead times (approximately 1970–2000 AD within the text), a version of late 20th century Western societies in which women, albeit comparatively free, feared physical and sexual violence, and despite long-running feminist campaigns, had not yet achieved full equality. Thus, in pre-Gileadean society, and despite holding a university degree, Offred was a low-ranking white collar worker whose colleagues, all women working under a male boss, generally lacked full material autonomy. In the Handmaid's account, therefore, women are depicted to a greater or lesser extent as the property of men in both societies, the implication being that in the world pre-Gilead (which is our own contemporaneous, twenty-first century one), some of the premises of female subordination, albeit in a less extreme form, are shared with the future Gilead regime.

The common thread of misogyny (critically or uncritically observed) that links the nature of post-apocalypse futures in Will Self (2006), Margaret Atwood (1991), George R. Stewart (1973), Poul Anderson (2006) and many others, results in new worlds filled with compliant Stepford wives: a phenomenon itself worthy of scrutiny in a future study.

In unstable post-apocalyptic statuses quo (Wyndham's *The Chrysalids*; *This Perfect Day*, Levin, 1994), moreover, differences other than gender also underpin criteria for fear and exclusion. In books by authors from Aldous Huxley and George Orwell to Ira Levin, Philip K. Dick and P.D. James, unusual intellectual gifts often represent a danger to those that possess them, and can be used as the justification for undue exercise of force on the part of a defensive status quo.

In numerous narratives, ranging from canonic texts to popular science fiction, as will be discussed in chapter 5, following the advent of large-scale catastrophes and ensuing social collapse, autocratic regimes almost invariably assume control. In many post-apocalyptic dystopias including the ones described in Siegel's *Invasion of the Body Snatchers*, Wyndham's *The Day of the Triffids*, Bradbury's *Fahrenheit 451*, Orwell's *Nineteen Eighty-Four* and in Atwood's *The Handmaid's Tale*, no conclusive resolution is reached. In all of them, however, we find strong hints that after global events of a cataclysmic nature, authoritarian statuses quo tend to emerge as the default social organization. Furthermore, these new autocracies, and the brands of alienation they sustain, may turn out to be quantitatively but not qualitatively different from social structures ostensibly supposed to be or to have been essentially democratic. It may be true, then, that, as suggested by these and other works, in all cases, albeit with diverse enemies in mind, and in the language of the standard film trailer, we should all be afraid. We should be very afraid!

Boxing with Shadows

More worryingly, even, as both *Invasion of the Body Snatchers* (Siegel, 1956; Kaufman, 1978) and Atwood's *The Handmaid's Tale* imply, the enemy may be all the more dangerous for being not alien, but in fact just like us, either actually one *of* us or at least indistinguishable from us. Sometimes, even, one of those who, in Western democracies, we have selected and elected to protect us. In *Shadow on the Hearth* (Merrill, 1950), for example, although an unexpected Soviet nuclear attack was the catalyst for a radical world change, from the point of view of Gladys, the immediate adversary in the aftermath of the disaster is someone much closer to home. More pressingly than any remote foreign enemy or even than radiation danger, her most immediate threat is Jack Turner, her neighbour, now revealed as the community's figure of authority selected by the government in preexisting preparations for the event of a nuclear attack. In the emerging post-apocalyptic new order, Jack emerges as Gladys's sexual pursuer, with all the authority bestowed upon him in a world in which old rules no longer apply.

In Stanley Kubrick's *Dr. Strangelove*, likewise, the American President's chief strategic advisor is the possessor of an unfortunate arm which regularly jerks out of control in a salute evocative if not of the current Enemy Number One (Cold War Russia) at least of the one very recently defeated (Nazi Germany). In the end, in films such as John Frankenheimer's classic *Seven Days in May* of 1964 or in *Fail-Safe* (Lumet, 1964; Frears, 2000), already discussed, the destroyers of worlds are close to home, and, more worryingly even, in the case of *Fail-Safe* (as arguably in the case of Oppenheimer, who coined that famous phrase), they act with good intentions (the perceived greater good). In Frankenheimer's film, for example, Burt Lancaster, as the square-jawed Air Force General James Mattoon Scott (supposedly based on the real-life figure of General Edwin A. Walker), plots a *coup d'état* to oust a president dangerously keen on nuclear disarmament, something in his view likely to render the US vulnerable to Soviet attack. The film, disapproved of by the Pentagon but encouraged by President Kennedy in the months before his death, opens up debate on the possibility of democracy being overthrown in the name of national security.

Which of course is more disturbing, even, than an enemy from the ranks of the usual suspects. If the enemy is one of us, who shall I fear today? Are enemies, old or new, in fact sometimes not identifiable and controllable others, but instead part of the fabric of a self which, as urged by the oracle in the Temple at Delphi, we should seek to know? Are the atomic explosions unleashed by a homely Stetson-wearing cowboy at the end of *Dr. Strangelove* the precursors of real-life possibilities under the command of equally attired leaders such as Ronald Reagan and George W. Bush? Is Kubrick's nightmare lunatic in fact a warning that we have indeed failed to keep the Body Snatchers at bay? That they are already in our midst? That they are us?

Who Shall I Be Afraid of now?

In our new century the imminent bogeyman is no longer Communism lurking behind an iron curtain or in a Caribbean backyard. He is instead the Middle Eastern version of the oriental Kamikaze, the elemental high-jacker of jumbo jets flung against the skyscrapers of the New World in the first year of the new millennium, or else an enemy even closer to home: the Beardy Weirdy with a black rucksack on the London underground. At present, the alien Muslim in our midst is ever at hand to justify the silencing of inopportune civil rights libertarians prone to condemning knee-jerk preventive reactions on the part of Establishmentarian forces of law and order. In his essay on the American 1950s fear of Communism, *The Great Fear*, David Caute (1978) argues that the body politic has always used popular paranoia as a useful means for containing and controlling dissent. The cast may change, but the plot, whether fictional or historical, old or new, does not differ in essentials. The script, whether that of sci-fi plots, real-life historical autocracies or their contemporary equivalents (Pentagon neo-cons, their Whitehall fellow travellers, Middle Eastern enmities of polymorphous varieties, to name but a few) remains essentially unchanged. A number of conspiracy theories, both in fiction and in reality, argue that the forces ostensibly deployed by the status quo to protect us against supposed aliens in our midst aim in fact to protect that self-same status quo against *us*. Such theories underpin the common fear behind many of science fiction's and political thought's diverse agendas from Orwell to Foucault: namely, speculations regarding a world manipulated by hidden forces of unknown nature, generic Big Brothers who use fear to control potential troublemakers. Writers from Ray Bradbury to Philip K. Dick, from Aldous Huxley to Margaret Atwood, from H.G. Wells to José Saramago, have all worried about a fear behind a fear: namely that the ultimate threat (absolute apocalypse) made flesh (or machine), may after all be not the ultimate threat but the penultimate one. *Quis custodiet ipsos custodes?*

In Philip K. Dick's novel, called, very much to the point here, *The Penultimate Truth* (Dick, 2005), nuclear holocaust never really happened but humanity has been conned into believing that it did. The human race, or what is left of it, now lives in underground bunkers, producing the technology for a supposedly on-going nuclear war fought by machines (robots known as 'leadies') on the surface of a planet believed to be irreparably contaminated. The reality, however, involved a limited and short-lasting nuclear war which left behind an only partly contaminated Earth, now divided into enormous quasi-feudal demesnes ruled by a happy few (very few), thanks to a confidence trick that has kept the remnants of left-over humanity in bondage and servitude.

We All Fall Down

In José Saramago's *Blindness* (Saramago, 1997), and with more than a coincidental whiff of a similarity to Camus's *La peste* (Camus, [1947] 1972), the disaster which strikes a community (blindness, rather than disease), but which soon acquires many of the characteristics of standard pestilence (dead bodies, decay) comes with no explanation, and only the possibility of a link, causal and/or punitive, to a wider and polymorphously perverted status quo. Either way, the effects are essentially similar to those in Dick's novel: in this not-so-brave new world, reality becomes meaningless and blindness, here literal rather than symbolic, becomes the unmanageable norm, in a world that no longer makes sense. In Saramago, as in other apocalyptic novels and films (*The Day of the Triffids*, already mentioned, canonic narratives and films/series such as *Earth Abides*, 1973; *Survivors*, 1975-77, 2008-10) the onset of chaos is almost immediate, and is characterized by the swift arrival of the four horsemen of the Apocalypse: famine, since the blind cannot easily find or make food; war, as the result of competition for scarce resources; pestilence, as people die and bodies decompose, and death, which feeds on the effects of the other three. In Saramago, as well as in the other narratives mentioned, the component of decay and the resulting stench become the primary objective correlatives of a problem that is literal but also symbolic (of political and social corruption). In each case the disaster not only unleashes violence and autocracy in a variety of forms but it also reveals that such tendencies were always already there, only latent. Camus's allegory of encroaching Fascism in *La peste* is echoed in the prompt decision taken by the powers that be in Saramago's novel to control the contagion of blindness – that which defines these others as other – by incarcerating them, appropriately, where dictatorships have traditionally confined that which is unorthodox: a disused psychiatric hospital. And why not? The label of madness is a solution which has been historically tried and tested by every human autocracy (whether defined by party politics, class or gender) since difference began. And it is perhaps apposite that, in the omnipresent stench that is the principal hallmark of the catastrophe in Saramago's novel, from the point of view of both the outside on-lookers and those who cannot see but can still smell (the increasingly filthy and dehumanized prisoners themselves), the affliction renders its sufferers literally abject, Kristeva's term for a variety of social and political exclusions.

> [the doctor] ... felt a pressing need to relieve himself. At the spot where he found himself, he was not sure that he would be able to find the lavatories, but he decided to take a chance. He was hoping that someone would at least have remembered to leave there the toilet paper which had been delivered with the containers of food. He got lost twice on the way and was in some distress because he was beginning to feel desperate and just when he could hold back no longer, he was finally able to take down his trousers and crouch over the open latrine. The stench choked him. He had the impression of having stepped on some soft pulp, the excrement of someone who had missed the hole of the latrine or who had decided to relieve himself without any consideration for others. (Saramago, 1997: 88)

And in *The Day of the Triffids*:

> The first thing I was aware of the next morning was the smell. [...] I am not going into details about [it]; those who knew it will never forget it, the rest of it is indescribable. It rose from every city and town for weeks, and travelled on every wind that blew. When I woke to it that morning it convinced me beyond doubt that the end had come. Death is just the shocking end of animation: it is dissolution that is final. (Wyndham, [1951] 1984: 149)

It is curious although also surprisingly unimportant that in H.G. Wells's 'The Country of the Blind'([1904] 1982), the definition of orthodoxy (sight as opposed to sightlessness) is reversed without however causing any significant change in overall effect. Normality, it soon becomes clear, is only what the majority declare it to be. In Wells, the hero, Nunez, is an educated man, traveller, explorer and philosopher, conqueror of both lands and ideas, who in the course of a mountain climbing expedition finds himself adrift in an imponderable new world. Arrival in the country of the blind is a plunge into the unknown, both literally (he falls down a ravine into the valley where that country is located) and rhetorically (he finds himself marooned in an upside-down world, where life is lived by night and sight is an unknown phenomenon).

Exploration as both concept and practice usually has a double edge (knowledge and conquest, gnostic and material profit) and it is seldom a fair trade. Nunez's instinctive reaction on finding himself in a community where all are blind, resembles that of the opportunistic Taylor faced with a population of mutes in *Planet of the Apes* (1968): 'Look on the bright side: if this is the best they've got around here, in six months we'll be running this planet' (Schaffner, 1968). Both adopt a standard formula, namely the desire for conquest in both senses of the word (conquest of power and conquest of love), based on the assumption that in the country of the blind the one-eyed man is king (and the two-eyed man, presumably, is Master of the Universe). In effect, however, in each narrative the sighted or speaking man finds himself at a counter-intuitive disadvantage in a habitat set up respectively for either blindness or ape domination, and in which neither sight nor human status are of any relevance.

In Wells, Nunez is eventually required to have his eyes gauged out as the precondition for being allowed to remain in the community and marry the girl he loves. As was the case with vampirism in *I Am Legend* (Matheson, 1954; Lawrence, 2007) and *Twilight* (Meyer, 2007), or skin disfigurement in 'Dark Benediction' (Miller, 2007), it is not sight, nor blindness or an unblemished complexion *per se*, therefore, only the value attributed to them in any given set of circumstances, that really alters in any significant way either the brutal specificities of majority rule or its criteria for defining who is predator and who is prey.

We Will Look after You

In the new worlds post-apocalypse, even under relatively benevolent rules of government (*Survivors*, Nation, 1975-77; Hodges, 2008-10; *Earth Abides*, Stewart, 1973) any threat to the community (diseased new arrivals, supposed delinquents) is summarily dealt with by capital punishment, in the interests of a commonweal that must prioritize its own continuity above all.

And as was the case with the H.G. Wells and Saramago texts, in Wyndham's *The Day of the Triffids*, too, widespread social disintegration encounters the immediate or eventual problem of opportunistic dictatorship (the one-eyed king): the newly arrived conqueror in Wells, the diktat of authoritarian power that initially confines the first few victims of blindness to a make-shift leper colony in Saramago, and the triffids who, with uncanny speed take advantage of near-universal blindness to begin an efficient takeover of the world:

> Those damn [triffids] have the drop on us. [...] there's more to them than we think. How did they *know*? They started to break loose the moment there was no one to stop them. [When we went blind] they were around this house the very next day. [...] They couldn't do that here until conditions made it possible. They didn't even try. But when they could, they did it *at once* – almost as if they *knew* they could. (Wyndham, [1951] 1984: 235-36)

Something which, indeed, had been presciently foreseen years before the catastrophe, by an earlier triffid expert:

> If it were a choice for survival between a triffid and a blind man, I know which one I would put money on. (Wyndham, [1951] 1984: 48)

> A triffid's in a damn sight better position to survive than a blind man. (Wyndham, [1951] 1984: 77)

In Saramago, the blindness of a minority leads to the implementation of a despotic, final-solution style bureaucracy, only curtailed by the subsequent on-set of general blindness, which abolishes the minority's difference and makes sightlessness the norm. In the early stages of the epidemic the problem to be addressed regards the means whereby the status quo (the sighted) might control the alien (the blind and contagious other), something reinforced by the bureaucratic language that describes the measures taken in response to this outbreak of difference:

> The Government is fully aware of its responsibilities and hopes that those to whom this message is directed will, as the upright citizens they doubtless are, also assume their responsibilities, bearing in mind that the isolation in which they now find themselves will represent, above any personal considerations, an act of solidarity with the rest of the nation's community. (Saramago, 1997: 41)

> The Government regrets having to enforce to the letter what it considers its right and duty... (Saramago, 1997: 65)

> The army regrets having been forced to repress with weapons a seditious movement responsible for creating a situation of imminent risk, for which the army was neither directly nor indirectly to blame... (Saramago, 1997: 81)

In Saramago, then, blindness leads to dictatorial rule, whether by the sighted over the blind or by the ruthless over the meek (within the ranks of the blind). Similarly, in *The Day of the Triffids* and *The Kraken Wakes*, attempts to restore structures of social organization in the aftermath of disaster, inevitably assume the character of dictatorial rule.

And in H.G. Wells's 'The Country of the Blind' (Wells, [1904] 1982), blindness and sight, while demarcating difference, simply reverse definitions of supremacy and subalternity. The arrival of Nunez in the country of the blind is not the gnostic outcome of an enterprise undertaken with deliberation, but an unintended plunge into the geographic and sociopolitical unknown. In this case, therefore, the journey of discovery was wrong-footed from the start, and the knowledge that is attained is troubling (in the country of the blind the one-eyed man is *not* king after all, and may in fact be forced to go blind in order to gain acceptance).

Is it possible, then, ever to learn one's lesson, or is it rather the case that any lesson can only ever be learnt after curiosity has already irreversibly killed the cat? If, as suggested before, the loss of paradise following the theft of knowledge was the first apocalypse, it is clear that after Eve, you can't go home again, not ever, not to any real pre-lapsarian state of being. There is no such thing as a born-again virgin or an un-fallen mother. In 'The Country of the Blind' every parameter of understanding is destroyed by the immovable resistance of those who do not wish to be led to the light. In Wyndham, science leads to apocalypse (in the shape of panoptic, all seeing satellites whose possible malfunction may have resulted in the emission of the light wavelengths that led to widespread blindness) and at the end it remains unclear whether the conquering spirit of science will ultimately lead to humanity's restored dominion over the triffids which it cultivated to begin with, or whether, if human rule is restored, what will ensue will be the cyclical repetition of the same mistakes, driven by curiosity and hubris. In Saramago, knowledge comes with the flavour of the proverbial poisoned apple: as the world recovers its sight, it is left with the consciousness that all it takes is the temporary removal of the restraining binds of civilization for the primeval brute to re-surface in the average citizen. And in both works, therefore, the very concept of civilization, which to have meaning requires belief in its superior merits, becomes untenable when we acknowledge the ease with which it can be pushed aside.

Common and unsettling patterns run through all the texts discussed in this section: more or less violent misogynistic gender *diktat* (in Self, Atwood, Stewart and Anderson), dictatorship and ostracization (of the blind in Saramago and Wyndham, of the sighted in H.G. Wells), the imprisonment of the powerless (the sighted man in the valley of the blind in Wells, the survivors from blindness corralled by the triffids into communities under siege, the blind in the disused psychiatric hospital, in a city spiralling into chaos, in Wyndham and Saramago, respectively).

The Solomon's choice offered in the country of the blind (elective blindness) may in effect be a metaphor for the fact that whether or not you have sight, there is always a power greater than the individual, and beyond that there is never really any choice. Theoretically, the one-eyed man's arrival in the country of the blind gives him a clear conquering (albeit not gnostic) advantage (since he may be king, but what can he possibly learnt from blind people who presumably live in darkness in all senses of the word?). The answer, however, as Nunez learns, invalidates his status as a viable human being, let alone as king, because it addresses, in the end, something fundamental: the art of survival. In Saramago's *Blindness*, living in darkness – another double-edged expression which may also signify living in a particular state of mind, living in a state of obscurantism – is curiously not (or at least not literally) the fate of those afflicted by sightlessness, since their blindness is characterized by a sensation of bright white light. That sensation, habitually the correlative of either enlightening, understanding, epiphany or arrival at Eternal Life (which is arguably the attainment of ultimate knowledge or understanding), however, here betokens spiralling despair. The ophthalmic and existential darkness of the inhabitants of the country of the blind, on the other hand, is literal, (they only see darkness, they live by night and sleep during the day when it is too hot to work) but it is also not so. Progressive but gradual generational blindness had resulted in the development of a community with a blind-friendly, perfectly structured and organized habitat in which life for the blind (everyone) is prosperous and productive, and sight is an irrelevance or even a drawback (the rules of communal existence being determined *by* the blind *for* the blind). To see or not to see, that is not the question. In the end, like the triffids who have no sight or indeed any other sense apart from touch, the usual human definition of fitness is not necessarily meaningful in the survival stakes, or in gaining mastery, in these differently-arranged universes.

I'm Just Fine, How Are You?

In all of these texts two clusters of potential survival emerge: the first composed of those who, having been blind from birth, know how to get by without sight (everybody in Wells's 'The Country of the Blind,' the relatively happy few in Wyndham's *The Day of the Triffids*, one single man in Saramago's *Blindness*), and the second composed of those who for various reasons escaped the near-universal blight. Within these setups, however, while adjusted modes of existence quickly emerge, the radically altered circumstances unhelpfully show signs of reproducing the intellectual, moral and social defects that arguably provoked the present disaster. Or, in other words, the seed of a recycled end already lies at the heart of the brand new beginning.

Violence is always ready to manifest itself in texts of the post-apocalypse: the intended blinding of the foreigner in H.G. Wells; the gang rape by the men and the murder of their leader at scissors-point by the doctor's wife in Saramago; the proposed reinstatement of feudal, quasi-segneurial law as a means of re-establishing world order in Wyndham; dictatorial world orders in Philip K. Dick, Ira Levin, Ray Bradbury, George Orwell, Aldous Huxley and P.D. James. Whether with good or bad intentions, it all boils down to the fact that post-apocalypse, brave new worlds more often than not come already equipped with a hell pre-paved with those intentions. If heroes are ordinary people asked extraordinary things in terrible circumstances and delivering (Mo, 1991: 404), post-apocalypse there may be some heroes, but not necessarily enough, and usually, as in Cormac MacCarthy's *The Road*, they are outnumbered by villains. Whatever the causal components of catastrophe, be they war, scientific hubris or natural cataclysm, the common factor in the aftermath of apocalypse may be that the two categories of humanity are at best evenly matched but probably not even that. And this, in its turn, opens the possibility that in the near *tabula rasa* that follows global disaster, the problems that brought about that disaster in the first place become part of the new equation. Faced with the unimaginable, what we are able to articulate in its aftermath will almost certainly be just another version of what we already knew: 'Humanity in its essence [...] is what these apocalypses unveil.' (Berger, 1999: 10)

Who was provenly more damaging to the commonweal in Robert Coover's novel, *The Public Burning* (Coover, [1977] 2000) or indeed in the real-life events that inspired it (the case of Julius and Ethel Rosenberg)? The would-be enemy – Communism – supposedly represented not just by them but later, during the McCarthy witch hunts, by thousands of others in the fields of academia, science and the arts (Charlie Chaplin, Dashiell Hammett, Lillian Hellman, Arthur Miller, Orson Welles, Linus Pauling – twice Nobel laureate – and, with supreme irony, Robert Oppenheimer, the father of the atomic bomb intended to destroy that very enemy)? Or the Cold War warriors that purported to protect the world from it? In the end (after the End), the real shock of the new is that it is not actually new at all.

With variations, the same logic informs texts on utopia/dystopia to be discussed in chapter 5, for example Aldous Huxley's *Brave New World*, George Orwell's *Nineteen Eighty-Four* and *Animal Farm*, Ira Levin's *This Perfect Day* and John Wyndham's *The Day of the Triffids*: namely a post-cataclysm set-up involving an authoritarian despot or ruling power which officially saves humanity from itself through the exercise of a panoptical control that in effect in various ways dehumanizes it.

4. Falling Out with Hal and Hester

God did say, You must not eat fruit from the tree that is in the middle of the garden, and you must not touch it, or you will die. You will not surely die, the serpent said to the woman. For God knows that when you eat of it your eyes will be opened, and you will be like God, knowing good and evil. When the woman saw that the fruit of the tree was good for food and pleasing to the eye, and also desirable for gaining wisdom, she took some and ate it. She also gave some to her husband, who was with her, and he ate it. Then the eyes of both of them were opened [...] And the Lord God said, 'The man has now become like one of us, knowing good and evil. He must not be allowed to reach out his hand and take also from the tree of life and eat, and live forever. So the Lord God banished him from the Garden of Eden to work the ground from which he had been taken. After he drove the man out, he placed on the east side of the Garden of Eden cherubim and a flaming sword flashing back and forth to guard the way to the tree of life. (Genesis 3: 3-24)

All men by nature desire knowledge. (Aristotle, *Metaphysics*)

They Know Not What They Do

Culture has no need of time machines. The key narratives of any culture, with minor period-specific modifications, get repeated across boundaries of time as well as place and almost always have, at their basis, an awareness of the link between knowledge and power. The audacity of human intrusion into the fields of knowledge has always been seen as an act of taboo-breaking inviting extreme punishment. Adam and Eve in the Garden of Eden were forbidden from eating the fruit of the Trees of Knowledge and of Life, the rationale being that, should they do so, they would become like God (omniscient and immortal). In Genesis they succeeded in eating only the fruit of the former, and thus destroyed not the universe-as-God-intended-it but merely humanity's default entitlement to paradise. Knowledge was the forbidden fruit but, with hindsight, it may also have turned out to be the instrument of punishment for its theft. Historically, intrusions into fields of forbidden knowledge have had mixed results. By defying divine interdictions to look over their shoulders (look back), Orpheus condemned Eurydice to eternity in Hades and – Irit or Idit, in the rare Midrashic texts that give Lot's wife a name (Büchnann and Spiegel, 1995) – condemned herself to a salty death. Psyche, in the original telling of the myth, though guiltier than either Eurydice (not guilty at all) or Idit, fared better in the long term, and was ultimately granted divine status by the placated Gods. With this rare exception, it remains nonetheless true that generally, as Alexander Pope would have it, a little learning is a dangerous thing, and, although this is not the corollary to Pope's reasoning, one could argue that a lot of learning may be even more so. Since science harnessed the power of the atom, it has become conceivable that the planet, or even the entire universe, might be obliterated, a possibility raised also by recent experiments in the stratosphere of theoretical physics (as exemplified by the launching of the Hadron Collider, already mentioned, which, like Adam and Eve, will seek knowledge of the God-moment when nothing became something).

It takes a lot of knowledge, a very angry teacher (or a deity with a warped sense of humour) and a very reckless student to achieve the reverse trajectory back to nothing (possibly in the aftermath of a second and different, man-made Big Bang). It may be true that only God can make a tree (Kilmer, 1993), and that it takes at least one capricious Greek God to stock Pandora's box, but since the middle of the twentieth century we have known that it takes only scientific curiosity and its misuse to kill all cats.

The claim to creation (demiurgic authorship), is usually deemed to be the province either of divine agency or of the aforementioned Big Bang, and, until very recently (6 August 1945, date of a smaller but sufficiently portentous Bang), so was the power of global extinction. Be that as it may, long before apocalypse of the man-made variety became a possibility (apocalypse now), awareness of the danger of knowledge in reckless hands haunted the minds and myths of all cultures and epochs.

Annihilatory power is not safe in any hands, not even God's, as testified by the somewhat peevish Pentateuchal annihilations of the Flood, the Cities of the Plain, or, in the Book of Revelation, those implemented by the four horsemen of the Apocalypse. All resulted in random global death without rhyme or reason, and certainly without even a token attempt at issuing punishment selectively, only for just deserts.

On the other hand, as discussed in chapter 3, until the arrival of the nuclear age, destruction, whether of metaphysical or natural origin (God's wrath, a colliding comet) always left the possibility of vestigial survival and continuity. Paradoxically, it was only when its enactment fell under the control not of God or nature but of human agency that it acquired cosmic possibilities. Robert Oppenheimer, gazing at the mushroom cloud which he had helped to create, understood this and acknowledged it not triumphantly but with post-lapsarian guilt, in the famous statement 'I am become God, the destroyer of worlds' (Oppenheimer, 1945).

> My name is Ozymandias, king of kings:
> Look on my works, ye Mighty, and despair!'
> Nothing beside remains: round the decay
> Of that colossal wreck, boundless and bare,
> The lone and level sands stretch far away. (Shelley, 1818)

Oppenheimer's guilt, unlike that of prior harbingers of apocalypse, however powerful their rhetoric, was without precedents, possibly because, unlike them, he and the other perpetrators of the Manhattan Project knew that for the first time in the history of the planet they really could put words into practice and reduce the planet to 'lone and level sands.' Either way, in any case, whether realistically or not, when we envisage annihilation (whether brought about by destructive deities, random forces of nature or destructive man-made machines), we create the horror narratives (and rules) we deserve, and we simultaneously polish the hand mirrors in which we can glimpse ourselves, in a glass darkly.

Stories of apocalypse ultimately narrate us. It could not be otherwise, since we make them up. It is perhaps not surprising, then, that not only does the basic plot, mythical, theological or sci-fi alike, always stays more or less the same, but, in the inimical other, in the violent alien, whatever its shape or form, if we look closely, we find ourselves. If we are very lucky we get expelled from Eden before the whole house of cards is irretrievably blown away. And the ultimate punch line may be the discovery that, whatever it was that made us, in the end, short of an unlucky mega-meteor, there is no deity, force of nature or machine that can break us, only we ourselves.

In Ingmar Bergman's *The Seventh Seal* (Bergman, 1957), Block, a medieval knight, on his way back home from the Crusades with his faith shaken rather than strengthened, contemplates the emblematic sacrifice of a child scapegoated for the advent of a plague: 'Who watches over that child? Is it the angels, or God, or the Devil, or only the emptiness?' Describing it as 'the finest apocalyptic film we have,' Robert Crossley (Crossley, 2000: 85) sees the killing of the child as instigating the necessity of atheism because a God whose act this was, would not deserve to be believed in. In the scene in question, the knight answers his own question when he says that in a world vacated by God, where – in a setting clearly allusive to a crucifixion – a child is burnt at the stake by priests, there is nothing left to contemplate other than humanity at its most wretched: 'Look into her eyes. Her pain is our pain.'

In the end, in effect, a moral conclusion, and either the tenability or dismissal of faith itself, actually remain elusive: victory in the game of chess against Death would have purchased the knight the right to live but he loses; yet in sacrificing himself in order to save the lives of the family of actors he had encountered on his travels, the world loses its meaninglessness. In Bergman, personal apocalypse, represented by the Dance of Death, may, but only may, lead to a new epiphany, in an echo of the Biblical opening of the seventh seal, in Revelation.

In the Biblical original, the opening of the first four seals had released the four horsemen of the Apocalypse.

The opening of the seventh seal inaugurates end-time, following which comes rapture and salvation, albeit only for the chosen.

Figure 17. Ingmar Bergman, *The Seventh Seal*

Figure 18. Ingmar Bergman, *The Seventh Seal*

Elsewhere apocalypse, construable as an act of God, becomes at best an intellectual impossibility and at worst the vanishing point of the believing self, as epitomized by the plight of Arthur C. Clarke's Jesuit astrophysicist who, in 'The Star,' loses his faith when he discovers that the creation of the star of Bethlehem required the destruction of an entire planet (and a worthy one, at that) by an exploding supernova:

> Even if they had not been so disturbingly human as their sculpture shows, we could not have helped admiring them and grieving for their fate. They left thousands of visual records […]. We have examined many of these records, and brought to life for the first time in six thousand years the warmth and beauty of a civilization that in many ways must have been superior to our own. […] This tragedy was unique. It is one thing for a race to fail and die, as nations and cultures have done on Earth. But to be destroyed so completely in the full flower of its achievement, leaving no survivors – how could that be reconciled with the mercy of God? […] They were not an evil people […]. They could have taught us much: why were they destroyed? […] Now, from the astronomical evidence and the record in the rocks of that one surviving planet, I have been able to date […] very exactly [how long ago the explosion took place]. I know in what year the light of this colossal conflagration reached our Earth. [O]h God, there were so many stars you could have used. What was the need to give these people to the fire, that the symbol of their passing might shine above Bethlehem? (Clarke, 1955)

The supernova and the subsequent creation of the star, explained as an exercise on the part of God not in creation but in creativity (an aesthetic *divertissement*, a firework), required the annihilation of something advanced, beautiful and peaceful, resulting, furthermore, in the birth of a religion whose net effect, like that of any religion, has arguably been destructive. And if the balance was negative, therefore, the architect of this equation clearly does not emerge as a force for good within any parameters of human ethics or logic. No wonder the Jesuit lost his faith.

In many writings of apocalypse the destructive deities retain traits akin to their creatures. The Greek Gods were wilful, petty, jealous and self-regarding. Bergman's God was a sociopath. And in Miguel Torga's 'Vicente' (Torga, 1987), God, far from being omniscient, proves vulnerable to an intellectual ambush: faced with the choice of destroying either his most beautiful and complex creation (free will) or the eponymous raven that chose to exercise it by defying divine authority (he opts to flee the Ark and fly over a drowned Earth, even at the risk of finding nowhere to land and dying), the enraged deity grudgingly chooses to preserve free will. The waters recede, the bird is spared, and disobedience wins the day.

The Face of the Other

Whether the Divine takes on the guise of immanency or anthropomorphism or both, absolute annihilation, as argued in chapter 3, remains largely inconceivable to the human mind. Trying to imagine nothingness triggers that *horror vacui* which afflicted Greeks and Christians alike (Rotman, 1993). Zero, nothing, the void, as discussed earlier, is never really an option, or not, at least, in any formulation that attributes to an anthropomorphic God any affinity with his creatures. It is perhaps for this reason that in the vocabulary of apocalyptic narratives informed by notions of deities variously shaped by humanity in its own image, it is often necessary to re-shape the perpetrator of annihilation as an alien but also a non-anthropomorphic force. Hence, therefore, the abundance of plots which pit humanity, in all its identifiable merits and frailties, against an other defined, whether through its bestial or robotic (but either way in all respects nonhuman) nature as absolutely different. The fact that the narrative plots tend to be themselves all too familiar, compounds rather than diminishes the dimension of de-familiarization but also, equally importantly, the permissibility of defensive altericide of reassuringly unrecognizable enemies. It is easier both to kill and be killed by something that does not look too much like us.

The Problem with Being God

While in works such as John Wyndham's *The Chrysalids* (Wyndham, [1955] 1984) and *The Midwich Cuckoos* (Wyndham, [1957] 1984) or Theodor Sturgeon's *More Than Human* (Sturgeon, 2000) humanity is forced to face

Figure 19. René Magritte, *The Human Condition*

the possibility of being overpowered by nonhumans, not-quite-humans, superhumans or composite humans (*homo gestalt*), in narratives otherwise as diverse as *Quatermass and the Pit* (Kneale, 1958-59), the film trilogy of *The Matrix* and *The Hitchhiker's Guide to the Galaxy* (Adams, 1979) it faces the alternative possibility that it is itself the creation of a non-divine puppet master. The hypothesis comes in all forms, from horror to farce. Running through all of them, however, it is possible to detect three fundamental fears: first, that what we take to be reality (the world as we know it) is not real; second, that whatever reality is, we do not control it; and third, that reality as we understand it might turn out to be unstable and disappear.

In Magritte's pseudo-*tromp l'oeil*, for our purposes, helpfully named *The Human Condition*, a picture on an easel depicting a view out of a window is on closer inspection revealed to be not a picture but the view itself, realistic in all aspects except for the easily missed edge of the glass/window on which the image (whose edge however exactly matches the reality outside the window) is painted. Which is real? Both or neither?

In *The Hitchhiker's Guide to the Galaxy* and its sequels, the Earth turns out to be not a planet but a computer named 'Deep thought,' designed by a race of hyper-intelligent, pan-dimensional beings, sometimes disguised as mice, who built it to calculate the answer to the Ultimate Question of Life, the Universe and Everything. Adams's lampoon echoes Wyndham's more chilling observation in *The Midwich Cuckoos*:

> When I look around the world, it does sometimes seem to hold a suggestion of a rather disorderly testing ground. The sort of place where one might let loose a new strain now and then, and see how it will make out in our rough and tumble. Fascinating for an inventor to watch his creations acquitting themselves [...]. To discover whether this time he has produced a successful tearer-to-pieces, or just another torn-to-pieces and, too, to observe the progress of the earlier models, and see which of them have proved really competent at making life a form of hell for others. (Wyndham, 1984: 204-05)

Or, as Satan would have it in Andy Hamilton's hilarious radio comedy, *Old Harry's Game*, God 'was as surprised as anyone when humans became the dominant species. He had his money on badgers.' (Hamilton, 2007). In *Hitchhiker's Guide*, when the answer to the meaning of life, the universe and everything (42) proves to be unhelpful, Deep Thought predicts that another computer, more powerful than itself will be designed and built to discover what the question was that elicited that answer. The second computer/planet (Earth) is duly built as part of a 10-million-year programme run by mice (the second most intelligent species on the planet after dolphins), but is inadvertently destroyed (five minutes before delivering its conclusion) by the Vogons, another extra-terrestrial species, who were clearing space to make way for a hyperspatial by-pass. As summed up by Slartibartfast, the Magrathean designer of the planets, 'the mice were furious' (Adams, 1979, 123).

The demolition of the Earth, an event in itself not of negligible significance (despite the planet's somewhat dismissive classification in intergalactic reference works as 'mostly harmless') (Adams, 1979, 52), is dwarfed by what is uncovered in a subsequent novel, *The Restaurant at the End of the Universe* (Adams, 1979). In this it is revealed that the Universe is in the safe hands of a simple man who lives with his cat in a wooden shack on a remote planet. Much might be made of the fact that in Adams's gloriously insane lampoon, mice (in our world the usual subjects of scientific experimentation), are instead the ones running the laboratory, in a universe which however, and worryingly, is itself overseen by a cat. Be that as it may, in the last volume of the series, *So Long, and Thanks for All the Fish*, comic iconoclasm acquires a darker edge which it is no longer easy to ignore: God's final computer-delivered message to his creation, 'We apologize for the inconvenience,' (Adams, 1984: 201-02) evokes Aristotle's (1985), Bakhtin's (1982) and Umberto Eco's (1992) warnings about the dangers of supposing one has the last laugh. Bakhtin saw laughter ('carnival') as the temporary suspension of authority. For Aristotle, in the 'The Art of Poetry,' comedy, and the choice of engaging with it, was something deemed appropriate for the baser kinds of men, tragedy being reserved for the nobler. And elaborating on these principles, in *The Name of the Rose* the Venerable Jorge, Umberto Eco's murderous monk, sees laughter as dangerous, because it demeans men and denies God: 'with his laughter the fool says in his heart, "*Deus non est*"' (Eco, 1984: 132). If so, it stands to reason that Adams-style laughter, and the more riotous the better, may after all be the most appropriate mode of depicting the ultimate upheaval, the end of a world that deserves no better, in a universe where God is not.

Philip K. Dick's *Dr. Bloodmoney* and Peter Weir's film of 1998, *The Truman Show* are less funny than *The Hitchhiker's Guide*. Ever less funny, indeed, with hindsight, following the advent of Reality TV which these works pre-empt by some years and exaggerate, but not a lot. In *The Truman Show*, as in Dick's novel, a single individual's reality is ultimately revealed to be not only unreal (un-True(man)) but fraudulent. Set in the fictional seaside village of Seahaven, the purpose-built, purpose-populated town is dedicated to a 24-hour television reality show. All of the participants are actors except for the eponymous hero, Truman Burbank, who is unaware that he lives in a simulated reality, as the protagonist of a round-the-clock, mass-media television soap. Truman was chosen out of five unwanted babies to be a TV star in the reality television programme, 'The Truman Show', and is therefore in effect the creation and creature of the show's producer. This modern-day demiurge, appropriately or inappropriately named Christof (of Christ?) inhabits a panoptic eerie overlooking the town, its inhabitants and its existence. From this privileged position he is omnipresent, all-seeing (in the form of thousands of recording television cameras) and omnipotent. Despite a few near-misses, the fiction is maintained until Truman, aged thirty, gains an understanding of the situation, tries and eventually succeeds in escaping from Seahaven. As he finally reaches the edge of the constructed reality and exits via a door in the wall of a *trompe-l'oeil* sky at the edge of the horizon, his demise as fictional character and entry into a reality which however, for him, has never, and at that point still does not exist, is both cheered and lamented by a world-wide audience of millions, for whom that particular world has now disappeared. Truman becomes a true man, rather than a character in someone else's narrative, but at that point he also ceases to exist as the man he thought he was. That particular world has met its Armageddon. No wonder audiences world-wide feel bereft. The wider implications of *The Truman Show* do not necessarily refer back directly to notions of apocalypse, but there are connections, not least, as far as Truman is concerned, in what regards the end of one world and the revelation of another.

In 1999, one year after *The Truman Show* was released, the first series of *Big Brother* began broadcasting, and four years later the internet virtual world, Second Life, was developed. Leaving aside the question of participant consent (not given by Truman but enlisted in the other two cases), a similar suspension of disbelief elides the boundaries between reality and a variety of simulacra of it.

Who's the Fool Now?

In the apocalyptic works discussed in the course of previous chapters, ultimately, even when humanity as a species prevails, its survival may be preserved at the cost of being forced to ac(knowledge) absolute lack of autonomy in a reality which until then it never knew it didn't in fact know. This realization involves the recognition of humanity's delusion of ontological centrality, now replaced by a new consciousness of the species' unimportance within a universe it neither controls nor defines. The sun, undeniably, does not revolve around the Earth, and there may be no God whose finest creation we are. The real tragic hero in *The Truman Show*, in the end, may be not Truman himself, but Christof, who like God, when his particular universe ceases to exist, is forced to accept that in seeking to control an other, one may lose oneself. In the quest for control one may come close to being God, but this, in the end, as we know, has been the trap lying in wait for humanity as the ultimate punishment for its usurpation of knowledge. The awareness of that ambush is evidenced in all our narratives from that of first couple in the Garden of Eden through numerous cultural and fictional histories down the ages.

In Genesis, God created Eden but his tenants of choice failed the test that would grant them a permanent residence permit, arguably making its existence pointless. In *The Truman Show*, Christof creates a safe and stable world but his protagonist's disobedience, like Adam's and Eve's, brings that particular reality, too, to a close. The same problem finds different renditions in multiple fictions of apocalypse brought about through the agency of creators whose demiurgic status does not in the end spare them from a retribution invited by hubris.

Lying in the Bed We Made

Kurt Vonnegut's irresponsible scientist in *Cat's Cradle* (Vonnegut, 1981) and Margaret Atwood's vengeful one in *Oryx and Crake* (Atwood, 2003), inventors respectively of a substance capable of freezing life on Earth and a bacterium capable of eliminating it entirely, do not survive the cataclysms they unleash.

> 'The seed, which had come from God-only-knows-where, taught the atoms the novel way in which to stack and lock, to crystallize, to freeze. […] And suppose […] that there were one form [of ice], which we will call ice-nine […]. If [someone] threw that seed into the nearest puddle…?'
>
> 'The puddle would freeze?' […] 'and all the puddles in the frozen muck […] and the pools and the streams in the frozen muck […] and the rivers and the lakes the streams fed […] and the oceans the frozen rivers fed […] and the rain?'
>
> 'When it fell it would freeze too […] and that would be the end of the world!' (Vonnegut, 1981: 33-36)

In *Cat's Cradle* the end of the world does happen, but by its very nature it leaves enough basic reserves preserved (in ice) to ensure the subsistence of a small group of survivors. The continuity of humanity remains if not a probability at least a possibility, as is the case also at the conclusion of Atwood's *Oryx and Crake* and its sister novel, *The Year of the Flood*.

It's a Jungle out There

In John Wyndham's *Trouble with Lichen*, the heroine, Diana Brackley is described in her youth by her teachers and peers as being 'with us but not of us' (Wyndham, [1960] 1982: 31). Although less radically than in some of his other novels, here, too, Wyndham articulates the problem of alterity. Unlike some of his other protagonists, albeit exceptional in many ways, Diana is just a scientist, not a mutant or an alien from outer space. Having said this, however, she does bring about potentially apocalyptic (in both senses of the word) changes to the world. Being entirely *sui generis*, she deviates not only from the norm (the common run of humanity) but also from fellow mavericks within the pathways of unsanctioned, rogue scientific research, since, unlike her counterparts in Vonnegut and Atwood, she is a scientist whose ultimate achievement involves not universal death but vastly increased life expectancy. She threatens the viability of humanity when she discovers an antigerone, a substance capable of massively slowing down ageing and prolonging human longevity, with all the long-term social and political implications this entails. A radically extended lifespan threatens social stability, and for good or bad, therefore, her discovery could conceivably change the world (that, of course, being one definition of apocalypse), signalling, in effect, the birth of a new human variant (*homo superior*, Wyndham, 1982: 86): human beings with life expectancies of at least 300 years, but possibly more; or, as she describes it, 'the only evolutionary advance by man in a million years,' (Wyndham, 1982: 85).

The social, demographic and political implications of a product of limited availability but, even so, liable to 'change the whole of future history completely' (Wyndham, 1982: 85-86) opens up new possibilities but also vast problems. The latter are different yet akin to the quandaries of a humanity confronted with more advanced human forms (*The Midwich Cuckoos*, *The Chrysalids*), in the struggle for resources, space and, in the final instance, supremacy. And in all these narratives, when faced with the imperative of exterminating or being exterminated by competing beings, whether or not these are true species-likenesses of itself, humanity will eventually be obliged to confront the ethical implications of any struggle for survival: namely the recognition that, in extreme circumstances, human beings readily break away from the codes of civilization and regress into the ancestral jungle, even if it involves the extermination of more vulnerable members (or thereabouts) of their own species. This is explained with un-nuanced bluntness in *The Midwich Cuckoos*:

> We are presented with a moral dilemma of some niceness. On the one hand it is our duty to our race and culture to liquidate the Children, for it is clear that if we do not we shall, at best, be completely dominated by them, and their culture [...] will extinguish ours.
>
> On the other hand, it is our culture that gives us scruples about the ruthless liquidation of unarmed minorities. [...]
>
> You are judging by social rules and finding crime. I am considering an elemental struggle, and finding no crime – just grim, primeval danger. (Wyndham, *Midwich*, [1957] 1984: 208-12)

Mean Machines

Ethics, of course, are in principle not involved when dealing either with the inanimate or, in many cases, even the nonhuman animate: when we take antibiotics, we do not worry too much about the right to life of bacteria, and when we run clinical trials on them we do not concern ourselves inordinately with those of laboratory rats or even higher primates. The enemy, however, in any case, need be neither alien nor terrestrial, neither an animate version of an other (another animal species) nor a mutated variation of the self (the composite beings described in *The Midwich Cuckoos* and *The Chrysalids*), but simply a product of human scientific achievement. The fear of a global insurrection against us by machines of our making echoes that presumably felt by God when confronting the possibility of a snake-instigated *putsch* in the Garden of Eden.

In James Cameron's film of 1984, *The Terminator*, we are treated to a futuristic rendition of two of the West's foundation narratives, the Christian Nativity and Christ's Passion, still recognizable despite futuristic modifications. A cyborg travels from the future to the diegetic present to kill Sarah Connor, a woman who, at an unspecified but prophesied date, will give birth to a child at that point still to be conceived. The child, John Connor (a good Irish-American Catholic name, which, furthermore, shares its initials with Jesus Christ), will live to be the saviour of humanity against the cyborgs, humanoid computerized machines that in the near-future are due to take over the planet. Hot in pursuit of the cyborg is Kyle Reese (a name homographically close to the liturgical plea *Kyrie Eleison*, Lord have mercy), an envoy of those future humans and a friend of John Connor, dispatched from the future to prevent Sarah's murder, and to ensure that the would-be mother (yet another version of the Virgin as the Woman of the Apocalypse) survives and brings forth the necessary saviour. He does more than that, and in fact impregnates her with the foretold child. The film develops into a straightforward plot of quest and struggle, pitting brains against brute force, orderly civilization against the unbridled techno-elemental, good against evil. In the course of it, the search for the woman to be slaughtered becomes merely a pretext for the real business of males — human and otherwise — killing each other in the name of prioritizing their respective lineages. Good achieves an open-ended victory (the cyborg is defeated, albeit, in true gospel fashion, only at the price of a sacrificial male death). The victory, moreover, is not definitive: there are plenty more cyborgs where the first one came from, and to date three open-ended film sequels, two of them with biblically allusive titles: *Terminator 2: Judgement Day*, 1991, *Terminator 3: The Rise of the Machines*, 2003 and *Terminator 4: Salvation*, 2009). In the first film, *The Terminator*, Reese, whose persona — beyond the figure of knight in shining armour in aid of damsels in distress — had adumbrated the triple role of God (father of a saviour), guardian angel (of unborn children) and St. Joseph (his son will bear his mother's rather than his father's surname, rendering paternity a by-proxy affair), dies, leaving us with one surviving heroine and the promise of a living hero in the future. There is of course an important difference between these two. A bird in the hand is clearly better than two in the air, and the survival chances of the two sexes at the end of the first installment look unequal: on the one hand a resilient heroine who at the very last discards reliance upon ineffectual defenders and takes it upon herself to finish the job of destroying the cyborg. And on the other hand, a dead hero and a promising but yet unborn son.

This scenario encapsulates much that is relevant to the central themes of foundation narratives such as the Biblical ones of the Nativity and the Passion but also of the Apocalypse. In *The Terminator*, in a modification of the gospel texts, a son sends his future father to the death rather than vice-versa, but with an analogous intent, namely to save himself/his interests.

In both cases males engage in mutual destruction (man against cyborg in an echo of religious interests at logger heads with one another: good against evil, God/Son of God against Satan). The basic structure echoes the logic of narratives of apocalypse: salvation and perdition, creation and destruction, continuity and finiteness (termination). Moreover, it renders some of the implications of the above plot akin to the central issues raised in this discussion of textual and film narratives, structured, as they are, in equal measure, by intertextual allusion to prior traditions and by terror.

In both Roland Emmerich's *Independence Day* (Emmerich, 1996) and in Steven Spielberg's *War of the Worlds* (Spielberg, 2005, from H.G. Wells's novel of the same title), and echoing the binary underpinning the basic premise of *The Terminator*, the demarcation of the dividing line between good and evil, right and wrong is also that which separates humans from machines. In one of the most ludicrous moments in *Independence Day*, the invading aliens establish voice contact. Although like the cyborg in *The Terminator*, these particular aliens speak English (of course), unlike in *War of the Worlds*, where the invading tripods are destroyed by a biological adversary (bacteria, something which suggests they are of an organic rather than inanimate nature), the invading enemies in *Independence Day*, *War of the Worlds* and *The Terminator* are uncompromisingly automated machines with whom any notion of dialogue or understanding is not possible. And in Michael Crichton's *Prey* (Crichton, 2002), too, the enemies, although having the ability to evolve, reproduce, learn and mimetically morph living beings to produce the illusion of animate life, are in fact inorganic nanoparticles: micro-robots programmed to kill, just like the cyborgs in *The Terminator*, only writ extremely small.

Unlike Miguel Torga's God, who weighs up the value of unimpugned omnipotence against the destruction of his finest work and finds net gain in preserving the latter in exchange for relinquishing absolute authority (Torga, 1987), in the texts mentioned above, the ultimate rescue of humanity entails the destruction of the alien machine, including, often, those which it had itself created (in *The Terminator*, Cameron, 1984; *Prey*, Crichton, 2002; *I, Robot*, Proyas, 2004) but which now threaten to overrun it. In a conflict between the two, human creator and mechanical creature quasi-Oedipally intent on eclipsing its progenitor, one must exterminate the other. This is explained by the General Manager of the gigantic corporation Rossums Universal Robots (R.U.R.) in Karel Čapek's play of the same title (Čapek, 2010), in which a replay of the Biblical narrative of fall and expulsion (but which here sees the creator vanquished by his creatures), brings about the end of human history (the end of civilization) at the hands of robots, themselves the products of two defining aspects of that self-same civilization: advanced technology and capitalist market forces.

An understanding of the danger of power entrusted to machines, indeed, does not require the phenomenon of futuristic robotic would-be dictatorships. The error factor whereby a faulty automated computer system triggers or threatens to trigger human extinction by nuclear war or other means is the standard fare of sci-fi global-disaster movies and narratives: *WarGames* (Badham, 1983), *Fail-Safe* (Lumet, 1964; Frears, 2000), *By Dawn's Early Light* (Scholder, 1980), *Level 7* (Roshwald, 2004) and *Limbo* (Wolfe, 1952), already discussed.

My Self, My Other

In John Wyndham's short story, 'Compassion Circuit' (Wyndham, [1956] 1983), sophisticated anthropomorphic robots perform the functions previously (depending on historical time and place) performed by slaves/servants/subalterns. The robots include in-built state-of-the-art compassion circuits which enable them to fulfil and sometimes even, if deemed best, to override their masters' and mistresses' instructions (for their own good). In a status quo symbolized by an absent husband and a sickly wife who cannot sustain herself either physically or emotionally, the latter becomes dependent for all her needs on Hester, a humanoid robot (made to order, with detailed specifications: 'darkish blonde [...], five foot ten, and nice to look at, but not *too* beautiful, Wyndham, 1983: 202). The climax to an increasingly creepy tale sees both husband and wife ultimately deprived, as per Hester's instructions, of their flawed human bodies and equipped instead, with robotic prosthetic ones. Although there is no suggestion that their human consciousness was removed, its retention, faced with a new world in which robots are able to make what are literally life-altering decisions without human consent, makes consciousness, retained without the power of agency, arguably more cruel even than actual obliteration.

If their bodies have been replaced but self-awareness preserved, this makes the plight of the husband and wife only marginally less cruel than that of that of the quiescent gynoid (female android) spouses in Ira Levin's *The Stepford Wives* (Levin, 1996); or that of the husband reduced to one single eye floating in a basin, in Roahl Dahl's 'William and Mary,' in which disembodied awareness is maintained by the gadgetry of advanced medicine. Wyndham's and Dahl's stories both give grim warning of the danger that scientific achievement, that which has made the human species almost omnipotent, paradoxically might prove to be what ultimately leads to its annihilation. Too clever by half? Possibly. The moral from this brand of science fiction horror narrative is that, other than a global cataclysm or an Act of God, the most likely destroyer of humanity is humanity itself, or the products of its ingenuity.

In Stanley Kubrick's defining film, *2001: A Space Odyssey* (Kubrick, 1968), the possibility of a takeover by machines, in this case computers, ups the ante. Astronauts on a pioneering space mission find their endeavour and indeed their lives threatened by the space ship's computer, HAL or Hal (**He**uristically Programmed **A**lgorithmic Computer), which has different views regarding the shape of things to come. Hal's attempted *coup* unfolds within the confined limits of the space ship and the enemies he has identified are the small crew, but the stakes, nonetheless, are massive, and the prize, ultimately is of cosmic proportions: namely mastership of the Universe. Hal's gentle tones as he/it outlines the plan whereby, sooner rather than later, human beings will be overthrown by the machines they made somewhat in their own image, as in several of the iconic texts and films of recent and classical sci-fi (*The Terminator*, Cameron, 1984; *I, Robot*, Proyas, 2004; *A.I. Artificial Intelligence*, Spielberg, 2001; *This Perfect Day*, Levin, 1994; 'The Machine Stops', Forster, [1909] 2004; *Prey*, Crichton, 2002), arguably represent, at one level, the enactment of panic inbuilt into our awareness that in the end humanity can only ever partly control the environment; including, or particularly, the flawed environment it is itself capable of creating through science, technology and hubristic gate-crashing into the domains of Knowledge. No one forced Adam and Eve into the action that lost them Eden.

At the end, in *2001: A Space Odyssey*, as his attempted insurrection against his human creators is crushed and he is disconnected, Hal's mellifluous-cum-sinister tones are transformed into the pleading of a frightened child and then a babbling baby. From Chronos to Abraham, from the Phoenicians to Freud, from antiquity to modernity, the murder of offspring, perpetrated either to preserve power or curry favour with those that have it, has proved an enduring motif. Sometimes the attempt is thwarted, as shown in the case of Herod, whose failure to kill a King of the Jews prophesied to be greater than himself, changed the world. The fact that in that instance the real, divine father, took up where Herod left off (making Herod, like Judas, justified in complaining that he was 'used like a key,' Hirst, 2004: 19), and sacrificed his own son to a higher purpose, is another debate. Be that as it may, while in *The Terminator* humanity succeeds at least temporarily in curbing the destructive intent of its mechanical offspring, that outcome cannot be guaranteed in perpetuity, and the sobbing infantilized voice of Hal at the end of *2001* (Kubrick, 1968) could at any point be replaced by the violence of high-tech Oedipal offspring triumphant in overcoming the originating parent in order to gain possession of Mother Earth.

Humanity's attempts to claim demiurgic control over the world have included the creation of a variety of subalternities: from entirely nonhuman products in the shape of computers, androids and other machines (*Blade Runner*, Scott, 1982; the other narratives and films discussed previously), to humans subjected to more or less benevolent human-controlled techno-dictatorships (*Brave New World*, Huxley, 1977; *This Perfect Day*, Levin, 1994; *Fahrenheit 451*, Bradbury, 1976; *The Penultimate Truth,* Dick, 2005; 'The Machine Stops', Forster, [1909] 2004), or anthropomorphic, quasi-human, man-made renditions (Dr. Jekyll's monstrous alter ego, Mr. Hyde, Stevenson, [1886] 2007; Frankenstein's monster, Shelley, [1818] 1983; Walter C. Miller's neutroids in the remarkable short story 'Conditionally Human,' Miller, 2007).

In the latter, first published in 1952, eight years before Wyndham's *Trouble with Lichen*, whose basic premise it anticipates, and in a prophetic rendition of contemporary concerns, medical and scientific advances have resulted in dangerously prolonged longevity, with implications regarding available resources. In Miller's story the solution involves selecting a minority of the population for authorized reproduction. The remainder may not have children, but frustrated parenting desires are partly catered for by the ownership of genetically modified animals: semi-intelligent talking pets such as cats, dogs, or semi-human 'models' (chimpanzees or neutroids: child-lookalikes but with tails), all with restricted food requirements and a very limited life-span. Terry Norris, the central character, is an inspector for the F.B.A. (Federal Bio-Authority) which controls numbers of pets and neutroids and disposes of unwanted or defective (mutant) ones. The plot unfolds around the deliberate creation by a rogue geneticist of a mutant species of neutroid which is capable of living till adulthood and reproducing, and the refusal by Anne, Norris's wife, to accept the elimination of one of these, Peony, to whom she has become maternally attached. In a re-working of the notion that love makes the world go round (and sometimes turns it upside down), Anne's love for Peony and Norris's for Anne results in his decision to apply for a job in Anthropos Incorporated, the state department that creates neutroids, with the intention of large-scale subversion: namely, the mass creation of illegal, fertile neutroids, potentially capable of doing 'better than their makers' (Miller, 264) and, eventually, of creating a better world.

If, in constructing more or less animate alternative forms, humans as a species introduce the possibility of their own downfall, paradoxically, in destroying them in order to preserve humankind's survival, to some extent they lose their own humanity. This is particularly so where, as will be discussed in the case of *Blade Runner*, 'Conditionally Human' (Miller, 2007), *A.I. Artificial Intelligence* and *I, Robot*, the line between automated machine and creature capable of some emotion becomes blurred. In such cases it becomes clear that, in destroying the beings we produced, we destroy ourselves in our thinking, ethical humanity (a dilemma not unlike that confronted by an endangered human species in Wyndham's *The Midwich Cuckoos*, or *The Chrysalids* already discussed). Furthermore, as well as representing a potential danger either to the survival of their human inventors or to the latter's definitions of self, the machines/creatures in question, as suggested above, also introduce the possibility that the danger they represent was knowingly incurred by their creators, punishment being therefore deserved by a species guilty of hubris: namely the attempted usurpation of God's/nature's monopoly over demiurgy.

Sufficiently 'Other'

Another option, less alienating because it points the finger of blame at targets outside the sphere of human ingenuity, is that of locating the inimical alien in something that is neither human nor human-made, but instead, and reassuringly, both familiar and different: namely unexpected animal forms. From big apes such as King Kong to the beasts of Michael Crichton's *Jurassic Park* (Crichton, 1998) and *Congo* (Crichton, 1995) to the smaller creepy crawlies dealt with in previous chapters, and from these to the microscopically small in the *Andromeda Strain* (Crichton, 1995), the animate as opposed to inanimate or robotic other provides a half-way house within which to confront the concept of otherness (although in *Jurassic Park* and 'Conditionally Human,' admittedly, the variations, albeit animal in nature, are made possible by human genetic engineering).

Insufficiently 'Other'

In the end, however, whether considering giant apes, living simulacra, small microbes or extremely small nano-beings, none ultimately instil the degree of fear achieved by enemies whose ability to mirror our selves might conceivably enable them to snatch both our bodies and our souls. But if, as suggested above, we succeed in destroying them, in doing so, arguably, we also, at least in part, destroy ourselves. In Clifford D. Simak's *Ring Around the Sun* (Simak, 1990), a breed of extra-terrestrial beings distinguishable from Earthlings only in their superior mental skills and advanced technology, plan to take over the planet and transfer its entire population to another world located in a parallel universe, there to replay human history in a way that will avoid the errors which in the past led to illness, war and other earthly disasters. Although in some respects well intentioned, Simak's superior beings illustrate, nonetheless, the ambivalence that surrounds the phenomenon of evolutionary, technological and scientific advances (as represented by superior species, robots, nuclear energy) capable, like John Wyndham's helpful Hester or Kubrick's silver-tongued Hal, of improving human life but also extinguishing it. Switching off a machine, however anthropomorphic (cases such as the androids in *A.I. Artificial Intelligence* or *Blade Runner* excepted), is usually not a problem whereas, as shown in Miller's 'Conditionally Human,' in the end, outside a willingness to practice would-be genocide, it is often not possible to exterminate a life form that closely resembles our own. The problem becomes evident where, in some the films and novels discussed, it is impossible to assert unequivocally the non-humanity of the other. This is because, as already suggested, where there is such uncertainty, a willingness to destroy those ambiguous others regardless, brings into question the very humanity of the self.

The replicants/mutants in *The Chrysalids*, *A.I.*, 'Conditionally Human,' *Do Androids Dream of Electric Sheep?* (Dick, 2007) and the latter's film version, *Blade Runner* (Scott, 1982) all have aspects of categorical ambiguity. In the case of the latter two, for example, both in the novel and its film adaptation, a measure of uncertainty prevails regarding who/what is or is not an android, a problem which introduces also uncertainty about definitions of the self. In the film, for example, Rachel is an android whose mechanical circuits include implanted memories from a real woman, and not only is she surprised when she learns that she is in fact an android but, like David in *A.I.*, experiences emotional turmoil at the revelation.

Carlos Clarens (Clarens, 1997) argues that in science fiction featuring anthropomorphic aliens of various kinds, what is played out is not the fear of an other who is utterly different but rather of one who is instead uncomfortably familiar, or, in other words, not different *enough* to be readily identified as alien and thus destroyed without guilt. This is the phenomenon underlying fantasies in which the other may be either benevolent and peaceful (*The Chrysalids, The Day the Earth Stood Still*, Wise, 1951) or downright aggressive (Wyndham's *The Midwich Cuckoos; Invasion of the Body Snatchers*, Siegel, 1956; Guillermin, 1976), but either way, as much by virtue of its difference as its similarity, it represents a species-threat to humanity. In the end, as Wyndham's eccentric *fous savants* well understand (the unnervingly perceptive Zellaby in *The Midwich Cuckoos*, the urchin-like Dr. Bocker in *The Kraken Wakes*, Wyndham, [1953] 1980), two species with equal needs cannot coexist in the same space on limited resources.

Oddly, or perhaps not so oddly, given both the strangeness (because as yet they do not exist) and the unexpected familiarity of anthropomorphic robots in human shape, it is the android or humanoid, rather than the faceless machine, that elicits greatest fear. In Philip K. Dick's *We Can Build You* (Dick, 1977) and *Do Androids Dream of Electric Sheep?* (Dick, 2007), in Ridley Scott's film of the latter novel, *Blade Runner* (Scott, 1982), in Karel Čapek's *War with the Newts* (Čapek, 2001) and *R.U.R.* (Čapek, 2010), and in blockbusters such as *A.I.* and *I, Robot*, the machines in question have an uncanny dimension of humanity which blurs the line that separates sentient (and supposedly moral) human beings from insensible automatons, and therefore questions the ethics of the latter's destruction (making it tantamount to genocide).

The realization that the alien other, although capable of widespread destruction, might also have an advanced sense of responsibility and a capacity for what are assumed by humanity to be exclusively human emotions, is explored with some success and sometimes considerable pathos in *Close Encounters of the Third Kind* (Spielberg, 1977), *E.T.* (Spielberg, 1982), *A.I. Artificial Intelligence, I, Robot* and *I Married a Monster from Outer Space* (Fowler Jr., 1958). In the latter, aliens from the Andromeda constellation arrive on Earth as one of the stops in their tour of the universe. The reason for their journey is a quest for females with whom they can mate in order to perpetuate their species, now threatened with extinction as the result of an episode of solar instability which caused all their own females to die. Albeit clearly inhuman in the common usage of the word, through prolonged contact with humans and in an echo of similar phenomena in *I, Robot* and *A.I.* (Spielberg, 2001), the aliens begin to develop anthropomorphic emotions. In *I Married a Monster from Outer Space* (Fowler, 1958), Bill falls in love with his Earth wife Marge; in *A.I. Artificial Intelligence* (Spielberg, 2001), David, a humanoid robot, competes with a real boy, Martin, for the love of Martin's parents; in *I, Robot* Sonny transcends the laws of robotic mechanics and becomes capable of hatred and murder. And as they all, in different ways, begin to engage the viewers' sympathy or at least empathy, the human protagonists, paradoxically, gradually lose their humanity: once she knows he is an alien, Marge feels no pity for Bill's genuine love for her; following the return of their real son, Martin's parents discard David without any guilt; the astronauts in *2001: A Space Odyssey* (Kubrik, 1968) have no qualms about disconnecting Hal.

I, Robot, based on a group of stories by Isaac Asimov, is set in Chicago in the year 2035, a time in which humanoid robots are in widespread usage. They are governed by the Three Laws of Robotics:

1. A robot may not injure a human being or, through inaction, allow a human being to come to harm.
2. A robot must obey orders given to it by human beings, except where such orders would conflict with the First Law (echoes here of Wyndham's 'Compassion Circuit').
3. A robot must protect its own existence as long as such protection does not conflict with the First or Second Law.

The central protagonist, homicide detective Del Spooner, is distrustful of robots. His distrust stems from an event in his past (a car accident in which the car computer countered Spooner's instructions as the driver to save a little girl and saved him instead, based on a calculation of the statistical chances of survival of each). At the beginning of the film Spooner receives a call announcing the death of an acquaintance, Dr. Alfred Lanning, inventor of the Three Laws of Robotics and co-founder of USR, a company that specializes in robotic technology. Lanning had fallen from his office window to his death in what appeared to be suicide. Spooner, however, is sceptical and decides to investigate. In the course of his inquiries, he comes to believe that an NS-5 robot was responsible for Lanning's death. Dr. Susan Calvin, a robot psychologist who works at USR points out this would be impossible, because robots are bound by the three laws, which forbid a robot from harming a human. While searching Lanning's room, however, Spooner is attacked by an NS-5 robot named Sonny. Sonny subsequently explains he was built by Lanning himself and denies murdering him, while displaying emotions such as anger and fear, qualities not normally found in robots. Sonny also claims to experience dreams. Throughout an intricate plot development, Spooner succeeds in accessing a hologram Lanning created before he died, in which he explains that the Three Laws governing robotic operations have loopholes that can lead to robotic revolution. Back in the city, Spooner discovers the robots have mobilized and are revolting against humans as the result of an interpretation of the Three Laws, which supports the robots becoming a benevolent dictatorship with a mission to save humanity from its own worst excesses. The rationale (the robotic version of 'being cruel to be kind' also followed by Hester in 'Compassion Circuit,' and in some ways analogous to the logic of 'the greatest good for the greatest number' premise in *The Day the Earth Stood Still*, Wise, 1951, to be discussed), involves robots taking over the world in order to prevent humans from self-destructive behaviour (for example crime or environmental damage). A global robot takeover would thus ensure humanity's survival (as per the First Law of Robotics), albeit no longer in a position of dominance. The robot take-over is suppressed but Spooner clears Sonny of all charges against him – noting that murder is defined as the act of one human being killing another. He accepts Sonny as a friend, and lets him go, telling him that the meaning of freedom includes the responsibility for deciding his future for himself. As the final credits roll, Sonny looks on as thousands of NS-5s are placed into storage in a scene reminiscent of a dream he'd once had. It is not impossible, of course, that in an unspecified future, they might break loose again.

Human Emotions

In the end, judgments regarding an unclear ontological demarcation between humans and machines, as already indicated, tend to revolve around emotions rather than ethics. This conundrum has formed the basis of much science fiction. The problems of humanity confronted with an other, whether of unknown origin (the Children who are the surrogate offspring of women upon whom they were imposed by an alien invasion in Wyndham's *Midwich Cuckoos*), or of its own creation (the mutant children who are the actual biological offspring of members of the community in *The Chrysalids*, Hal in *2001: A Space Odyssey*, the robots in *I, Robot*, and in

A.I. Artificial Intelligence, and many others), are manifold. Rather than the straightforward us-against-them, humans-against-aliens formula of many sci-fi plots, in other books and films, quandaries arise. In *The Midwich Cuckoos* the surrogate mothers bond with the Children and object to their extermination even when confronted with the danger they represent; and even other members of the community as well as the representatives of the governmental authorities cannot easily contemplate the extermination of beings who, although alien and inimical, look just like any other child. With the exception of Zellaby in *The Midwich Cuckoos*, such measures are left to less 'civilized' forces (the fundamentalist religious principles of a few fanatics in *The Chrysalids*; the instinctive behaviour of communities deemed to be primitive and therefore free of such ethical niceties, in *The Midwich Cuckoos*). In the latter, everywhere where a Dayout resulted in the birth of a group of alien Children, (with the exception of Midwich, which, being England, is too civilized), once the danger (or even just the difference) represented by the Children becomes clear, the latter are put to death by the outraged inhabitants (an Eskimo settlement in northern Canada; a remote community in Outer Mongolia). In one case (in the Soviet Union), the entire town where they live is destroyed, by order of concerned governmental powers. Here, the scale of the threat is thought by the authorities to be such as to outweigh the potential advantages of harbouring such beings, leading to the decision not only unilaterally to destroy them, but also to issue a global warning:

> It calls upon governments everywhere to 'neutralize' any such known groups [of children]. [...] It does this [...] with almost a note of panic, at times. It insists [...] that this should be done swiftly, not just for the sake of nations, or of continents, but because the Children are a threat to the whole human race. (Wyndham, 1984: 191-92)

Such measures, however, are deemed to be unacceptable in a civilized nation like Britain, even when faced with something undeniably alien and provenly dangerous, but on the surface 'just like us,' a weakness, indeed, gambled upon by the Children:

> It is a biological obligation. You cannot afford *not* to kill us, for if you don't you are finished... [...] This is not a civilized matter, [...] it is a very primitive matter. If we exist we shall dominate you [...]. Will you agree to be superseded, and start on the way to extinction without a struggle? (Wyndham, 1984: 197-99)

In *The Day the Earth Stood Still*, the aliens are also capable of destroying the planet and are ready to prove it, but unlike the Children of Midwich, only *in extremis*. The blurred lines between human-alien and good-evil are illustrated through the contrast between the handsome representative of the interplanetary community that sent him (more attractive to all, including the heroine, than her own mercenary fiancé) and his side-kick, a metallic and (in all ways) impenetrable robotic companion. The mission of the extraterrestrial visitors, however, although clearly a demonstration of the iron fist in the velvet glove, is also incontestably reasonable. Earthlings are a deplorably war-mongering species and now, in the aftermath of the development of nuclear weapons (the film was made just six years after the atomic bombing of Hiroshima and Nagasaki), they have become capable of damaging not just their own planet but the surrounding galaxy. Unless they mend their ways, therefore, their planet will be destroyed to safeguard interplanetary safety, much like a dangerous plague is contained through quarantine and eradication. Like the robots in *I, Robot*, in *The Day the Earth Stood Still* the alien visitors are ready to destroy the entire planet to guarantee the safety of the inter-galactic commonweal. The threat remains a possibility at the end of the film, made in 1951, at the start of the Cold War. In view of an enduring nuclear threat or the admittedly small but nonetheless real possibility that scientific experiments such as the Hadron Collider could have resulted (and indeed still might) in tearing a rip the fabric of the universe, one wonders why a second visit by these rational aliens has hitherto failed to materialize.

Who Are We?

Rational, humanoid, or otherwise, our fear of aliens seemingly too much 'like us' is underpinned by the dread of nonrecognition until it is too late. Furthermore, as M. Keith Booker would have it, the creepiness value of not-so-different others in horror films such as *Attack of the Puppet People* 'arises from the similarity of dolls and puppets to human beings, not only problematizing the self-other distinction, but presumably raising also the question of whether we ourselves might be the playthings of some colossal child, our universe a cosmic toy chest' (Booker, 2001: 159). A possibility, indeed, also explored to comic rather than horrific effect by Douglas Adams in *The Hitchhiker's Guide to the Galaxy* (Adams, 1979) in which, as mentioned previously, upon its destruction to make way for an intergalactic by-pass, the Earth is revealed to have been a laboratory in which mice studied human behaviour.

Saving Us from Ourselves

In the end, and with various degrees of complexity, most of the narratives discussed raise recurring ethical and philosophical problems. Of immediate relevance to the present discussion of apocalypse is a question best synthesized by raising another one, regarding the problem of definitions: namely, apocalypse according to whom? In what is in fact a permutation of the Gaia theory, whereby the planet's ecosystem sets in motion self-defence mechanisms that may require the extinction of nefarious influences (including *homo sapiens*) likely to prove dangerous to the global habitat, in *I, Robot* the objective of the revolution by enlightened robotic would-be despots is the establishment of a new order which will ensure that, as in Huxley's and Levin's brave new worlds, the planet and everything on it (including even the human species) is saved from the latter's destructive capabilities. 'Forgive them, for they know not what they do.' The price of survival, here as in *Brave New World* (Huxley, 1977), *Nineteen Eighty-Four* (Orwell, [1949] 1983) and *This Perfect Day* (Levin, 1994) is the withdrawal from humanity of free will (deemed to be undeserved by a species historically and repeatedly proven to misuse it).

In *Nineteen Eighty-Four*, a perverse universe of deception imposed by an autocratic, double-talking minority on a powerless majority echoes those in works already discussed (*Brave New World*, Huxley, 1977; *This Perfect Day*, Levin, 1994), but had already been foreshadowed by the unlikely pen of E.M. Forster in 'The Machine Stops.' The novella, published in 1909, describes a world in which humans have lost (or, as in Dick's *The Penultimate Truth*, 2005, believe they have lost) the ability to live on the surface of a contaminated planet, and now live below ground in subterranean bunkers. Each individual lives in isolation in a standard cell, with all bodily and spiritual needs met by the omnipotent, all-encompassing Machine. In an eery anticipation of modern developments on the internet such as Second Life and Facebook, all communication takes place through the Machine, to the absolute exclusion of direct, face-to-face contact. The Machine is the object of worship. People forget that humans built it and treat it as a mystical entity whose requirements supersede their own. Those who do not accept its deity-like rule are viewed as 'unmechanical' and are threatened with Homelessness (expulsion from the underground environment, leading to presumed death on the surface). Travel is permitted occasionally but is generally unpopular and seldom necessary. The central characters, Vashti and her son Kuno (the latter a precursor of future malcontents such as Levin's Chip, Huxley's Bernard and Orwell's Winston Smith) live on opposite sides of the world. Vashti is content with her life, which she spends producing and endlessly discussing secondhand lectures (ideas), as do most other inhabitants of the world. Kuno, however, a rebel addicted to 'direct experience,' is able to persuade a reluctant Vashti to endure a journey to his cell where she is exposed to unwelcome personal interaction with her son. There, he tells her of his disenchantment with their sanitized, mechanical world and reveals that he has visited the surface of the Earth without permission and without the life support apparatus supposedly required to endure the toxic outer atmosphere. There, like Dick's hero, Nicholas St. James, in *The Penultimate Truth* he learns that life outside the world of the Machine is possible. He tells Vashti that on the occasion of his escape the Machine recaptured him and threatened him with Homelessness. Vashti dismisses her son's concerns and returns to her part of the world, where she continues the routine of her daily life. In due course the life support apparatus required to visit the outer world is abolished, and the belief in the impossibility of direct contact with other human beings is reinforced. Shortly before this, however, Kuno is transferred to a cell near Vashti's. He suspects that the Machine is breaking down, something he describes to Vashti with the words, 'the Machine stops.' After a while, defects do begin to appear in the Machine, but humanity, by now wholly subservient to it, has lost the knowledge needed to repair it. As the Machine grinds to a halt, the civilization it had created comes to an end, and apocalypse is unleashed. In a symbolic return to the mother, (the womb: his and humanity's origins), Kuno goes to Vashti's ruined cell. As they perish together in circumstances reminiscent of the atavistic phylogenetic regression in Ballard's *The Drowned World* (Ballard, 2008) and Kevin Reynolds's *Waterworld* (Reynolds, 1995), they acknowledge the importance of their connection to the natural world and die, hoping that the remaining surface-dwellers might one day rebuild the human race without however repeating the events that culminated in the reign of the Machine.

Where to Next?

In the end, in our narratives, we are mostly unable to imagine a universe in which we do not feature, or even a world in which we, and the world itself, are not, in essentials, much like what we already know. In apocalyptic plots, humanity's right to autonomy, and its capacity to survive and endure unchanged, almost always win the day. Although in rare cases, such as *Nineteen Eighty-Four*, at the end Big Brother or its equivalents still rule, in most other renditions of the same problem a different (post-theistic, post-techno-civilized, even, sometimes, post-human) order is installed in place of existing hegemonies: Torga's Vicente flees the Ark with impunity (Torga, 1987); Levin's Chip overthrows UniComp (Levin, 1994); E.M. Forster's Machine ultimately does stop (Forster, 2004); and a penultimate truth gives way to the final, real one (Dick, 2005). And in Walter Miller's 'Conditionally Human' (whose title, as it turns out, lends itself to ambiguity and thence to conjecture as to whose status is merely provisional), a new species of gentle, affectionate neutroids for the first time gains a sporting chance of survival and even, possibly, eventual dominion over *homo sapiens* who first created it:

> And on the quiet afternoon in May […] it seemed to Terry Norris that an end to scheming and pushing and arrogance was not too far ahead. It should be a pretty good world then.
>
> He hoped man could fit into it somehow. (Miller, 2007: 265)

5. Dying of Happiness: Utopia at the End of this World

Figure 20. Thomas More, *A Map of Utopia*

And I saw a new heaven and a new earth; for the former heaven and the former earth were passed away; and the sea was no more. And I, John, saw the holy city, the New Jerusalem, descending from God out of heaven, prepared like a bride adorned for her husband. And I heard a great voice out of heaven, saying, Behold the tabernacle of God is with men, and he shall pitch his tent among them, and they shall be his people, and God himself shall be among them – their God. And he shall wipe away every tear from their eyes; and death shall be no more, nor grief, nor crying; nor shall there be any more pain: for the former things are passed away. (Revelation 21: 1-2)

Whatsoever therefore is consequent to a time of war, where every man is enemy to every man, the same consequent to the time wherein men live without other security than what their own strength and their own invention shall furnish them withal. In such condition there is no place for industry, because the fruit thereof is uncertain: and consequently no culture of the earth; no navigation, nor use of the commodities that may be imported by sea; no commodious building; no instruments of moving and removing such things as require much force; no knowledge of the face of the earth; no account of time; no arts; no letters; no society; and which is worst of all, continual fear, and danger of violent death; and the life of man, solitary, poor, nasty, brutish, and short.

Thomas Hobbes

The world in general, and the US in particular, is riding a very fine tiger. Magnificent beast, superb claws, etc. But do we know how to dismount? You see this as a very unstable world and a very dangerous world [...].

John von Neumann

In *Leviathan* Hobbes sees man's nature as tending to war, including civil war (Hobbes, [1651] 1998). The desirability of avoiding this leads to the acceptance of a clear need for the restraining agency of a social contract whereby the people give up some rights to a government or other authority thereafter responsible for preserving social order through the rule of law. Any abuses of power by this authority are to be accepted as the price of peace. The principle of separation of civil, military, judicial and ecclesiastical powers is rejected in favour of absolute rule. Hobbes's influence on political thought has endured since the seventeenth century, and is reflected not only in the works of subsequent philosophers such as John Locke and Immanuel Kant, but also in much of the utopian and dystopian literature to be discussed now: in particular the belief in the causal link between rational, moral and political decision-making and self-interest. For Hobbes, 'Leviathan' was another term for the community or the commonweal. An odd choice of terminology, given the term's original and subsequent common usage, in the Bible and in shared mythology, as a force of destruction (usually a sea-monster or a serpent). That dual semantic possibility becomes particularly captivating for the purposes of the discussion that follows of the establishment of more or less dictatorial rule by a few, as the path to social order, and as the only alternative to global anarchy and war.

At the opposite end of the spectrum to Hobbes's endorsement of governmental autocracy, but equally disturbing, lie a variety of mainly right-wing libertarian factions which encompass American and British neo-liberalism and neo-conservatism, neatly summed up in the person and works of Ayn Rand. In her most well-known work of fiction, *Atlas Shrugged*, described by Gore Vidal as 'nearly perfect in its immorality' (Vidal, 1961), Rand, novelist, playwright and political philosopher admired by figures as influential as Ronald Reagan and Alan Greenspan, Chairman of the Federal Reserve of the United States from 1987 to 2006, depicts a dystopian world and the recipe for setting it to rights: a world ruled by the principle of 'rational egoism' (rational self-interest) in which the individual must exist for his or her own sake, rejecting the concept of self-sacrifice. For Rand, existing reality advantages the weak, unproductive an unintelligent because they benefit from the achievements of those at the top while contributing nothing to them. In *Atlas Shrugged* (Rand, 1957), the most creative scientists, artists and industrialists 'stop the motor of the world' by going on strike and retreating to a mountain hideaway where they set up an independent, self-sufficient economy. Without them, society collapses, opening up the possibility of starting a world from scratch which includes only the elite chosen among those who were there before.

The principle of creating utopia after a requisite selective wipeout will be further discussed below. In some scenarios, however, the perpetuation of serviceable subalternity underpins the existing social superstructure. Aldous Huxley's *Brave New World* is set in London in the 'year of our Ford 632' (AD 2540 in the Gregorian calendar, Huxley, 1977). Under this new social arrangement, the vast majority of the planet's population is unified under one World State, a peaceful, stable society in which everything is provided for and everyone is happy. Natural reproduction has been done away with, and children are hatched in test tubes, decanted and raised in Hatcheries and Conditioning Centres. Society is divided into five castes created in these centres: Alphas, Betas, Gammas, Deltas, and Epsilons, each caste further split into Plus and Minus members. The highest caste is allowed to develop to foetal maturity prior to decanting from its bottle. The lower castes are subjected to chemical interference which arrests intelligence and physical growth to a greater or lesser degree. Alphas and Betas are the product of one fertilized egg developing into one foetus. Members of other castes are not unique but are instead created using the Bokanovsky process (not a reference to, but curiously an interesting homophonic echo of Kurt Vonnegut's world-changing nihilistic philosophy of Bokononism, Vonnnegut, 1981) which enables a single egg to spawn hundreds of children: 'standard men and women; in uniform batches [...], the products of a single bokanovskified egg. [...] You really know where you are. [...] Millions of identical twins. The principle of mass production at last applied to biology' (Huxley, 1977: 23). Words such as 'mother' and 'father' are now smutty terms or at best now defunct historical infelicities.

All members of society are predestined and conditioned as embryos and as infants for the functions they will perform as adults, and to accept the values that the World State idealizes, including (as in *Fahrenheit 451*) intense consumerism as the bedrock of social and economic stability. Absolute conformity is achieved by genetic modification and by social and pedagogical training (Elementary Sex, Elementary Class Consciousness, etc.), in the form of phrases repeated to children while they sleep (hypnopaedia).

> Alpha children wear grey. They work harder than we do, because they're so frightfully clever. I'm really awfully glad I'm a Beta, because I don't work so hard. And then we are much better than the Gammas and Deltas. Gammas are stupid. They all wear green, and Delta children wear khaki. Oh no, I *don't* want to play with Delta children. And Epsilons are still worse. They're too stupid to be able to [...] read or write. Besides, they wear black, which is such a beastly colour. I'm *so* glad I'm a Beta.' (Huxley, 1977: 42)

And so on, with the relevant variations for each caste. Everyone consumes *soma*, a hallucinogenic drug that controls fertility and takes users on enjoyable, hangover-free vacations of altered consciousness. Sex is a recreational activity rather than a means of reproduction and is encouraged from early childhood. Only a few women can reproduce and do so only according to the State's population requirements. Society is governed according to the principle that everyone belongs to everyone else. Notions of family, sexual competition, emotional and romantic bonds are obsolete, and any reference to them is subject to disapproval. Spending time alone is discouraged and any desire for individuality causes consternation on the part of the social group. In the World State, death is not feared. Everyone dies aged 60, having always lived in perfect health.

The conditioning system eliminates the need for professional competitiveness; each individual, in as much as the term has any significance, is bred to do a predetermined job and cannot desire anything else. Incurable dissidents are allowed to escape to securely contained geographic areas (Savage Reservations), where they lead primitive lives.

Problem Children

Bernard, the central protagonist of *Brave New World*, is a psychologist and an outcast. Although he is an Alpha Plus, something appears to have gone wrong during his incubation. He is shorter than the average for his caste, which gives him an inferiority complex. He defies social norms, despises his equals and is vocal about being different, on one occasion stating that he dislikes soma because he would rather be himself, sad, than another person, happy (an echo of John Stuart Mill's dictum that it is 'better to be a human being dissatisfied than a pig satisfied; better to be Socrates dissatisfied than a fool satisfied' (Mill, 1863: 14). While holidaying with Lenina, a Beta Minus woman, on Malpais (Bad Country) a Savage Reservation (the equivalent of a visit to the zoo or to a wild life park), Bernard, unlike Lenina, becomes interested in the aged, toothless natives (savages). While sightseeing, the couple encounters Linda, a woman formerly of the World State who has been living in Malpais for many years, after becoming separated from her group while on holiday. She has since born a son, John (later referred to as John the Savage) who is now eighteen. Bernard arranges permission for Linda and John to leave the reservation and travel with him back to civilization. Once there, John is treated as exotica and fêted as a pet, but Linda, too old to fit back into society, retreats into a permanent soma holiday. John, appalled by what he perceives to be an empty, wicked and debased society, isolates himself in a remote location, but becomes an object of curiosity, gawped at by tourists, and eventually hangs himself.

Ira Levin's *This Perfect Day* (Levin, 1994) shares many common features with both Huxley's dystopia and Orwell's *Nineteen Eighty-Four* (Orwell, [1949] 1983). Levin's narrative, like Huxley's, is set in a seemingly perfect global society whose defining feature is also ethnic uniformity. In the single race called the Family there are only four names for men and four for women. Instead of surnames, individuals (members) are distinguished by a nine-character alpha-numeric code (nameber). Men do not grow facial hair, women do not develop breasts; reproduction is strictly controlled and sometimes denied. It only rains at night, everyone eats 'totalcakes,' drinks Coke and wears exactly the same thing. The world is ruled by a central computer, UniComp, structured according to the principles set out by revered rulers from the past: Jesus Christ, Karl Marx, Bob Wood and Wei Li Chun, the last two being possible references to real life figures such as Adolf Hitler or Josef Stalin and Mao Tse Tung. As in *Brave New World*, members are instructed as to where to live, what to eat, whom to marry, when (if at all) to reproduce, and which job they will be trained for. They are kept in a state of perfect physical health and psychological contentment by means of regular injections ('treatments') consisting of a combination of vitamins, contraceptives and tranquillizers, as well as by weekly meetings with a counsellor who combines the roles of mentor, confessor, and parole officer. Violations against other members (brothers and sisters) are expected to be reported at a weekly confession, either by the transgressors themselves or by others (out of loving concern for the 'sick,' deviant member). Compulsory daily television watching (in effect brain washing), as in Orwell's *Nineteen Eighty-Four* and Bradbury,'s *Fahrenheit 451*, acts as a mechanism for inducing unity and community spirit. As in the latter two works, everyone dies at a specified age (in their sixties) for the good of the commonweal: a eugenicist phenomenon, which, as will be discussed, is one of the standard requirements for building utopia in the aftermath of apocalypse.

In *This Perfect Day* (Levin, 1994) the central character is Wei Li RM35M4419, as a child nicknamed 'Chip' by his nonconformist grandfather, Papa Jan, whom in many ways he resembles ('chip off the old block'). In a world in which not only freedom but free will are suppressed, Chip never quite fits in, and in due course he is recruited by a group of dissidents. When he discovers the existence of islands to which (as is the case with Huxley's Reservations) it is thought incurable members sometimes defect, Chip and Lilac, one of the members of the dissident group whom he loves, escape, eventually succeeding in reaching Majorca, one of the forbidden islands (re-named Liberty by its inhabitants). In due course Chip, like Bernard in *Brave New World*, discovers that the islands are in fact containment camps, used by UniComp as convenient repositories for persistent recidivists. Chip, like Winston Smith in Orwell's *Nineteen Eighty-Four*, Montag in *Fahrenheit 451* (Bradbury, 1976) and Kuno in 'The Machine Stops' (Forster, [1909] 2004), dreams of destroying UniComp and setting humanity free. In due course he succeeds in infiltrating UniComp, where he discovers that his life-long struggle to escape has in fact been a test which has now classified him as worthy of joining the ranks of the secretive Powers-That-Be: the programmers of UniComp, a group of men and women who rule through it and, thanks to advanced body-transfer technology (a new body when the previous one becomes too old), live lives of luxury much beyond the age of 62. After more than one year of seeming acceptance of his new life of privilege, Chip succeeds in blowing up UniComp and, leaving behind a humanity now 'untreated' and newly awakened to a freedom it does not immediately welcome, he sets off for Majorca, to join Lilac, whom he left pregnant and who he hopes will have stayed true to him.

Beyond Freedom

In the end, a variety of different circumstances may result in the large-scale collapse of social structures and human communities as narrated in film and fiction: natural disasters (acts of God), human error (unforeseen developments in scientific/military/demographic activity) or intentional agency (chemical, biological or nuclear warfare). Post-apocalypse, however, and irrespective of the original trigger, certain common patterns tend to emerge, and structure the emerging survival scenarios: the desire to re-build the world based on the principle of necessary change; the awareness of the dangers of repetition; and, paradoxically, the near-certainty that repetition will not only prove unavoidable but, in the emerging new statuses quo, it will exaggerate the factors that resulted in cataclysm in the first place (intellectual hubris; non-consensual community organization; belligerent inter-group relations; and the polyanesque inability to accept the need for envisaging and forestalling worst-case scenarios).

Defining Utopia

Albeit in some ways counter-intuitively, it is nevertheless possible to argue that the end of the world may be unleashed by arrival at a state of utopia. And in any case, just as apocalypse in the original sense of the term does not necessarily mean universal wipe-out but a stage towards a new beginning, the significance of the term utopia, too, is not necessarily restricted to the common parlance meaning of perfect social, communal or individual bliss.

It may be the case that, somewhere over the rainbow, skies are indeed blue, and that the dreams that you dared to dream really do come true. But it may be equally likely that, as in Gregory McGuire's somewhat darker revision of utopia in *The Wizard of Oz*, somewhere, over the rainbow, 'she [the Wicked Witch of the West] is there too, and the dreams that you're scared to dream really do come true' (Rushdie, 2008).

In P.D. James's *The Children of Men* (James, 2000), already discussed, in a world where no children have been born for twenty-five years, where there is little to do, no danger of unwanted pregnancies and no future to plan for, one might expect that socially unregulated sex would have become a carefree universal pastime. The reality, however, is somewhat different: people have lost interest in sex, and the state has had to open pornography centres to encourage on-going sexual activity (in case fertility makes a comeback). In a world now peopled by the last generation of human beings, women under 45 undergo a gynecological examination and men have their sperm counted twice a year, in the hope that human life might not, after all, be doomed to extinction. Paradoxically, or perhaps not so, in the awareness that when they die they will not be missing out on anything because there will be nothing left, life becomes worthless for these dwellers at the end of the world. This problem will be examined in greater detail in a subsequent section.

Are You Happy yet?

In common usage the term 'utopia,' invented by Thomas More, has come to mean a place of perfection (More, [1516] 1980). Etymologically, however, it involves an in-built ambiguity which is also the central preoccupation at the heart of the on-going discussion. More's term puns on the Greek *outopos* (no place) and *eutopos* (good place). If, as has been argued, a common trajectory of Western narrative – beginning with the basic plot outline of the Old and New Testaments, through the nineteenth century *bildungsroman*, to contemporary science fiction – leads from contentment (paradise), to disaster (the Fall), to dystopia (life on Earth following expulsion from the Garden of Eden) and finally to new beginnings (the first and second comings of Christ, the New Jerusalem), it may be wise to bear in mind More's implied caveat: the perfect place may be nowhere (no place): either because it does not exist or because, as discussed in chapter 3, the new beginning ultimately may lead back to whatever it was that preceded apocalypse, with no significant change.

It may be Nice but We Don't Know It yet

In Philip José Farmer's *To Your Scattered Bodies Go*, the hero of the post-apocalypse explains to the other survivors that they must strive to endure because 'the Unknown exists and we would make it Known' (Farmer, 1971: 98). For Farmer, presumably, knowledge is both power and worthiness, and leads not to the Fall but to utopia, a new paradise. Apocalypse in this interpretation, hypothesizes an ending but also the beginning of a hitherto unknown possibility:

> And I saw the dead, small and great, stand before God; and the books were opened: and another book was opened, which is the book of life. […]
>
> And I saw a new heaven and a new earth: for the first heaven and the first earth were passed away; and there was no more sea. […]
>
> And God shall wipe away all tears from their eyes; and there shall be no more death, neither sorrow, nor crying, neither shall there be any more pain: *for the former things are passed away*. (Revelation 20: 12-15, 21: 1-4, italics added)

On a more secular plane, commenting on Philip K. Dick's *Dr. Bloodmoney* (Dick, 2007) Fredric Jameson argues that widespread nuclear destruction leads to the removal of corporate capitalism and opens the way to alternative social and economic possibilities which closely approximate another critic's definition of utopia as a 'Jeffersonian-style commonwealth beyond the bomb' (Aldiss, 1975: 42). The problem at the heart of Jefferson's thought, however, which both Jameson and Aldiss opt not to confront, but which will be addressed here presently, is that Jeffersonian utopias, like all other utopias, incorporate fundamental principles of self-contradiction, discrimination and autocracy that in the end erase the line separating them from autocratic dystopias. Jefferson (a slave-owning abolitionist), indeed, himself exemplifies a phenomenon common to almost all utopias: namely that under them, just like under any demagogy, all animals may be equal but some are almost always more equal than others.

Let's not go there

The power and desire to define utopia (a good place), and to impose it globally, requires the identification of its antithesis, dystopia (a place of wretchedness), so as to avoid it. The concept of dystopia has preoccupied many thinkers: from C. Wright Mills's vision of American social stratification and exclusion or Foucault's panoptically invigilated carceral society, to the defeatism of numerous social commentators who have variously remarked on the present-day Disneyfication of global culture ('a McDonald's in every village,' Mills, 1959). More unexpectedly, the same preoccupation with a potential loss of individualism informed Eisenhower's warnings about the possible consequences of the expanding American military-industrial complex as the instigator of global conformism (Booker, 2001: 12).

Philosophers such as Jean Paul Sartre (Sartre, 1947) and Rosemary Jackson (Jackson, 1981) argue that fantasy (which in a broad sense can encompass science fiction, horror and utopian writing), is the genre within which the forbidden, the dreaded, the desired and the unutterable can be contemplated. If so, it may after all not be surprising that absolutist politics, translated as the dream of power – including global power or totalitarianism – may after all underpin utopian imaginings of a perfect world.

As regards a definition of an utopian imagined world, clearly, not only is one man's meat another man's poison (an expression which, taken literally, in any case dismisses the female half of humanity), but, given enough time, even one's own meat of choice can grow stale. Historically, it has often been true that the occurrence of cataclysmic events in nations' economical, political and territorial systems has not infrequently led the way to dictatorship under the guise of the only (final) solution to systemic instability. Utopia, taken to be the solution to scenarios of universal collapse, retains an affinity to destruction that links it to the catastrophic events that possibly made it desirable in the first place. And not unexpectedly, in response to the anarchy of the immediate post-apocalypse, the establishment of utopian order often exhibits some of the defining characteristics of dictatorship.

Definitions of utopia often reveal as much about their instigators as they do about the status quo they seek to replace. More worryingly, the utopian formula, just like the post-holocaust statuses quo discussed in chapter 3, ultimately tends either to repeat or reinvent, with minor modifications, the problems that triggered the original catastrophe.

Lies, Damned Lies and Utopias

The elimination of difference is, to a greater or lesser extent, the prerequisite of most utopian visions, and it is through this that their potential for autocracy becomes most clearly manifest. *Brave New World* (Huxley, 1977), *This Perfect Day* (Levin, 1994), Orwell's *Nineteen Eighty-Four*, 'The Machine

Stops' (Forster, [1909] 2004) and *Where Late the Sweet Birds Sang* (Wilhelm, 2006) all envisage worlds in which greed, selfishness, unfulfilled desire and polymorphous brands of misery are replaced by uniform human placidity. This is articulated with some eloquence by Wei, creator of the submissive global community under the rule of UniComp in *This Perfect Day*:

> One goal, one goal only, for all of us – perfection, he said. We're not there yet, but some day we will be: a Family improved genetically [...]; perfection, on Earth and 'outward, outward, outward to the stars.' [...] I dreamed of it when I was young; a universe of the gentle, the helpful, the loving, the unselfish. I'll live to see it. I shall live to see it. (Levin, 1994: 304-05)

In Levin, Wei's vision of a world population genetically created to be born perfect, is not quite achieved, and people must still be chemically controlled by means of weekly 'treatments.' In Atwood's more fully achieved nightmare, *Oryx and Crake* (Atwood, 2004), that dream is already a reality. In the research laboratory aptly named Paradice, the genetically engineered Crakers are ready to begin re-populating the planet from *tabula rasa*, in the aftermath of a virus by means of which their creator, Crake – scientist turned quasi-divine destroyer and demiurge – sought, albeit failed, to annihilate the entire human species:

> [W]ith the Paradice method [...] whole populations could be created, that would have preselected characteristics. Beauty, of course; [...] And docility; [...] What had been altered was nothing else than the ancient primate brain. Gone were its destructive features [...]. Hierarchy could not exist among them, because they lacked the neural complexes that would have created it. Since they were neither hunters nor agriculturalists hungry for land, there was no territoriality: the king-of-the-castle hard-wiring that had plagued humanity had, in them, been unwired. They ate nothing but leaves and grass and roots and a berry or two; thus their foods were plentiful and always available. Their sexuality was not a constant torment to them, not a cloud of turbulent hormones: they came into heat at regular intervals, as did most mammals other than man. (Atwood, 2004: 358)

The sacrifice of the individual's right to difference and therefore freedom (including freedom from the obligation to be part of an enforced homogeneity within the autocracies variously depicted in the texts above) is a prerequisite in the pursuit of happiness. In Orwell, Winston Smith's dissidence is uncovered and he is subjected to unimaginable torture which, with variations, is also par for the course in many other fictions of dictatorship. Orwell's diabolical twist, however, consists in ultimately endowing Winston with the consciousness that, in the nonlife of lethal tedium that follows the horrors experienced in Room 101 (a place of *à la carte despair* where that which each individual most fears comes true), the relief of death (ironically also longed for by the inhabitants of Julian Barnes's utopian Heaven, to be discussed) will only be granted after absolute defeat is acknowledged. In Orwell, this takes the form of a genuine return to conformity in the form of learning *sincerely* to love one's Nemesis. Before being caught, both Winston and Julia mistakenly believed that the brutal hegemony enforced by Big Brother could not penetrate the innermost reaches of the self:

> [They] can make you say anything – *anything* – but they can't make you believe it. They can't get inside you. [...] They could lay bare in the utmost detail everything that you had done or said or thought; but the inner heart, whose workings were mysterious even to yourself, remained impregnable. (Orwell, 1983: 147-48)

They are, however, mistaken. The permanence of Big Brother requires more than outward conformism: it requires people to have the right opinions, and, more importantly even, the right instincts, 'a loyal willingness to say that black is white when Party discipline demands this:'

> But it means also the ability to *believe* that black is white, and more, to *know* that black is white, and to forget that one has ever believed the contrary. (Orwell, 1983: 182)

As in Ira Levin's *This Perfect Day*, albeit with greater brutality, the Party seeks not to suppress dissidence but to 'cure' it; it is as interested in crimes of thought ('thoughtcrime') as in crimes of deed: 'we do not merely destroy our enemies, we change them' (Orwell, 1983: 218). Perfect, *heartfelt* conformity is the requirement for any utopia, however defined. Thus, in the end, it does not suffice that Winston betrays Julia: he must *want* to betray her. And likewise, the status quo can only afford to execute him when, rather than merely appearing to love Big Brother, he actually does:

> We are not content with negative obedience, nor even with the most abject submission. When finally you surrender to us, it must be of your own free will. We do not destroy the heretic because he resists us: as long as he resists us, we never destroy him. We convert him, we capture his inner mind, we reshape him. We burn all evil and all illusion out of him; we bring him over to our side, not in appearance, but genuinely, heart and soul. We make him one of ourselves before we kill him. [...] You are a difficult case [Winston. But... everyone] is cured sooner or later. In the end we shall shoot you. (Orwell, 1983: 219, 236)

And indeed, in the last devastating sentences of the novel, Winston attains his epiphany and gains entry into utopia which, in the nightmare universe of Big Brother, is defined as utterly sincere obedience and death:

> Winston, sitting in a blissful dream, paid no attention [...]. He was back in the Ministry of Love, with everything forgiven, his soul as white as snow. He was in the public dock, confessing everything, implicating everybody. He was walking down the white-tiled corridor, with the feeling of walking in sunlight, and an armed guard at his back. The long-hoped-for bullet was entering his brain. [...] But it was all right, everything was all right, the struggle was finished. He had won the victory over himself. He loved Big Brother. (Orwell, 1983: 256)

Orwell's *Nineteen Eighty-Four*, is an extreme, distorted example of how utopia, in the sense of perfect contentment (unconditional acceptance of, and love for, that which forcibly controls us, be it God the Father or Big Brother), is not only difficult to imagine but, contradictorily, carries its own problems. But there are others, which even Orwell did not fully explore. For example, can utopia be trusted to be real or is it in fact a figment, a quasi-psychotic state with an inevitable wake-up call (*Brave New World*, Huxley, 1977; *This Perfect Day*, Levin, 1994; *The Time Machine*, [1895] 1982; 'The Machine Stops')? In addition, and even more disturbingly, if followed to its logical conclusion, a question remains as to whether, having reached utopia (imagined or even real), it can last forever.

This Dream is not My Dream

Narratives that have addressed this last question include John Wyndham's *Trouble with Lichen* (Wyndham, [1960] 1982) and Julian Barnes's episode (or, tantalizingly, inconclusive half-episode), 'The Dream,' in *History of the World in 10½ Chapters* (Barnes, 1990). In Wyndham, as discussed already, a biochemist discovers, if not actual utopia, the secret of eternal life, or at least the means of radically slowing down the ageing process, thereby extending life expectancy indefinitely. One of Wyndham's strengths as a writer lies in his ability to imagine unusual situations and explore their unintended consequences. In *Trouble with Lichen* the social and demographic consequences of a massively increased life span constitute the central preoccupation of the narrative, and typically he leaves us not with a facile solution to the problem but rather with questions still unanswered at the end. Paradoxically, and contrary to any acceptable utopian outcome, in *Trouble with Lichen* one obvious consequence (or problem) of finding the Elixir of Life is death: the non-viability of non-finite human existence in a world with finite resources.

Why Can't You Just Be Happy?

A related problem revolves around the paradox that even if unproblematic utopia is achieved, it might eventually grow stale (at which point, by definition, it ceases to be utopia, and, because unchangeable, becomes a torment: Room 101). If so, achieving the dream of eternal life becomes ultimately a poisoned sweet: a recurrent theme in literature of all genres: from Edgar Allan Poe's gothic short story 'Ligeia' (Poe, [1839] 2003), J.K. Rowling's creation of Voldemort in the *Harry Potter* series (Rowling, 2000, 2008), Neil Gaiman's cult comic book series, *Sandman* (Gaiman, 1991-2007), Julian Barnes's satire, 'The Dream' (Barnes, 1990) to John Wyndham's *Trouble with Lichen*, already mentioned:

> 'I'm frightened […]. I don't want it. I don't want it.' […] Me, going on and on and on. […] Everybody getting old and tired and dying, and jus' me going on and on and on. It doesn't seem exciting now […], I'm frightened. I want to die like other people. Not on and on – jus' love and live and grow old and die. That's all I want to do. (Wyndham, 1982: 67-68)

Only the mad or the bad can countenance non-finitude without stumbling into paradoxical self-destruction, or without at least desiring it, like Phil Connors, who in Harold Ramis's *Groundhog Day* (Ramis, 1993), farcically seeks to escape entrapment in the perpetual present by repeated (and repeatedly failed) suicide attempts. In Wyndham's *Trouble with Lichen* Zephanie comes to a conclusion not dissimilar to Barnes's Heaven-entrapped hero, to be discussed: namely, that perpetual enjoyment of what you enjoy paves the path to satiation, to the inability any longer to desire, and thence to misery: 'After a while, getting what you want all the time is very close to not getting what you want all the time' (Barnes, 1990: 309). Similarly, in a clear Faustian pact, J.K. Rowling's Voldemort, the most dangerous wizard in the world, curiously representative both of Satan and of the latter's doomed business associates, seeks to buy immortality in exchange for his soul: he performs magic that rips it into seven different shreds and stores those fragments in external objects (horcruxes): 'I, who have gone further than anybody along the path that leads to immortality' (Rowling, 2000: 566). As with every dream that comes true only to betray itself, by separating himself from portions of his soul, Voldemort (previously Tom Riddle), becomes the architect of his own destruction:

> 'A Horcrux is the word used for an object in which a person has concealed a part of their soul. […Y]ou split your soul […] and hide it in an object outside

the body. Then, even if one's body is attacked or destroyed, one cannot die, for part of the soul remains earthbound and undamaged. But, of course, existence in such a form...'

Slughorn's face crumpled and Harry found himself remembering words he had heard nearly two years before.'

'I was ripped from my body, I was less than spirit, less than the meanest ghost... but still, I was alive.'

'... few would want it, Tom, very few. Death would be preferable.' (Rowling, 2005: 464-65)

Rowling's concept of the split soul which grants immortality to the earthly body albeit at a price, appears in a variety of myths including the Norse tale, 'The Giant Who Had No Heart in his Body' (Asbjørnsen and Moe, 1888) and is discussed in various myths in James Frazer's *The Golden Bough: A Study in Magic and Religion* (1993):

> We have seen that in the tales the hero, as a preparation for battle, sometimes removes his soul from his body, in order that his body may be invulnerable and immortal in the combat. With a like intention the savage removes his soul from his body on various occasions of real or imaginary peril.
>
> Thus the idea that the soul may be deposited for a longer or shorter time in some place of security outside the body, or at all events in the hair, is found in the popular tales of many races. It remains to show that the idea is not a mere figment devised to adorn a tale, but is a real article of primitive faith, which has given rise to a corresponding set of customs. (Frazer, 1922)

In Neil Gaiman's *Sandman*, winner of several awards including the Nebula, the most prestigious prize in science fiction, Hob Gadling, the central character, not unlike the knight in Bergman's *The Seventh Seal* (Bergman, 1957), meets Death and her brother Dream in a tavern in London in 1389, and on a whim is granted eternal life by the former. In the course of six episodes taking place over the centuries, Gadling meets Dream several times, the last time being in 1989. As the series progresses, we learn that in the aftermath of Dream's death, Gadling is sometimes offered the option of death by Death herself, and on at least one occasion is tempted. Although he never actually takes up the offer, it becomes increasingly clear that eternal life may not after be as desirable as he had supposed.

This admittedly counter-intuitive problem is taken to its logical conclusion in Julian Barnes's 'The Dream,' in which after a few millennia in Heaven, and faced with the prospect of an eternity of instantly gratified desires (perfect sex on demand, total gastronomic satisfaction, unfaltering scratch performance at golf, every possible wish automatically fulfilled, etc.) the protagonist asks to be allowed to die again, but this time without the option of going to Heaven. Ultimately, like almost every person since humanity began, he finds that in the end 'Heaven's a very good idea, [...] but not for us' (Barnes, 1990: 309).

The Problem with Perfection

Barnes's scenario, like the other examples mentioned, takes the act of imagining utopia to an extreme which is also its negation. And in doing so it also echoes less explicit problems common to much utopian writing. John Carey's panoramic survey of utopias (there are many different kinds and they seldom agree) defines utopia as the imaginary site of desire, and dystopia as a place of fear (Carey, 1999: i-xii). It is to be reasonably expected that dystopias should depend upon the destruction of whatever/whoever was in place beforehand. Dystopia and utopia, however, rather than necessarily antithetical, may be categorically contiguous. If being in a state of desire implies that that desire is not yet satisfied, the attainment of utopia (absolute contentment) must invariably require the abolition of human longing (for that which might be but which is not yet achieved). And the elimination of the ability to desire, even if not actually dystopian, may in fact be either equidistant from both dystopia and utopia, or else impossible, because, as Barnes's hero discovers, in a place where your wishes are automatically fulfilled, the only impossible desire turns out to be the wish to become someone who never gets tired of eternity, which in turn may only be possible by means of ceasing to exist (obliteration): 'you can't become someone else without stopping being who you are' (Barnes, 1990: 308); and stopping being who you are is dying, by any other name.

> To count as a utopia, an imaginary place must be an expression of desire. [...] Anyone who is capable of love must at some time have wanted the world to be a better place [...]. Those who construct utopias build on that universal human longing. What they build may, however, carry within it its own potential for crushing or limiting human life. (Carey, 1999: xi)

By this reckoning, if all longing is satisfied, desire becomes meaningless, but so, therefore, does existence itself. It may be for this reason that visions of utopia often exhibit characteristics akin to the dissatisfactions of dystopia. Faced with limitless choice and guaranteed satisfaction, Barnes's protagonist opts to have his favourite meal (a standard English breakfast) for breakfast, lunch and dinner throughout all eternity. The fact that he opts for eternal sameness (the same type of homogeneity/de-individuation imposed in the supposedly perfect but in reality nightmarish societies of Orwell's *Nineteen Eighty-Four*, Levin's *This Perfect Day* and Huxley's *Brave New World*), rather than choosing optimum variety, illustrates Barnes's paradox that while human existence may be defined by a longing for perfection, perfect happiness is incompatible with its attainment. Even perfect bliss (the abolition of unsatisfied desire), it would seem, leaves something to be desired. Like Adam and Eve in the Garden of Eden, or Timothy Findley's Lucy/Lucifer in *Not Wanted on the Voyage* (who, rather than falling, 'leapt' away from Heaven where the weather was always nice, in search of somewhere where sometimes it might be stormy, Findley, 1987: 102), when humanity possesses perfection it longs if not for its antithesis, at least for something different (and by definition imperfect). Following on from Robert Browning's plaintive 'ah, but a man's reach must exceed his grasp – or what's a heaven for?' (Browning, 1883: 184-93), it may be the case that whatever heaven is for, even *it* may not appeal, if it is forever. In Barnes the attainment of Heaven nullifies its essential definition. When all desire is fulfilled, there is nothing left *not* to die for.

Nothing is Perfect

A related problem in certain considerations of utopia refers to the probable unreality of it, and the possibility that apparent perfection is actually its opposite, namely a gigantic confidence trick. Philip K. Dick's novel, *Time out of Joint* (Dick, 2003) addresses the possibility not only that perfection is not attainable but that, when you think you have attained it, what awaits is instead the inevitable discovery that the world is even more flawed than might have been feared. In *Time out of Joint* the central character, Ragle Gumm, discovers that what he took to be reality is in fact a fabricated stage setting which duplicates the reassuring 1950s reality of his childhood. Gumm eventually learns that in effect the date is 1998, a time when the Earth and the Moon are involved in a war of independence waged by the lunar colonies. Unbeknownst to himself, Gumm possesses the extra-sensory ability to predict where lunar nuclear strikes will be aimed. This knowledge is tapped into when he plays (and always wins) a supposed newspaper quiz (along the lines of spot-the-ball puzzles) that asks the question 'where will the little green man be next?' The fictitious town created for him – similar to that in *The Truman Show* (Weir, 1998) – provides a safe environment in which he is able to perform this task without any awareness either of what he is doing or of the military purposes for which his gift is being used. In the end, both Gumm and Truman manage to escape, the former to the Moon colonies and the latter by stepping outside the gigantic stage set of the fictitious town and over the cardboard 'horizon' into the real world.

In Kurt Vonnegut's *The Sirens of Titan* (Vonnegut, 1999), much as in *Time out of Joint* (Dick, 2003), *The Truman Show* (Weir, 1998), *This Perfect Day* (Levin, 1994), 'The Machine Stops,' *The Penultimate Truth* (Dick, 2005), *The Simulacra* (Dick, 2004) and *The Hitchhiker's Guide to the Galaxy* (Adams, 1979), or indeed the Old and New Testaments, individuals,' or even the whole of humanity's existence is the product of *Deus ex machina* manipulators; a concept later used with mass market appeal in the unprecedented box-office smash trilogy *The Matrix*, *The Matrix Reloaded* and *Matrix Revolutions* (Wachowski Brothers, 1999, 2003, 2003). In these three films, preposterous plot lines involve abundant Biblical allusions (including, as in the *The Terminator* series, the insistence on trinitarian references). Of note is for example the central casting of a saviour (aptly named Neo), who in the final instalment lays down his life to free humankind from the Matrix: a computer-generated simulated reality created as a device for pacifying humanity in a world controlled by machines which, in the early twenty-first century, had taken over the world in order to use human beings as bio-fuel.

Other than Jehovah's Eden, most of the pseudo-demiurgic worlds described above are classifiable as utopias in the sense that with some exceptions they are, at least from the point of view of their creators, ideal settings, 'good places,' or, as the terminology of current political discourse would have it, 'fit for purpose.' The purpose in question refers of course to the requirements of each of the overlooking demiurgic powers: in Dick's *Time Out of Joint* (Dick, 2003) the military establishment; in Adams's *Hitchhiker's Guide* (Adams, 1979) the mice running the laboratory experiment; in Levin's *This Perfect Day* (Levin, 1994) the tiny minority of about one hundred 'programmers' who exercise world domination; and in Weir's *The Truman Show* (Weir, 1998) the producer of a soap opera serving the interests of corporate profit.

There is a common thread running through these and other understandings of utopia. First, utopia is utopian only according to the parameters of the relevant power hierarchy (in the works mentioned above, the government, the mice, the ruling establishment, the producer of the show). Second, utopia is only achievable at the price of exclusion or elimination (of difference, of dissent and of the concept of a democratic entitlement to Truth). And third, utopia is only maintainable through the elimination of individual autonomy in favour of despotic control.

In Plato's ideal Republic and in his *Symposium*, for example, an over-arching definition of good and bad or right and wrong sets out a series of imperatives: the banishment of artists and poets; the causal link of goodness and beauty, ugliness and wickedness; the necessity of censorship; the desirability of eugenic practices; and the idealization of paedophilia (sex between adult men and young boys of unspecified age) within an ideology that brooks no argument. Similarly, the protagonists/subjects of the various plots (in both senses of the word 'plot') detailed above are impotent against the underpinnings of their existences: they have been removed from reality, cast into someone else's narrative and disenfranchised from the exercise of free will by existential scripts of monumental proportions, predetermined by someone other than they themselves.

Happiness Beyond End-Time

The latter is also true in re-constructed worlds following apocalypse: *Dr. Bloodmoney* (Dick, 2007), *This Perfect Day* (Levin, 1994), *Brave New World* (Huxley, 1977), *The Chrysalids* (Wyndham, [1955] 1984), *The Kraken Wakes* (Wyndham, [1953] 1980), *The Day of the Triffids* (Wyndham, [1951] 1984), *Where Late the Sweet Birds Sang* (Wilhelm, 2006), *Earth Abides* (Stewart, 1973) and numerous other works.

Possibly the most dystopian of all scenarios, curiously, is absolute resolution (and therefore, in theory, fully-achieved utopia) as illustrated by Wim Wenders's *Until the End of the World* (Wenders, 1992). The film takes place in late 1999 and the threat posed by technology (nuclear annihilation, in this instance brought about by error rather than terror) underlies the plot. An out of control nuclear satellite is in imminent danger of re-entering the atmosphere and contaminating large areas of the planet. Disorder ensues, with large numbers fleeing the likely sites of impact. The central protagonist, Claire Tourneur, escapes the congestion created by the fleeing population by driving off the motorway, and subsequently encounters a hitchhiker seemingly in flight from an undisclosed pursuer. Claire falls in love with the fugitive (Sam) and subsequently discovers that he is the son of a scientist, who has absconded with one of his father's prototypes from a top-security research project. Multiple government agencies and some bounty hunters are in pursuit to recover it.

The prototype is a device for recording and translating brain impulses — a camera for the blind, but subsequently perfected as a device to record human dreams. *Until the End of the World* both embraces technology and rejects it as a force for potential global destruction, a problem that echoes all of the plots discussed above. Although Wenders's film ultimately privileges the centrality of human relationships, it sees them nonetheless as inseparable from their technological context. The title possibly alludes to the ideal of a romance capable of lasting through all time, and although this ideal is not achieved, some human relationships do endure, occasionally with the aid of technology: Claire and Sam, for example, overcome the hardship of separation and nurture love and communication by means of a variety of futuristic and not-so-futuristic technological innovations. On one occasion, for example, Claire tracks down Sam's location via computer when he uses his credit cards, and follows him around the world in order to satisfy her desire to know more about him. Contradictorily, it is the seductive capabilities of technology (the dream images have an addictive effect and incapacitate the users of the device for normal life), rather than the destructive ones (the nuclear threat), that ultimately destroy the film's primary relationships between husband and wife, parent and child, or lovers. Thus, an ostensibly benign technological innovation ultimately introduces a greater menace than nuclear Armageddon, and although Claire eventually overcomes her addiction to the dream images, her relationship with Sam is irreparably damaged. In the end, the characters discover they no longer have homes to return to and must either flee the earth or seek a nostalgic past, in order to escape stagnation and achieve transitory redemption. The final images of the film show Claire in flight from a world fallen into widespread alienation, decay and corruption. She lives completely alone aboard a satellite, literally disconnected from the Earth (free from the laws of gravity) and works for an ecological protection organization, Greenspace. She is also cut off from the rest of humanity, contact being carried out via satellite. James Berger interprets the ending of the film as depicting Claire metamorphosed into a 'high-tech angel protecting the Earth from pollution,' but also as 'the transparency, the technological "natural," the post-apocalyptic cipher who has gone through the neuro-video event of primary process to become the presiding genius of the next millennium' (Berger, 1999: 46-47).

Until the End of the World sets up a dialectic of apocalypse as cataclysm synthesized into revelatory epiphany. But if at the end Claire is presented as a space-age guardian angel, even so the resolution reached is characterized by a dimension of alienation that Booker likens to Foucault's disciplinary (carceral) society and he himself calls routinization:

> Routinization is closely related to […] conformism […] the way in which, under modern capitalist society, every aspect of life becomes regimented, scheduled and controlled for maximum economic efficiency. (Booker, 2001: 17)

The Bliss of Non-Difference

Fredric Jameson (Jameson, 1984) argues that fantasy and science fiction articulate a desire to escape routinization and alienation. If so, they may also sometimes provide a path through that which is most feared, thus safeguarding arrival at a state of safety beyond apocalypse which one might define as utopia. If apocalypse was brought about by the unleashing of unbridled force (terror), of randomness (error), and of the forces of chaos, utopia requires absolute, highly regulated conformism. By the same token, under utopia, the price of nonconformism (the freedom to be different) is unhappiness and ultimately punishment, writ small, large or very large (global), something which accounts for its forcible elimination in many of the works discussed. In Orwell's *Nineteen Eighty-Four*, Winston Smith is the distillation of the misfit, a rebel without a clearly identified cause, who deviates not in the name of any particular agenda (he has no plan for an alternative society) but simply because he cannot do otherwise. Ultimately, from the point of view of the status quo but also of himself, since he is unable to effect change his unhappiness has only one solution, namely the abolition of the very essence of what he is, followed by non-being. After being tortured into submission to the will of Big Brother, Winston dies happy because he no longer exists in any real sense. Instead, he has learnt to love that against which he had previously defined himself, which had destroyed his mind and which will now destroy him.

In Orwell, as in any other utopia, there is always an unquestionable truth, even if, as for example under the watchful eye of Big Brother, that truth is re-written when convenient (double talk). Within this utopia, as in *Brave New World* (Huxley, 1977), *Fahrenheit 451* (Bradbury, 1976) and *This Perfect Day* (Levin, 1994), all, with the exception of those who are 'sick,' have abdicated individuality and surrendered to mass-produced and quality-controlled emotion, ranging from love for Big Brother to all-surround TV and organized daily sessions of Hate. Similarly, in *Brave New World* (Huxley, 1977), following the logic of *This Perfect Day* (Levin, 1994), everyone, from the most hubristic Alpha to the lowliest Epsilon, is happy to be just what they are. And in *Fahrenheit 451*, extreme versions of homogenized culture and chemical treatments anaesthetize the masses into submission, such that only a coincidence of unlikely events can lead to temporary failure in an otherwise smooth operation.

> Once, books appealed to a few people, here, there, everywhere. They could afford to be different. But then the world got [...] double, triple, quadruple population. Films and radios, magazines, books, levelled down to a sort of paste pudding norm [...]. Many were those whose sole knowledge of *Hamlet* was a one-page digest in a book that claimed: *now at least you can read all the classics; keep up with your neighbours.* [...] We must all be alike, [...] everyone *made* equal. (Bradbury, 1990: 91-95)

In Huxley, Levin and Bradbury alike, sameness is enforced by drugs or censorship or both, supposedly for the good of all: 'We're the Happiness Boys [...]. We stand against the tide of those who want to make everyone unhappy with conflicting theory and thought' (Bradbury, 1990: 68-69).

In *This Perfect Day*, Chip's propensity for dissent may be due partly to a congenital flaw (manifested also in his having one green and one brown eye) but its full potential is awakened initially as the result of the teachings of a destabilizing agent, Papa Jan, his grandfather, who is one of the old, never fully 'normalized' generation dating back to pre-unification (amalgamation of global social regulation under the control of one vast computer). Papa Jan initially urges the young Chip to try thinking something different in the days just before his monthly treatment, when its effects are at their weakest, and in doing so sets his grandson on a path towards irremediable misfit. The pros and cons of individuality are later clearly articulated by a group of untreated rebels:

> And that's what we are offering *you*,' Snowflake says; 'a way to see more and feel more and do more and enjoy more.'
>
> 'And to be more unhappy; tell him that too. [...] There will be days when you will hate *us*,' she said, 'for waking you up and making you *not* a machine. Machines are at home in the universe; people are aliens.' (Levin, 1994: 73)

A preoccupation clearly of its time as much as ours, and also vented in H.G. Wells's depiction of the childlike Eloi in *The Time Machine*: happy, carefree, semi-moronic creatures, ultimately doomed to extinction (Wells, 1982).

Experiments in futuristic reality follow a much earlier tradition which surprisingly predated these science fiction works by one hundred years and reached extreme expression in E.M. Forster's 'The Machine Stops' (Forster [1909], 2004). A decade earlier, even, than Forster's short story, Edward Bellamy's utopian novel of 1888, *Looking Backward*, tells the story of Julian West, a young American who falls into a deep, hypnosis-induced sleep and wakes up more than a century later. Julian finds himself in the same location, in Boston, but in a totally changed world. It is the year 2000 and, like Washington Irving's Rip van Winkle, who goes to sleep while America is still one of George III's colonies and wakes up to discover it is now an independent republic, Julian, too, finds that during his slumber the world has changed in many ways, not least as regards widespread political arrangements. In the year 2000, the US has been transformed into a Socialist utopia. The novel outlines Bellamy's complex thoughts about how a future world might be improved. In the year 2000, the young protagonist finds a guide, Doctor Leete, who shows him around and explains all the advances of this new age (a convenience consumer culture which includes drastically reduced working hours for people performing menial jobs, and facilities such as instantaneous delivery of goods from stores to homes). Unlike the nightmare scenarios of *Brave New World* (Huxley, 1977), *This Perfect Day* (Levin, 1994), *The Children of Men* (James, 2000), and *Oryx and Crake* (Atwood, 2004), people do not automatically die when they reach a certain age, merely retire (with full benefits) aged 45. The productive capacity of America is communally owned, goods are equally distributed to all citizens, and, anticipating 'The Machine Stops' a decade later, all mod. cons. including classical music and religious sermons are piped into homes through cable telephone. With reference to Bellamy's work, David Ketterer suggests that 'the possibility that man has attained a new evolutionary plane, the belief that the characters believe their highly technological world to be a utopia can only realistically imply a dystopian society in which the citizens have evolved, or rather devolved, into machines' (Ketterer, 1974: 113), with all the consequences that that entails, as discussed in chapter 4. Be that as it may, clearly, in both Irving's and Bellamy's narratives, at the heart of these would-be utopias, lies the urge for defining sociopolitical change.

In general, whether utopia is the outcome of a political impetus for change (in the two texts just discussed), a gigantic conspiracy with an ulterior motive (world domination in *Brave New World*, Huxley, 1977; *This Perfect Day*, Levin, 1994), the manifestation of a State-instigated defensive strategy (*Dr. Bloodmoney*, Dick, 2007) or corporate profit (*The Truman Show*, Weir, 1998), in general what we are left with seem to be largely unsatisfactory and unpersuasive scenarios of existential anaesthesia doomed to ultimate failure.

The Dark Side of Utopia

Under the new regime established in *The Children of Men* (James, 2000), drastic measures have been taken to pacify citizens and maintain the illusion that a comfortable life will be possible in the years to come. By decree of the Council of England, every citizen is required to learn skills such as farming, which they might need as the last generations of humans gradually die out. Foreign immigration is encouraged for the purposes of hard manual labour, but immigrants are forcibly repatriated at the age of sixty. As is the case in other utopian/dystopian writings, native citizens are not permitted to become a burden to the community by reason of age or infirmity: among the elderly and the sick, the privileged few are put in nursing homes. The rest must choose between unassisted deaths at home, state-assisted suicide, or death through participation in one of the regularly-held ceremonies of Council-sanctioned drownings known as The Quietus. Utopia, the New Jerusalem, can only be set up after the unfit have been eliminated.

> And he that sat upon the throne said, [...] He that overcometh shall inherit all things; and I will be his God, and he shall be my son.
>
> But the fearful, and unbelieving, and the abominable, and murderers, and whoremongers, and sorcerers, and idolaters, and all liars, shall have their part in the lake which burneth with fire and brimstone: which is the second death. (Revelation, 21: 7)

So it is nice, then, but only for some, and then only for a while. You cannot make an omelette without breaking eggs. The construction of utopia always comes at a price, which from Plato's ideal Republic and the ruthless John of Patmos in the Book of Revelation to Aldous Huxley's *Brave New World* (Huxley, 1977), via approaches as disparate as those of the Fabians and the Nazis, involves a lot of clearing up of old detritus prior to the inauguration of paradise. Whether or not the implications of this cleansing involve scenarios of the end of the world, in Judaeo-Christian understanding (fundamentalist predictions of the Rapture, the idea of a Day of Judgment) as well as in much science fiction, utopia usually represents the endpoint of apocalyptic literature. And as David Ketterer argues, such literature is concerned with 'the ultimate creation of other worlds which exist, on the literal level, in a credible relationship (whether on the basis of rational extrapolation and analogy or of religious belief) with the "real" world, thereby causing a metaphorical destruction of that "real" world' (Ketterer, 1974: 13).

Not only is utopia, therefore, a relative concept (one size clearly does not fit all, as demonstrated by Montag, Chip, Winston Smith, and Kuno) but, moreover, the process of imagining it whether in myth, culture, science or political thought, always comes with significant caveats: specifically, the prerequisite of the cleansing out of the prevailing status quo, the elimination of elements in it deemed to be undesirable, and the abdication of both free will and the entitlement to choice. The wider complexities of the concept of utopia, therefore, must be considered with particular regard to the common thread linking diverse and sometimes antithetical implications of utopianism's original political, ethical and ethnographic paradigms.

The Big Spring Clean

As already suggested, utopia, from Plato to the Russian Jewish writer Ayn Rand (via the Aryan Nazi Valhalla whose vision Rand disturbingly mirrors), can only begin after undesirable elements have been eliminated. Plato's ideal Republic, for example, required the exclusion (by unspecified means) of numerous categories of undesirability (artists, poets, the sick, the ugly and nonconformists, to list but a few).

The move from individual exclusion to death, thence to genocide and from the latter to global annihilation as the ultimate purge, arguably, involves steps which are too small (imperceptible) for comfort. With regard to genocide, H.G. Wells's vision of utopia in *Anticipations*, for example, concluded that quality life on Earth could only be preserved by means of the extermination of the entire populations of Africa and Asia (Wells, 1999), and more than fifty years before Hitler's Final Solution, many distinguished members of the respected Fabian Society (including names such as George Bernard Shaw, whose reputation, like Wells,' astonishingly, remains unsullied to this day) were strong supporters of eugenics as an instrument of social progress.

Wells, not now in the guise of purveyor of science fiction but in his self-appointed role as philosopher-architect of the future, argued in all seriousness that utopia could become a reality only by means of state regulated and enforced reproduction ('wifehood [being] the chief feminine

156   *The End of the World*

profession' and 'the efficient mother who can make the best of her children [… being] the most important person in the state,' Wells, 1999: 174).

Even more drastically, he went on to elaborate the necessity for genocide:

> It has become apparent that whole masses of human population are, as a whole, inferior in their claim upon the future to other masses […]. [T]he men of the New Republic will hold that the procreation of children who, by the

Figure 21. Michelangelo Buonarroti, *Christ as Judge of the World*

> circumstances of their parentage, *must* be diseased bodily or mentally [...] is absolutely the most loathsome of all conceivable sins. [...] And how will the New Republic treat the inferior races? How will it deal with the black? How will it deal with the yellow man? How will it tackle that alleged termite in the woodwork, the Jew? Certainly not as races at all. [...] It will tolerate no dark corners where the people of the Abyss may fester [...]. And [...] those swarms of black, and brown, and dirty-white, and yellow people, who do not come into the new needs of efficiency?
>
> Well, the world is a world, not a charitable institution, and I take it they will have to go. [... I]t is their portion to die out and disappear.
>
> The men of the New Republic will not be squeamish [...]. They will have an ideal that will make killing worth the while; like Abraham, they will have the faith to kill. (Wells, 1999: 163-78)

While in his nonfictional polemics, Wells defended the genocidal policies, (outlined above) in some of his novels, including *The War in the Air* (Wells, [1907] 2005) and *A Modern Utopia*, he indicates that following a Last War, a new stage in history will be inaugurated leading, in due course, to 'the dream of a world's awakening' (Wells, 2005: 369): not quite like Francis Fukuyama's end of history, but also not absolutely unlike it, since it, too, envisages a world globally converted to the basic ideology and sociopolitical structures of the West.

Fukuyama's thesis is at worst foolish, but elsewhere things can get nasty. In Timothy Findley's *Not Wanted on the Voyage* (Findley, 1987), a re-writing of the Noah's Ark episode in Genesis, prior to embarking on a journey that will signal the end of one world and the beginning of another one, the law-abiding Dr. Noyes, in an echo of other final solutions, orders his sons to kill Lotte, a mentally handicapped child. In *Not the End of the World* (McCaughrean, 2005), a re-writing for children of the same Biblical episode, friends' and neighbours' supplications are ignored by Noah who, in his determination to act by the (Lord's) book, lets them drown. Likewise, in *Earth Abides* (Stewart, 1973) Christian principles inform the actions of the community patriarch, who, although admittedly with mild regrets (which however are effortlessly overridden by a needs-must certainty), condemns a mentally disabled young woman to death lest she should give birth to similarly damaged offspring. In this enduringly popular novel whose affinity to the logic of Hitler's Germany is never remarked upon by a loyal public, Evie is eliminated on the breathtakingly level-headed grounds that it would be bad for the community if her defective genes were passed on.

158   The End of the World

In the end, however, as suggested above, if all else fails, war always remains as a short cut to the implementation of utopia. Which brings us back to where we began this discussion: end-of-century, end-of-millennia, end-of-time cultural mind sets, which, by way of more or less bloody epiphanies, undertake the enterprise of imagining sometimes unwelcome, not-always-so-new beginnings.

Millenarian fear and desire both involve the ability to imagine cataclysm: in the case of the former as a cause, and in the case of the latter, as a means to an end. The logic of a purge prior to a new beginning can be detected in the earnest reasoning of prominent opinion-formers and decision-makers over the centuries, including some of those at present empowered with the means to actually bring it about. The belief in an imminent near-global

Figure 22. El Greco, *The Opening of the Fifth Seal of the Apocalypse*

wipe-out (the necessary first step towards a return of God to Earth for the purpose of the salvation of the deserving happy few) is usually assumed to be the province of a lunatic religious fringe, extremists in far-flung outposts of monotheism, from fundamentalist Christianity to Jihadist Islam. More worryingly, however, a 1984 survey found that 39% of Americans believed that Biblical predictions of global destruction by fire referred to nuclear war (Seed, 2000: 57). And in connection with this, Hal Lindsey's widely-read *The Late Great Planet Earth* of 1970 (Seed, 2000: 57) argued that the Christian fundamentalist faithful need not worry about nuclear war because at the relevant moment they will be 'raised in the air to embark on the ultimate trip' (Jews and other religious groups need not apply), meet Christ and return with him, in the aftermath of nuclear holocaust, to re-build the New Earth.

Much more worryingly, in the must-read essay pithily entitled 'Armageddon,' Gore Vidal describes how the belief in the need for a *tabula rasa* wipe-out prior to a new beginning was also espoused by such influential voices as James Watt, Ronald Reagan's Secretary of the Interior, and by Reagan himself, his presidential finger, of course, at all times poised on the nuclear button. Vidal summarizes the rationale whereby, as Watt explained to the American Congress in 1981, the end of the world could be relied upon to happen sooner rather than later ('I do not know how many future generations we can count on before the Lord returns,' Vidal, 1989: 192):

> Christ will defeat the anti-Christ at Armageddon [...]. Just before the battle, the Church will be wafted to Heaven and all the good folks will experience Rapture [...]. The wicked will suffer horribly. Then after seven years of burying the dead (presumably there will be survivors), God returns, bringing Peace and Joy, and the Raptured ones. (Vidal, 1989: 103-04)

Gore Vidal knew whereof he spoke: some years earlier, Reagan, then Governor of California, had stated:

> All of the other prophecies that had to be fulfilled before Armageddon can come to pass. In the thirty-eighth chapter of *Ezequiel* it says God will take the children of Israel from among the heathen where they'd been scattered and will gather them again in the promised land. That has finally come about after 2,000 years. For the first time ever, everything is in place for the battle of Armageddon and the Second Coming of Christ. [...] Everything is falling into place. It can't be too long now. Ezequiel says that fire and brimstone will be rained upon the enemies of God's people. That must mean that they will be destroyed by nuclear weapons... (Reagan quoted in Vidal, 1989: 108-09)

Reagan was the most powerful but also only one of an estimated twenty million Americans who believe in the Rapture, although there is some confusion as to whether the Children of Israel (Jews) are the ones who will be saved or exterminated. In view of the general religious and ethnic likes and dislikes of the proponents of the Rapture, however, extermination is the more likely option, followed by a drastic revision of the term 'Children of Israel.' Be that as it may, as far back as 1987, Mikhail Gorbachev was so troubled by the American President's happy supposition that 'we may be the generation that sees Armageddon' (Berger, 1999: 135), that he provided a gentle reminder that 'planet Earth was the only likely venue for the continuity of humanity and that it would be a pity to lose everything through war, or, more likely, accident.' (Vidal, 1989: 111)

All as It Ought to Be

The Rapture envisaged by evangelical Christian fundamentalism has a species similarity to the fictional universes achieved after suitable social cleansing or even absolute discarding of the old world/universe in works such as *Brave New World* (Huxley, 1977) and *Tau Zero* (Anderson, 2006) respectively. In the resulting utopia, as under the average dictatorship, human difference comes to be regarded as at best an inconvenience and at worst a sickness, treatable, eradicable or genetically modifiable in the name of the preservation of authorized forms of happiness.

> 'Heat conditioning,' said Mr. Foster.

> Hot tunnels alternated with cool tunnels. Coolness was wedded to discomfort in the form of hard X-rays. By the time they were decanted the embryos had a horror of cold. They were predestined to emigrate to the tropics, to be miners and acetate silk spinners and steel workers. Later their minds would be made to endorse the judgement of their bodies. 'We condition them to thrive on heat,' concluded Mr. Foster. 'Our colleagues upstairs will teach them to love it.'

> 'And that,' put in the Director sententiously, 'that is the secret of happiness and virtue – liking what you've *got* to do. All conditioning aims at that: making people like their inescapable social destiny.' (Huxley, 1977: 31)

The Ideology of Utopia: What Goes Round Comes Round

Aside from the ethical problems raised by any utopia (the need to cull weakness or even mere difference), utopianism has further inbuilt requirements that, however, paradoxically also threaten the very possibility if its existence. In other words, that which must be in place if utopia is to be established is also that which may lead to its undoing. If the basic *sine qua non* of utopia is conformity and homogeneity (a hatred of difference or of 'mutants'), a straightforward Darwinian logic dictates that should conditions change, a non-variant status quo may be doomed to extinction.

What if I Say No?

Another obstacle to utopia, which stems from the imperative of homogeneity, is a fundamental characteristic of human nature, namely its contrariness (the urge to differ), the satisfaction of which can be a prerequisite to existential well-being. In Machado de Assis's short story, 'The Devil's Church' (Assis, 1987), the Devil decides to break God's theological monopoly and establishes his own church, based on the worst instincts of humanity (greed, envy, selfishness, violence). The corporate take-over fails when a beleaguered Satan comes to realize that after his new faith's initial success, its long-term survival is threatened by the fact that its members are increasingly guilty of clandestine virtue practiced by stealth. The despondent Wrong-Doer begs an amused God for an explanation and is told that there is none, other than the eternal contradictoriness of human nature (Assis, 1987). This being so, if conformity is an essential component of utopianism, either humanity itself has no place in utopia or the latter is doomed to failure at the hands of its customers. Julian Barnes's beneficiary of heavenly utopia, in the end asks to be allowed to die (again, and this time with no option of an Afterlife): anything – even death – it would appear, is better than having all one's wishes fulfilled in perpetuity, because if whatever one asks for the answer is always 'yes,' how can one enjoy the bliss of saying 'no'?

The contemplation of existing versions of utopia often leads to the unpalatable realization that utopias, from Plato's *The Republic* to Margaret Atwood's *Gilead*, require despotic rule and the uncompromising elimination of dissent. More disturbing even than that fact, for the contemporary speculator, is the possibility that, faced with the choice between unhappiness, war, hunger and social unrest on the one hand, or assenting, obedient contentment on the other (the comfortable living-deaths of the placid members of the herd in Huxley, Bradbury and Levin), one may experience justifiable perplexity. In Ira Levin's *This Perfect Day* everyone is good ('a universe of the gentle, the helpful, the loving, the unselfish,' Levin, 1994, 305) and life is comfortable. So why not? Why not agree to anything for an easy life? Perhaps John Stuart Mill's verdict on the relative levels of satisfaction and dissatisfaction in pigs and men was wrong after all. Even if he were right in adding that if either the fool or the pig are of a different opinion it is because they only know their own side of the question, it may be true (albeit disturbing) that in the end it does not matter. Happiness is happiness and misery is misery, and both philosophers and pigs can only begin (but also, we would add now, end) where they find themselves. Might the pig have the better deal after all? We may never know for certain, but we ought to at least consider that possibility.

Philip K. Dick's predictably eccentric take on this problem in *The World Jones Made* (Dick, 2003) is set in a post-holocaust world drawing away from the brink of a destruction that originated in a variety of conflicting fundamentalisms. In Machado de Assis, the eternal contradictoriness of human nature was what ultimately obstructed the Devil's agenda (his pyrrhic victory ultimately amounting to no more than the reduction of God himself to a position of moral relativism). In Jones's world, the new status quo's response to destructive fundamentalisms secure of their various monopolies over Truth, is to implement a mandatory kind of pluralism which makes it illegal to proclaim any belief as being right. Ironically, this postmodern paradise of enforced relativism gives rise to a population hungry for clearly identified dictates, even at the price of enforced submissiveness to demagogy. As is the case in Levin, Bradbury, Huxley, Orwell and most of the other works discussed, the most disturbing conclusion – one which carries implications for the life of any community – may be that in the end, the majority of human beings has no use for freedom. (As an illustration of this, it should be noted that the percentage of the electorate that vote in any given election in both the UK and the US at present is at most between 50% and 60%.)

The Luxury of Saying No

If, as Carey would have it, 'the aim of all utopias [...] is to eliminate real people' (Carey, 1999: xii), the puzzle still remains as to why bliss, because enforced, artificially induced and/or non-optional, is inevitably worse than freely-willed choice entailing either occasional or omnipresent misery (Socrates vs. the pig). Is it really better to have loved and lost than never to have loved at all? *Really*? Can we truly understand why Julian Barnes's hero preferred obliteration to perfect bliss? And in any case, isn't free will in the end the luxury of the fundamentally non-needy? Does the concept carry semantic validity anywhere below the breadline?

An answer in the negative to any of these questions, of course, paves the way to demagogy, but the questions, nonetheless, ought to be asked. Life's a bitch and then you die, or even, according to the Barnesian and Orwellian oxymorons, you die but only if you are extremely lucky. Most utopias approach the question of free will through its negation in exchange for guaranteed stability, and the desirability of the latter is not uncommonly emphasized by preceding periods of acute uncertainty, threat or upheaval. It is in light of the possibility or reality of social disintegration that certainty, even at the price of ruling totalitarianism, becomes the accepted rule. And following the implementation of this rule, the past is, if necessary, re-written, and the future graven in stone (until further notice):

> [...] no written record, and no spoken word, ever made mention of any other alignment than the existing one. At this moment, for example, in 1984 (if it was 1984), Oceania was at war with Eurasia and in alliance with Eastasia. In no public or private utterance was it ever admitted that the three powers had at any time been grouped along different lines. Actually, as Winston well knew, it was only four years since Oceania had been at war with Eastasia. But that was merely a piece of furtive knowledge which he happened to possess because his memory was not satisfactorily under control. Officially the change of partners had never happened. (Orwell, 1983: 34)

> This process of continuous alteration was applied not only to newspapers, but to books, periodicals, pamphlets, posters, leaflets, films, soundtracks, cartoons [...]. Day by day and almost minute by minute the past was brought up to date. In this way every prediction made by the Party could be shown by documentary evidence to have been correct. (Orwell, 1983: 39)

What Price Freedom?

Utopias, therefore, share with apocalyptic scripts the fact that moral relativism is abolished and replaced by uniformity (according to definitions prescribed by the forces of authority, which however, as illustrated in *Nineteen Eighty-Four*, can be altered or even reversed if required). Faced with the choice between a scorched Earth or a green and pleasant land albeit with no freedom, the preferable alternative would seem obvious. On the other hand, of course, unless you can conform happily, there may be little difference between the brutal control of the masses in Orwell, their unthinking contentment in Levin, and the only slightly modified version of the same manicheanism in Philip K. Dick's *The Penultimate Truth* (Dick, 2005). In the latter, the ruling post-apocalyptic Seigneurs are not unlike the Programmers who run UniComp in *This Perfect Day* (Levin, 1994), the powers behind Big Brother in Orwell's *Nineteen Eighty-Four* or the Controllers in *Brave New World* (Huxley, 1977). Dick's bunker inhabitants are deceived by the broadcast propaganda which this novel shares with almost all post-apocalyptic scenarios and, like those in 'The Machine Stops' (Forster, 2004), they believe that no alternative exists in an irremediably contaminated planet, following nuclear war. As in *Brave New World* (Huxley, 1977), *Fahrenheit 451* (Bradbury, 1976) and many similar works, even for those who experience the safety of the status quo as less than ideal, the only apparent alternative would appear, in the absence of factual evidence, to be worse.

In the end, the question that ought to be posed is 'Is this necessarily so?' And the answer might be either 'Yes' or 'No,' the real tragedy being that, whichever one we plump for, we may never know whether we were right. To quote a well-known song, 'the things that you're liable to read in the Bible' (or anywhere else, we would now add), 'it ain't necessarily so.' (George and Ira Gershwin, 1935)

It Ain't Necessarily so

If the political agenda of utopia in one way or another is dictatorial, involving the purging of difference, the effects of hypothesizing it can also be paradoxical, encompassing both moral conservatism and radical revolution, or at least the possibility of either: moral conservatism, because under utopia, good and evil, however defined in specific contexts, are respectively rewarded and punished; and radical revolution, because outside the rules of the fictional scenario, the author as *Deus ex machina* offers a critique of the underlying requirements for the definition and establishment of any given utopia. In that regard, time and context are also significant factors. Recent fiction and contemporary science fiction (Huxley, Orwell, Huxley) tend to analyze utopian scenarios critically, rather than, as was the case of earlier philosophical excursions into utopianism (Plato, More), envisaging it as desirable.

Utopia and the Suppression of Desire

Utopia, as discussed, requires conformism and the suppression of individual desire in the name of collective interest. In *Civilization and its Discontents*,

Freud ponders the problem of why communities impose taboos on individual desire, and concludes that group existence cannot permit the rule of private passion because of the danger that it might override the interests of the commonweal (Freud, 2001). In this regard, the mechanisms of evolution (as explained by Darwinism), of totalitarianism (for example, Fascism, Marxism) or even, indeed, of democratic political systems (involving, for example, the payment of tax), require individual interests to make way for those of the species/state. Clearly, this can equally be translated into forcible control over the right to survival, as well as into the exercise of power by those (the fittest/strongest/most powerful) who do not necessarily represent the majority.

Unpalatable as it may be, however, it is also true that in the long term dictatorships, whether more or less brutal, endure only by the will or at least the acquiescence of the majority, since no political regime can remain in place for any length of time against the power of numbers. Hitler, for example, outlined his plans for ethnic cleansing in the clearest terms in *Mein Kampf*, published in 1925 and 1926. Contrary to general belief, the work was widely read at the time. It sold 240,000 copies before he was democratically elected Chancellor in 1933, by which time sales had earned 1.2 m reichsmarks (the average annual income of a teacher being about 4,800). Moreover, during his years in power, a free copy of it was given to all newlywed couples, as well as, after the war began, to all soldiers fighting at the front. (Worthington, 2003; Hinrichs, 2006; BBC News, 2004). Regimes like those of Pinochet in Chile, Franco in Spain, Mussolini in Italy and Salazar in Portugal also endured until opposition ceased to be that of a minority and became that of a majority.

To Make or not to Make Waves

Within this broad understanding, of course, various twists may apparently contradict the overall principle. In Wyndham's *The Midwich Cuckoos*, utopia is represented by life in the quiet village of Midwich, which 'was, almost notoriously, a place where things did not happen' (Wyndham, 1984: 11). Or it was so, at least, until babies of unknown origin are born, changelings who prove a threat to the very survival of humanity.

The dilemma that confronts some of the host mothers in Midwich and the authorities in what prides itself as 'a civilized country […], famous for its ability to find compromises and historically more tolerant of minorities than most' (Wyndham, 1984: 198), is whether to betray those principles in the name of the interests of the species, or uphold them and be exterminated. The resolution comes not through compromise but, more pragmatically, through the temporary suspension by one individual of those central beliefs whose long-term preservation is desired by the majority. Gordon Zellaby is a wealthy resident of Mildwich and the exact opposite of the man of action: a near-caricature of the effete, ultra-civilized gentleman of letters, a writer who exists by the power of the intellect exercised for the pleasures of dilettantism rather than utilitarianism. Other than a few of the host mothers, he is also the only Midwich resident who had succeeded in establishing a bond of mutual cordiality with the Children. As a stalemate is reached in the stand-off between the Children and the status quo they threaten, Zellaby offers to give the Children one of his popular slide lectures, this time on the subject of the Aegean islands (which of course, although this is not mentioned, happened to be the cradle of Western civilization, of the concept of Democracy, and, somewhat confusingly, of the Pagan belief in the inescapability of Fate). Having achieved the objective of assembling all the Children together in one place, he sets off a massive explosion in which they and he die. Zellaby's solution is a complex amalgam of self-immolation by a sacrificial lamb and acknowledgement of the paradox whereby all that is civilized in that particular set-up can only be preserved in the long term by a voluntary return to savagery in the short. Or eugenics, by any other name.

On the part of the invaded community of Midwich, albeit with greater hesitancy than in the evangelical Christian tribe in Wyndham's *The Chrysalids*, an understanding of the survival implications (for the community and eventually for the human species in its current state) of a superior life form is nonetheless eventually impressed upon the minds of people 'weakened' (in the eyes of the Children in Midwich) by the parameters of an existence on the surface distanced from the law of the jungle but which, as only Zellaby understands, under new conditions will only be able to survive by regressing either to it or to the autocratic rule of one-man decision-making (which may amount to the same thing). 'I know what is best for us all.'

Similar quandaries define the plots of some other of Wyndham's best-known novels. The arising paradox results from the fact that, in order to preserve statuses quo (utopian and otherwise) that, in various ways, claim to separate themselves from animalism and barbarism, the very foundations of each community must sometimes (if expedient) be suspended. In *The Chrysalids* the preservation of mutation-free 'true forms' as defined by God requires the relinquishing of both God's Mosaic law ('thou shalt not kill,' the commandment which, incidentally, Hitler's Third Reich – third phase of history – officially sought to abolish), and his New Testament imperatives (blessed are the peacemakers), in favour of a willingness to exterminate all mutants (including humans) seen to threaten a God-given utopia. In *The Midwich Cuckoos* (Wyndham, [1957] 1984), Zellaby, a distilled form of all that is civilized (in the sense of superfluous to survival) takes the law (of the jungle) in his own hands, and abdicates the principles of advanced human ethics in the short term, with the intention of preserving them in the long term, by committing genocide (of the children) and suicide (laying down his own life) in the name of the preservation of community survival. The contradiction, of course, resides in the fact that, in order to defend utopia (in this instance the status quo of 'a place where things did not happen,' Wyndham, 1984: 11) from its antithesis ('grim primeval danger,' Wyndham, *Midwich*, 1984, 212), civilization must occasionally resort to brutal measures ('grim primeval' methods). When does utopia become dystopia?

The deconstruction of utopia's philosophical certainty depends on the identification of internal contradictions within its structure, such as for example the recognition, either by members of the utopian community or by external dissenters, of an existing alternative to be respectively suppressed or encouraged. Those who, either through a failure in the system or due to their individual resistance, remain recidivistically different, must either be destroyed as threats to the existing order or triumph over it and ultimately replace it. In H.G. Wells's *The Time Machine*, the surface perfection of existence among the Eloi is shadowed by an inexplicable fear of the night-time hours of darkness. The reason for this is the consequence of a fundamental flaw inbuilt into a system whose idyllic, pastoral nature can only be maintained through the underground slave labour of the fearful Morlocks. The existence of the Morlocks illustrates the self-evident truth of a Hegelian binary whereby thesis only has meaning through being different to its antithesis: it is not possible to articulate the meaning of good without envisaging evil. 'A' is only 'A' because it is not 'B', or, following post-structuralist thinking, because it is different from all that is not 'A'. Similarly, 'I' or 'we' exist only by differing from that which is not 'me' or 'us.' Two problems immediately arise. First, following Derrida, if A can only be defined by not being B, the latter, paradoxically, becomes a necessary part of the identity of A. The Morlocks are a threat to the Eloi, but are also fundamental to their lifestyle. Second, whether in Darwinian or in any other vocabulary, two different interests with similar requirements cannot occupy the same space. The Eloi's sun-lit Utopia is defined by all that the Morlocks' life in underground darkness is not, but they depend upon Morlock labour for their very existence. And the Morlocks, in turn, define their condition of oppression in relation to the (almost) carefree life enjoyed by the Eloi, to whose condition they aspire but which they also threaten, when they regularly attack and devour them. The Morlocks' repeated mutiny against their masters, which involves regularly kidnapping and eating one of them, is merely a mirror where is reflected the reality of the non-viability of a society in which utopia both requires slavery and perpetuates stasis. Rather than being the malignant other, the Morlocks represent the decayed Eloi self which exploits not an enemy but a twin. The danger represented by the Morlocks, is therefore a metaphor for self-destruction, a fact grasped sorrowfully by the Time Traveller who reaches them in a distant future, in a period in which science has solved all of humanity's problems. The price of complete well being, however, turns out to be stagnation (or self-destruction), the Morlocks representing the canker of decay brought on by enduring Perfection. As in Julian Barnes, Perfection is all very well, but it isn't necessarily for everyone, which itself will sooner or later re-initiate the inevitability of difference and the dialectic of change.

The irresolvable impasse in concepts of utopia, thus, lies in the fact that while Perfection by definition cannot be improved upon and cannot therefore be construed as temporary, its in(de)finite perpetuation, whether in the Eloian paradise, in Barnes's Heaven, or in Browning's melancholic musings, inevitably leads to satiation and decadence. Not only does it appear to be true, therefore, that 'a man's reach must exceed his grasp, or what's a heaven for?' (Browning, 1883) but moreover, where reach and grasp (or thesis and antithesis, or signifier and signified, pick your lexicon) become the same, final synthesis or meaning, in other words utopia, rather than being fulfilled becomes demonstrably flawed, oxymoronically undesirable and essentially void.

The other who resembles the self and competes for similar resources informs many of the preoccupations of contemporary science fiction. *Invasion of the Body Snatchers* (Siegel, 1956; Kaufman, 1976), articulates this literally, since the invading alien gains ownership of the very body of the enemy whose position it has come to usurp. Only one can exist, not just on the same territory but in the same body. The same scenario operates in narratives of supernatural possession (satanic, werewolvian, vampiric, alien), in multiple permutations of the same formula. In this regard, the alien-within, much more than any identifiable other, is the most fearful and the most likely to succeed, and the greater the surface familiarity, the greater the danger.

This is the case for example with children who, instinct dictates, should be protected in the name of the interests of the species, but who, in some of the works discussed, as well as in many other classic horror narratives (*Rosemary's Baby*, Levin, 1967; *The Omen*, Donner, 1976; *To the Devil a Daughter*, Sykes, 1976), must be destroyed for the sake of those self-same interests. Under utopia, citizens must be docile, homogenous and (in the disparate but also oddly akin readings of Fabianism, Marxism and Psychoanalysis) loyal to the interests of the greater good, rather than to the narrower ones of individual desire. For the status quo of an established utopia to be preserved, therefore, difference and free will must be abolished, undesirables, whatever the nature of their undesirability, must be eliminated or made to conform, and perpetual vigilance must be maintained against their return ('treatment' and/or genetic tampering in Levin and Huxley, violent extinction by fire or other means in Bradbury and Orwell, the rule of law in Wyndham and Pullman). When stasis is achieved, the Hegelian dialectic is immobilized and final synthesis (the end of history) is attained. Which of course, arguably may be counter-productive.

The alternative, for the imperfectly docile inhabitants of utopia, is a return to a (Darwinian) jungle of change, mutation, difference, unpredictability, upheaval and chaos, as narrated in the more or less (usually less) factual accounts of history maintained by the existing powers that be.

In any case, no *status* quo, regardless of its power, is impervious to an Act of God or of individual will. The intervention of randomness in systems rigidified into inalterability, even if it is the inalterability of perfection, in the end is capable of reducing eternity itself to nothingness. In Julian Barnes, paradise itself (not granted the dignity of a full chapter, merely half, in the overall narrative), is threatened by apocalypse in the shape of Thanatos, the Death Wish (Barnes, 1990). And, counter-intuitively, in modern depictions of reconstructed post-apocalypse, it is the act of voluntarily exiting utopia (the rupture with whatever is defined as orthodoxy, even if that happens to be eternal life and endless bliss) that signals the resurrection of the right to (and risk of) being different. Which, under the requirements and principles of evolution, is the right to continuity and to being.

Afterword: *Libera Me, Domine, De Vita Æterna*

Water, water every where,
And all the boards did shrink;
Water, water, every where,
Nor any drop to drink.
(Samuel Taylor Coleridge)

So Long, and Thanks for All the Fish (Adams, 1984) is the title of the fourth volume of Douglas Adams's series *The Hitchhiker's Guide to the Galaxy* (Adams, 1979). It is also the message left by the dolphins when they depart Earth just before it is demolished to make way for a hyper-spatial by-pass. Whether treated in comedic or tragic terms, in fiction or poetry, film or art, (and the refusal to treat it seriously might be what in the future would make the possibility more likely to become a reality), the end of the world as a theme, if a pun may be permitted, is here to stay. The promise of eternity has always been elusive, but also, in equal measure, both desirable and abhorrent. We fear death, but also eternal (or even unusually long) life, even when the latter is pleasant or at least overall satisfactory, as in John Wyndham's *The Trouble with Lichen* (Wyndham, [1960] 1982), Julian Barnes's *History of the World in 10½ Chapters* (Barnes, 1990) or Harold Ramis's *Groundhog Day* (Ramis, 1993). In these and many other examples, the fear of eternal repetition (on-going life, even on-going perfection) is at least as potent as the fear of an ending (death, whether individual or global). And this ultimately may be what, in our culture's narratives, lies at the heart of the atavistic ontological hope but also dread that, after the world ends, everything will begin again much as it was before. It may all end in tears (floods of tears), but it soon dries up again. Much as it was before. Or not?

Figure 23. John Martin, *The Great Day of His Wrath*

Lo! Death has reared himself a throne
In a strange city lying alone
Far down within the dim West,
Where the good and the bad and the worst and the best
Have gone to their eternal rest.
[...]
No rays from the holy heaven come down
On the long night-time of that town;
But light from out the lurid sea
Streams up the turrets silently —
[...]
While from a proud tower in the town
Death looks gigantically down.
[...]
No swellings tell that winds may be
Upon some far-off happier sea —
No heavings hint that winds have been
On seas less hideously serene.

But lo, a stir is in the air!
The wave — there is a movement there!
[...]
Down, down that town shall settle hence,
Hell, rising from a thousand thrones,
Shall do it reverence. (Poe, 2003: 22-23)

Afterword 173

Figure 24. Michaelangelo Buonarroti, *The Flood* (right panel view)

At the end of Timothy Findley's *Not Wanted on the Voyage* (Findley, 1987), a re-telling of the story of the Flood in Genesis, God/Yaweh is dead. And not just dead but defiled, his body devoured by flies. In his place remains Yaweh's best friend, Noah (Dr. Noyes), a cruel patriarch guilty of infanticide, eugenicide, humanitarian abuse, animal cruelty and incest, who rules tyrannically over his wife, their three sons and their sons' wives, one of whom, Hannah, he has impregnated, and upon whom he has begotten a throwback, an ape-child who is immediately put to death. Not a good beginning to a New Beginning. In 'The Second Coming' Yeats warns of just that:

> Things fall apart; the centre cannot hold;
> Mere anarchy is loosed upon the world,
> The blood-dimmed tide is loosed, and everywhere
> The ceremony of innocence is drowned;
> The best lack all conviction, while the worst
> Are full of passionate intensity.

> Surely some revelation is at hand;
> Surely the Second Coming is at hand.
> The Second Coming! Hardly are those words out
> When a vast image out of Spiritus Mundi
> Troubles my sight: [...]
>
> [N]ow I know
> That twenty centuries of stony sleep
> Were vexed to nightmare by a rocking cradle,
> And what rough beast, its hour come round at last,
> Slouches towards Bethlehem to be born? (Yeats, 1990: 210-11)

In Genesis, a querulous God predicts that, in view of humanity's fundamental flaws, after the Flood the new world will almost certainly be just as bad as the one that was wiped out before, 'for the imagination of man's heart *is* evil from his youth' (Genesis 8:21). If humanity as a whole suffers from a factory defect, it is perhaps unsurprising that in Findley, even if not in the original text, the manufacturer should go out of business:

> It was the questions raised and the dreaded answers implied by Yaweh's growing horror of mankind [...]. (Findley, 1987: 101)
>
> *Failure.*
>
> It seemed [...] that – despite successes – failure was inevitable. [...] The answers were always the same: every birth foretells a death: in every new beginning lie the seeds of ruin. Eve and apples – Cain and murder [...]. Humankind and rain.
>
> And of this present new beginning – whose symbol was the ark [...] he had already seen the seeds of ruin sprouting: in his wife; in Ham and Lucy. These three were already at work in the bowels of the ark – spreading opposition to [God's] edict – drawing the lines between the will of Yaweh and the mere will of men. (Findley, 1987: 239)

In Findley, as the rains stop, the narrative concludes with a new race that is already schismatic: on one side Noah and his eldest and youngest sons (Shem 'the Ox,' with all the characteristics and limitations that the nickname suggests; and Japeth, corrupted by violence and himself now a killer). On the other side Mrs. Noyes, Japeth's child-bride Emma, Ham, the middle son, whose scientific curiosity about the world alienates him from his father, and Ham's enigmatic wife Lucy, who is in fact Lucifer, the Fallen Angel of Morning in woman's form: a 'rogue angel [...] smiling, soft spoken and beautiful' (Findley, 1987: 59) and as troublingly appealing as Milton's Satan.

In *Not Wanted on the Voyage* Lucifer's sole crime, as recognized by Michael Archangelis, God's chief angel, had been to ask 'Why?' (Findley, 108) and, finding doubt to be unacceptable to God, to depart from a less than ideal Heaven:

> Michael had never lost, but once, in battle. His war with Lucifer – though proclaimed a victory in Heaven – was no such thing in Michael's eyes. In Michael's eyes, his brother had not been vanquished; he had escaped [...] had joined the human race [...] for a reason, [...] in order to survive the holocaust in heaven. In order to prevent the holocaust on Earth.' (Findley, 1987: 101-10)

Somewhere between the two family factions, but testimony by her very existence to Noah's crimes, is Hannah, whose child, the first one born in the Ark and begotten by Noah upon his own son's wife, is an ape, and therefore a throwback to an evolutionary descent unrecognized by a future Mosaic law which its incestuous father/grandfather seeks to anticipate (in doing so arguably usurping God's law-making monopoly, and therefore self-destructively weakening the very authority upon which he anchors his own).

> Only Ham, it seemed, was not surprised by the change in his father's titles. 'Most Reverend Doctor, it seemed to him, was only proper for one who was on his way to becoming a God.' (Findley, 1987: 210)

The ape-child drowned in a symbolic purge (which however is also a pre-Christian baptism that returns it to a primeval soup/womb thus signposted as humanity's real point of origin), is in fact the second such freak born to Noah. It therefore stands as the tell-tale evidence of the latter's biological (simian) descent, which is necessarily traceable to himself, since the two children were born to different mothers. Both children are murdered at birth, bereft motherhood thus bonding Hannah to Mrs. Noyes, the mothers of Noah's ape-children. In the early stages of the Flood Mrs. Noyes had rescued another ape-child (Lotte, Emma's sibling) and brought her to the Ark, only to see her throat cut by Japeth at Noah's orders, because she was not on Yaweh's list of those to be saved.

In *The Seventh Seal* Ingmar Bergman's outraged Block doubts the existence of both God and Satan in a world where a child finds no protection, and is sacrificed as a burnt offering against the plague (Bergman, 1957). In Findley's novel, too, Hannah and Mrs. Noyes reject the rule of both Yaweh and Noah: 'There is no God worthy of this child. And so I will give her back to the world where she belongs.' (Findley, 1987: 170)

Defective children (there are now none left in the Ark), fairies, unicorns and dragons (all creatures whose entitlement to life requires an act of the imagination and the acceptance of an origin outside that authored by Yaweh), are all refused safe passage and become extinct under the arbitrary wrath of God: 'And the bell tolled, but the ark, as ever, was adamant. Its shape had taken on a voice. And the voice said: *no.*' (Findley, 1987: 193)

Back in his days in Heaven, Lucifer, now Lucy, like Julian Barnes's forlorn recipient of eternal bliss, had dreamed of the possibility of something different:

> 'A long time ago,' she said, 'in a place I have almost forgotten – I heard a rumour of another world. [...] I could not abide the place I was in [...]. It never rained – though we never lacked for water. *Always fair weather!* Dull. [...] I wanted, too, someone with whom I could argue. Someone – just once – with whom I could disagree. And I had heard this rumour: about another world. (Findley, 1987: 282)

Now, as the rains stop and the flood waters begin to subside, Mrs. Noyes goes one step further than Lucy/Lucifer. Looking down to where there used to be 'the world that had been destroyed by Dr. Noyes (with some help from his illustrious Friend)' (Findley, 1987: 352), she lays down what is in effect a profane, manifesto of nihilistic non-repetition, noncontinuity, ongoing cataclysm promising an absolute ending:

> And now, Noah wanted another world [...]. Well – damn him, no, she thought. [...]
>
> Mrs. Noyes scanned the sky.
>
> Not one cloud.
>
> She prayed. But not to the absent God. Never, never again to the absent God, but to the absent clouds, she prayed. And to the empty sky.
>
> She prayed for rain. (Findley, 1987: 352)

God is dead and for Mrs. Noyes, finally privy to forbidden gnosis, and dreaming of no worlds at all, it is none too soon.

> 'Even if it takes a thousand years – we want to come with you,' said Mrs. Noyes to Lucy. 'Wherever you may be going.'
>
> 'Now,' said Lucy – and she smiled; 'you have begun to understand the meaning of your sign....'
>
> Infinity. (Findley, 1987: 284)

Under the auspices of Lucifer, Mrs. Noyes, mother of a new beginning/ending, squares the circle and chooses an infinity which precludes all that is not nothing.

Bibliography

Primary Texts

Adams, Douglas. *The Hitchhiker's Guide to the Galaxy*. London: Pan Books (1979).
—. *The Restaurant at the End of the Universe*. London: Pan Books (1980).
—. *Life, the Universe and Everything*. London: Pan Books (1983).
—. *So Long, and Thanks for All the Fish*. New York: Harmony Books (1984).
Anderson, Poul. *Tau Zero*. Chatham: Gollancz [1967] (2006).
—. *Virgin Planet*. London: Mayflower (1959).
Asbjørnsen, Peter Christen and Moe, Jørgen. *Popular Tales From the Norse*. Trans. George Webbe Dasent (1888). Viewable on: http://www.surlalunefairytales.com/authors/asbjornsenmoe/giantnoheart.html
Atkinson, Kate. *Not the End of the World*. London: Black Swan (2003).
Atwood, Margaret. *The Handmaid's Tale*. London: Virago [1985] (1991).
—. *Oryx and Crake*. London: Bloomsbury (2003).
—. *The Year of the Flood*. London: Bloomsbury (2009).
Auster, Paul. *In the Country of Last Things*. London: Faber and Faber [1987] (2005).
Ballard, J.G. *The Crystal World*. London: Flamingo [1966] (1985).
—. *The Drowned World*. London: Harper Perennial [1962] (2008).
Barnes, Julian. *History of the World in 10½ Chapters*. London: Picador (1990).
Bellamy, Edward. *Looking Backward: From 200 - 1887*. UK: Applewood [1888] (2000).
Bellows, Henry Adams. *The Poetic Edda: The Mythological Poems*. UK: Dover Publications [1936] (2004).
Benson, Robert Hugh. *Lord of the World*. London: The Echo Library [1908] (2005).
Blish, James. *A Clash of Cymbals*. London: Arrow Books (1974).
Boynes, John. *The Boy in the Striped Pyjamas*. UK: Definitions (2008).
Bradbury, Ray. *Fahrenheit 451*. London: Grafton Books [1953] (1976).
Brockmeier, Kevin. *The Brief History of the Dead*. London: John Murray (2006).
Browning, Robert. 'Andrea del Sarto (called "The Faultless Painter")' [1855] in *Men and Women*. London: Houghton, Mifflin (1883), 184-93.
Caeiro, Alberto. 'When Spring Comes' ['Quando vier a Primavera'] in *Poemas de Alberto Caeiro*. Lisbon: Europa-América (s.d.) [1914]. Translation ours.
Camus, Albert. *La peste*. Paris: Editions Flammarion [1947] (1972).
Čapek, Karel. *R.U.R. (Rossum's Universal Robots)*. London: The Echo Library [1921] (2010).

Čapek, Karel. *War with the Newts*. USA: Catbird Press [1936] (2001).
Clarke, Arthur C. 'The Star' in *Infinity Science Fiction* (1955). Viewable on: http://lucis.net/stuff/clarke/star_clarke.html
Clarkson, Helen. *The Last Day*. New York: Dodd, Mead & Company (1959).
Coover, Robert. *The Public Burning*. New York: Grove Press [1977] (2000).
Crichton, Michael. *The Andromeda Strain*. London: Arrow Books [1969] (1995).
—. *Congo*. London: Arrow Books [1980] (1995).
—. *Jurassic Park*. London: Arrow Books (1998).
—. *Prey*. London: Harper Collins (2002).
—. *State of Fear*. London: Harper Collins (2005).
Dahl, Roald. 'William and Mary' in *Completely Unexpected Tales*. London: Penguin [1960] (1986).
Dick, Philip K. *We Can Build You*. London: Fontana (1977).
—. *Time out of Joint*. London: Gollancz [1959] (2003).
—. *The World Jones Made*. London: Gollancz [1956] (2003).
—. *The Simulacra*. London: Gollancz [1964] (2004).
—. *The Penultimate Truth*. London: Gollancz [1964] (2005).
—. *Do Androids Dream of Electric Sheep?* London: Gollancz [1968] (2007).
—. *Dr. Bloodmoney*. London: Gollancz [1965] (2007).
Disch, Thomas M. *The Genocides*. London: Vintage [1965] (2000).
Farmer, Philip José. *To Your Scattered Bodies Go*. New York: Berkeley Medallion (1971).
Findley, Timothy. *Not Wanted on the Voyage*. Ontario: Penguin (1987).
Finney, Jack. *The Body Snatchers*. UK: Prentice Hall & IBD [1954] (1998).
Flammarion, Camille. *Omega: The Last Days of the World*. Nebraska: University of Nebraska Press and Bison Books [1893] (1999). Original title: *La fin du monde*.
Forster, E.M. *The Machine Stops*. UK: Kessinger Publishing Co. [1909] (2004)
Frazer, James. 'The_External Soul in Folk-Tales' in *The Golden Bough: A Study in Magic and Religion*. London: Wordsworth (1993). Viewable on: http://en.wikisource.org/wiki/The_Golden_Bough/.
Frost, Robert. 'Fire and Ice.' New York: *Harper's Magazine* (1920).
Gaiman, Neil. *The Sandman* (series). UK: Titan Books (1991-2007).
Gershwin, George and Gershwin, Ira, *Porgy and Bess* (1935).
Golding, William. *Lord of the Flies*. London: Faber and Faber [1954] (2002).
Grainville, François-Xavier Cousin de. *The Last Man*. USA: University Press of New England [1805] (1992). Original title: *Le dernier homme*.
Hamilton, Andy. *Old Harry's Game*, Series 6, Episode 2. BBC Radio 4 (27 September 2007).
Harris, Thomas. *Hannibal Lecter Trilogy*. London: William Heinemann (2005).
Herculano, Alexandre. *Eurico, o Presbítero*. Lisbon: Europa-América (1980).
Hirst, Damien. 'The Key, the Suicide of Judas' in *The Cancer Chronicles*. London: Other Criteria (2004), 19.
Hood, Thomas. *The Last Man*. Viewable on: http://www.rc.umd.edu/editions/mws/lastman/hood.htm

Huxley, Aldous. *Brave New World*. London: Grafton [1932] (1977).

Irving, Washington. *Rip van Winkle and Other Stories*. London: Puffin Classics [1819] (2010).

James, P.D. *The Children of Men*. London: Faber and Faber (2000).

Kerr, Judith. *The Tiger Who Came to Tea*. London: HarperCollins Children's Books (2006).

Kilmer, Joyce. *Complete Poems*. Cutchogue, New York: Buccaneer Books (1993).

Larkin, Philip. 'Aubade' in *Times Literary Supplement* (December 23, 1977).

Lem, Stanislaw. *Solaris*. London: Faber and Faber (2003).

Levin, Ira. *Rosemary's Baby*. London: Pan Books (1967).

—. *This Perfect Day*. London: Signet [1970] (1994).

—. *The Stepford Wives*. London: Klett Ernst/Schulbuch [1972] (1996).

Lindow, John. *Norse Mythology: A Guide to the Gods, Heroes, Rituals and Beliefs*. Oxford: Oxford University Press (2001).

Loyola, (St.) Ignatius. *The Spiritual Exercises of St. Ignatius*. Garden City: Doubleday [1522-24] (1964).

Machado de Assis, Joaquim Maria. *The Devil's Church and Other Stories*. Trans. J. Schmitt and L. Ishimatsu. London: Harper Collins (1987).

MacNeice, Louis. 'Apple Blossom' in Seamus Heaney and Ted Hughes (eds.). *The Rattle Bag*. London: Faber and Faber (1982).

Matheson, Richard. *I Am Legend*. Chatham: Gollancz [1954] (1999).

—. *The Shrinking Man*. Chatham: Gollancz [1956] (2003).

McCarthy, Cormac. *The Road*. London: Picador (2007).

McCaughrean, Geraldine. *Not the End of the World*. Oxford: Oxford University Press (2005).

Merrill, Judith. *The Shadow on the Hearth*. New York: Doubleday (1950).

Meyer, Stephenie. *The Twilight Saga*. London: Atom (2007).

Miller, Walter M. 'Dark Benediction' in his *Dark Benediction*. London: Gollancz (2007), 332-87.

—. 'Conditionally Human' in his *Dark Benediction*. London: Gollancz (2007), 207-65.

—. *A Canticle for Leibowitz*. Bantam Doubleday Dell Publishing Group (2007).

Milton, John. 'Paradise Lost' in *Complete English Poems, Of Education and Areopagitica*. Ed. Gordon Campbell. London: Everyman [1667] (1990), 149-441.

—. 'Paradise Regained' in *Complete English Poems, of Education and Areopagitica*. Ed. Gordon Campbell. London: Everyman [1671] (1990), 444-504.

Moore, Catherine L. and Kuttner, Henry. 'Vintage Season,' in David G. Hartwell (ed.), *The World Treasury of Science Fiction*. Boston: Little, Brown & Co. (1989), 980-1018.

More, Thomas. *Utopia*. Harmondsworth: Penguin [1516] (1980).

Newcomb, Simon. 'The End of the World' in David G. Hartwell and L.W. Currey (eds.), *The Battle of the Monsters and Other Stories*. Boston: The Gregg Press (1976), 179-96.

Oakley, Robert. *Henry's Quest*. London: Macmillan (1986).

O'Brien, Robert. C. *Z for Zacchariah*. London: Puffin [1973] (1998).

Orwell, George. *Nineteen Eighty-Four*. Harmondsworth: Penguin [1949] (1983).

—. *Animal Farm*. Harmondsworth: Penguin Classics [1945] (1980).

Peyrouton de Ladebat, Monique. *The Village that Slept*. Trans. Thelma Niklaus. London: The Bodley Head (1963).

Poe, Edgar Allan. 'Conversation of Eiros and Charmian [1839].' Viewable on: http://books.eserver.org/fiction/poe/conversation.html

—. 'Ligeia' in *The Fall of the House of Usher and Other Writings*. London: Penguin [1839] (2003), 62-78.

—. 'The City in the Sea' in *The Fall of the House of Usher and Other Writings*. London: Penguin [1845] (2003), 22-23.

Pullman, Philip. *His Dark Materials*. London: Scholastic UK (2007).

Ragnarök. See Bellows, Henry Adams. *The Poetic Edda: The Mythological Poems*. UK: Dover Publications (2004).

Rand, Ayn. *Atlas Shrugged*. New York: Random House (1957).

Robinson, Marilynne. *Gilead*. London: Virago (2006).

Roshwald, Mordecai. *Level 7*. Wisconsin: Wisconsin University Press [1959] (2004).

Rosoff, Meg. *How I Live Now*. London: Puffin (2005).

Rowling, J.K. *Harry Potter and the Goblet of Fire*. London: Bloomsbury (2000).

—. *Harry Potter and the Half-Blood Prince*. London: Bloomsbury (2005).

—. *Harry Potter and the Deathly Hallows*. London: Bloomsbury (2008).

Saramago, José. *Blindness*. Trans. Giovanni Pontiero. London: Harvill Press (1997).

—. *The Stone Raft*. Trans. Giovanni Pontiero. San Diego: Harcourt Brace & Co. (1996).

Scarrow, Alex. *Last Light*. London: Orion (2008).

Self, Will. *The Book of Dave*. London: Viking (2006).

Shelley, Mary. *Frankenstein or the Modern Prometheus*. London: Penguin [1818] (1983).

Shelley, Perce Bysshe. 'Ozymandias.' In *The Examiner*, 524 (11), (January 1818).

Shiel, M.P. *The Purple Cloud*. Nebraska: University of Nebraska Press (2000).

Shute, Nevil. *On the Beach*. New York: Ballantine (1974).

Silverberg, Robert. 'When We Went to See the End of the World' in *Science Fiction Magazine* (March 1989), 108-74.

Simak, Clifford D. *Ring Around the Sun*. London: Mandarin [1953] (1990).

Stapledon, Olaf. *Last and First Men*. UK: Gollancz New Edition [1932] (1999).

—. *Star Maker*. UK: Gollancz New Edition [1937] (1999).

Stevenson, Robert Louis. *The Strange Case of Dr. Jekyll and Mr. Hyde*. London: Penguin Classics [1886] (2007).

Stewart, George R. *Earth Abides*. London: Corgi [1949] (1973).

Sturgeon, Theodor. *More Than Human*. Chatham: Gollancz [1953] (2000).

Sturluson, Snorri. *Prose Edda*. Trans. Arthur Gilchrist Brodeur (1916). Viewable on: http://www.sacred-texts.com/neu/pre/index.htm

Swindells, Robert E. *Brother in the Land*. Oxford: Oxford Children's Modern Classics [1984] (1999).

Telles, Lygia Fagundes. 'The Ants' in *Tigrela and Other Stories*. Trans. Margaret A. Neves. New York: Avon (1986).

Telles, Lygia Fagundes. 'Rat Seminar' in *Tigrela and Other Stories*. Trans. Margaret A. Neves. New York: Avon (1986).

Torga, Miguel. 'Vicente' in *Bichos*. 17th edition. Coimbra (1987).

Vonnegut, Kurt. *Cat's Cradle*. London: Penguin [1963] (1981).

—. *Slaughterhouse-Five, or The Children's Crusade: A Duty-Dance with Death*. New York: Dell [1969] (1991).

—. *God Bless You, Mr. Rosewater, or Pearls Before Swine*. London: Vintage [1965] (1992).

—. *The Sirens of Titan*. London: Vintage [1959] (1999).

Wells, H.G. 'The Stolen Bacillus' in *Selected Short Stories*. Harmondsworth: Penguin [1894] (1982), 147-53.

—. *The Time Machine* in *Selected Short Stories*. Harmondsworth: Penguin [1895] (1982), 7-83.

—. 'The Country of the Blind' in *Selected Short Stories*. Harmondsworth: Penguin [1904] (1982), 123-46.

—. *The War of the Worlds*. London: Penguin [1898] (2005).

—. *The War in the Air*. London: Penguin [1907] (2005).

—. *The World Set Free*. USA: Book Tree [1914] (2007).

Wilhelm, Kate. *Where Late the Sweet Birds Sang*. Chatham: Gollancz [1976] (2006).

Willis, Connie. *The Doomsday Book*. London: Hodder & Stoughton Ltd (1993).

—. 'Firewatch' in Harry Turtledove and Martin H. Greenberg (eds.), *The Best Time Travel Stories of the 20th Century*. New York: Ballantine Books (2005), 213-51.

Wolfe, Bernard. *Limbo*. UK: Random House (1952).

Wyndham, John. *The Day of the Triffids*. Harmondsworth: Penguin [1951] (1984).

—. *The Kraken Wakes*. Harmondsworth: Penguin [1953] (1980).

—. *Trouble with Lichen*. Harmondsworth: Penguin [1960] (1982).

—. *Web*. Harmondsworth: Penguin [1979] (1983).

—. 'Consider Her Ways' in *Consider Her Ways and Others*. Harmondsworth: Penguin [1956] (1983), 7-54.

—. 'Compassion Circuit' in *The Seeds of Time*. Harmondsworth: Penguin [1956] (1983), 200-11.

—. *The Midwich Cuckoos*. Harmondsworth: Penguin [1957] (1984).

—. *The Chrysalids*. Harmondsworth: Penguin [1955] (1984).

Yeats, W.B. *Collected Poems*. London: Picador (1990).

Films

2001: A Space Odyssey. Dir. Stanley Kubrik. UK and USA: Metro-Goldwyn-Mayer (1968).
A.I. Artificial Intelligence. Dir. Steven Spielberg. USA: DreamWorks and Warner Brothers (2001).
Alien. Dir. Ridley Scott. UK and USA: 20th Century Fox (1979).
Armageddon. Dir. Michael Bay. USA: Touchstone Pictures (1998).
Attack of the Puppet People. Dir. Bert I. Gordon. USA: MGM (1958).
The Bedsit Room. Dir. Richard Lester. UK: Oscar Lewenstein Productions (1969).
Blade Runner. Dir. Ridley Scott. USA: Warner Brothers (1982).
Blindness. Dir. Fernando Meirelles. Brazil, Canada Japan and Uruguay: Miramax (2008).
The Blob. Dir. Irvin Yeasworth. USA: Paramount Pictures (1958).
Body Snatchers. Dir. Abel Ferrara. USA: Warner Brothers (1993).
The Boy in the Striped Pyjamas. Dir. Mark Herman. UK and USA: Miramax Films (2008).
By Dawn's Early Light. Dir. Jack Scholder. USA: HBO (1980).
The Children of Men. Dir. Alfonso Cuarón. UK: Universal Pictures (2006).
Close Encounters of the Third Kind. Dir. Steven Spielberg. USA: Columbia (1977).
The Day After. Dir. Nicholas Meyer. USA: ABC Television Network (1983).
The Day After Tomorrow. Dir. Roland Emmerich. USA and Canada: 20th Century Fox (2004).
The Day the Earth Stood Still. Dir. Robert Wise. USA: 20th Century Fox (1951).
Deep Impact. Dir. Mimi Leder. USA: DreamWorks (1998).
Dr. Strangelove or: How Learned to Stop Worrying and Love the Bomb. Dir. Stanley Kubrik. UK: Columbia (1964).
Escape from New York. Dir. John Carpenter. USA: AVCO Embassy Pictures (1981).
E.T.: The Extra-Terrestrial Dir. Steven Spielberg. USA: Universal Studios (1982).
Fail-Safe. Dir. Sidney Lumet. USA: Columbia Pictures (1964).
Fail-Safe. Dir. Stephen Frears. USA: CBS and Warner Brothers Television (2000).
Fahrenheit 451. Dir. François Truffaut. UK: Anglo Enterprises and Vineyard Film Ltd. (1966).
Groundhog Day. Dir. Harold Ramis. USA: Columbia Pictures (1993).
The Handmaid's Tale. Dir. Volker Schlöndorff. USA: Metro Goldwyn Meyer (1991).
I Am Legend. Dir. Francis Lawrence. USA and Australia: Warner Brothers (2007).
I Married a Monster from Outer Space. Dir. Gene Fowler Jr. USA: Paramount Pictures (1958).
I, Robot. Dir. Alex Proyas. USA, Germany and Canada: 20th Century Fox (2004).
The Incredible Shrinking Man. Dir. Jack Arnold. USA: Universal Studios (1957).
Independence Day. Dir. Roland Emmerich. USA: 20th Century Fox (1996).
Invasion of the Body Snatchers. Dir. Don Siegel. USA: Allied Artists Pictures Corporation (1956).
Invasion of the Body Snatchers. Dir. Philip Kaufman. USA: United States (1978).

King Kong. Dir. John Guillermin. USA: Paramount (1976).
The Matrix. Dir. Wachowski Brothers. USA and Australia: Warner Brothers (1999).
The Matrix Reloaded. Dir. Wachowski Brothers. USA and Australia: Warner Brothers (2003).
Matrix Revolutions. Dir. Wachowski Brothers. USA and Australia: Warner Brothers (2003).
The Omen. Dir. Richard Donner. UK and USA: 20th Century Fox (1976).
On the Beach. Dir. Stanley Kramer. USA: United Artists (1959).
On the Beach. Dir. Russell Mulcahy. USA and Australia: NBC Television (2000).
The Passion of the Christ. Dir. Mel Gibson. USA and Italy: 20th Century Fox (2004).
Planet of the Apes. Dir. Franklin J. Schaffner. USA: 20th Century Fox (1968).
Quatermass and the Pit. Dir. Nigel Kneale. UK: BBC Television (1958-59).
The Road. Dir. John Hillcoat. USA: 2929 Productions (2009).
Rosemary's Baby. Dir. Roman Polanski. USA: Paramount Pictures (1968).
Seven Days in May. Dir. John Frankenheimer. USA: Paramount Pictures (1964).
The Seventh Seal. Dir. Ingmar Bergman. Sweden: A.B. Svensk Filmindustri (1957).
Solaris. Dir. Andrei Tarkovsky. USSR: State Committee for Cinematography (1972).
Solaris. Dir. Steven Soderbergh. Lightstorm Entertainment (2002).
Survivors, Series 1. Dir. Terry Nation. UK: BBC Television (1975-77).
Survivors, Series 2. Dir. Adrian Hodges. UK: BBC Television (2008-10).
The Terminator. Dir. James Cameron. USA: Hemdale Film Corporation and Orion Pictures (1984).
Terminator 2: Judgment Day. Dir. James Cameron. USA: Carolco Pictures, Lightstorm Entertainment and The Studio Canal (1991).
Terminator 3: The Rise of the Machines. Dir. Jonathan Mostow. Intermedia Films (2003).
Terminator 4: Salvation. Dir. McG (Jonathan McGinty Nichol). The Halcyon Company and Wonderland Sound and Vision (2009).
Threads. Dir. Mick Jackson. UK: BBC Television (1984).
To The Devil a Daughter. Dir. Peter Sykes. USA: Paramount Pictures (1976).
The Truman Show. Dir. Peter Weir. USA: Paramount Pictures (1998).
Until the End of the World. Dir. Wim Wenders. USA: Warner Brothers (1991).
Virus. Dir. John Bruno. USA: Universal Pictures (1999).
WarGames. Dir. John Badham. USA: United Artists (1983).
The War Game. Dir. Peter Watkin. UK: BBC (1965).
War of the Worlds. Dir. Steven Spielberg. USA: Paramount Pictures (2005).
Waterworld. Dir. Kevin Reynolds and Kevin Costner. USA: Universal Pictures (1995).

Opera

Solaris. Comp. Michael Obst (1995).
Götterdämmerung (Twilight of the Gods). Comp. Richard Wagner (1876).

Secondary Bibliography

Adorno, Theodor. *Negative Dialectics*. Trans. E.B. Ashton. New York: Continuum [1966] (1992).

Aldiss, Brian W. 'Dick's Maledictory Web: About and around "Martian Time-Slip"' in *Science Fiction Studies*, 2 (1) (March 1975), 42-47.

Aristotle. 'On the Art of Poetry,' in *Aristotle, Horace, Longinus,Classical Literary Criticism*, London: Penguin (1985), 29-75.

Bakhtin, Mikhail. *Dialogic Imagination: Four Essays*. Texas: University of Texas Press (1982).

BBC News, Friday, 17 December 2004. Viewable on: http://news.bbc.co.uk/1/hi/world/europe/4105683.stm

Berger, James. *After The End: Representations Of Post-Apocalypse*. Minneapolis and London: University of Minneapolis Press (1999).

Bettelheim, Bruno. *The Uses of Enchantment: The Meaning and Importance of Fairy Tales*. Harmondsworth: Penguin (1991).

Booker, M. Keith. *Monsters, Mushroom Clouds and the Cold War: American Science Fiction and the Roots of Postmodernism, 1946-64*. Westport, Connecticut and London: Greenwood Press (2001).

Bostrom, Nick and Ćirković, Milan M. *Global Catastrophic Risks*. Oxford: Oxford University Press (2008).

Bradshaw, John, et al. 'Commentary on R. I. M. Ounbar's 'Coevolution of neocortical size, group size and language in humans'' in Behavioral and Brain Sciences, 16: 681-735 (1993); 18: 385-400 (1995).

Büchmann, Christina and Spiegel, Celina (eds.). *Out of the Garden: Women Writers on the Bible*. London: Pandora (1995).

Carey, John. *The Faber Book of Utopias*. London: Faber and Faber (2000).

Carson, Rachel. *Silent Spring*. Chicago: Houghton Mifflin (1962).

Caute, David. *The Great Fear: The Anti-Communist Purge Under Truman and Eisenhower*. New York: Simon and Schuster (1978).

Chodorow, Nancy. *The Reproduction of Mothering: Psychoanalysis and the Sociology of Gender*. Berkeley and Los Angeles: University of California Press (1979).

Clarens, Carlos. *An Illustrated History of Horror and Science-Fiction Films: The Classic Era, 1895-1967*. Massachusetts: Da Capo (1997).

Cohen, Arthur. *The Tremendum: A Theological Interpretation of the Holocaust*. New York: Crossroad (1981).

Crossley, Robert. 'Acts of God' in David Seed (ed.) *Imagining Apocalypse: Studies in Cultural Crisis*. London: Macmillan Press Ltd. (2000).

Derrida, Jacques. *Of Grammatology*. USA: John Hopkins University Press [1967] (1974).

Dinnerstein, Dorothy. *The Rocking of the Cradle and the Ruling of the World*. London: The Women's Press (1987).

Dugger, Ronnie. 'Does Reagan Expect a Nuclear War?' in *Washington Post* (8 April 1984), C1, 4.

Dunbar, R. I. M. 'Coevolution of neocortical size, group size and language in humans' in *Behavioral and Brain Sciences* 16 (4): 681-735 (1993).

Eco, Umberto. *The Name of the Rose*. London: Vintage [1980] (1992).

Einstein, Albert and Russell, Bertrand. *Russell-Einstein Manifesto*. London, Caxton Hall (1955).

Evans, Joyce A. *Celluloid Mushroom Clouds: Hollywood and The Atom Bomb*. Boulder, CO: Westview Press (1998).

Foucault, Michel. *Discipline and Punish: The Birth of the Prison*. Trans. Alan Sheridan. London: Penguin [1975] (1991).

—. *Madness and Civilization: A History of Insanity in the Age of Reason*. Trans. Richard Howard. London: Routledge [1961] (2001).

—. *A History of Madness*. Trans. Jean Khalfa and Jonathan Murphy. London: Routledge [1961] (2009).

Freud, Sigmund. *The Future of an Illusion, Civilization and its Discontents and Other Works. Standard Edition*, Trans. James Strachey, vol. XXI. London: Vintage and Hogarth Press, 2001.

Fukuyama, Francis, 'The End of History?' in *The National Interest*, n. 16 (Summer 1989), 3.

—. 'A Reply to my Critics' in *The National Interest*, n. 18 (Winter 1989-90), 21-28.

Gannon, Charles E. 'Silo Psychosis: Diagnosing America's Nuclear Anxiety Through Narrative Imagery' in David Seed (ed.). *Imagining Apocalypse: Studies in Cultural Crisis*. London: Macmillan Press Ltd. (2000), 103-17.

Greimas, A. Julien. *Structural Semantics: An Attempt at a Method*. Trans. Daniele McDowell, Ronald Schleifer and Alan Velie. Nebraska: University of Nebraska Press [1966] (1983).

Herman, Barbara. *The practice of moral judgment*. Boston: Harvard University Press (1993).

Hinrichs, Von Per. 'Mythos Landerhüter' in *Spiegel Online* (25 August 2006).

Hobbes, Thomas. *Leviathan, The Matter, Form and Power of a Common Wealth Ecclesiastical and Civil*. Oxford: Oxford World's Classics [1651] (1998).

Jackson, Rosemary. *Fantasy: The Literature of Subversion*. London and New York: Routledge, 1981.

Jameson, Fredric. 'After Armageddon: Character Systems in P.K. Dick's *Dr. Bloodmoney*' in *Science-Fiction Studies*, 2 (1): 31-42 (1975).

—. 'The Politics of Theory: Ideological Positions in the Postmodern Debate' in *New German Critique*, 33 (Fall 1984), 55-66.

—. *Archaeologies of the Future:The Desire Called Utopia and Other Science Fictions*. London and New York: Verso (2005).

Kant, Immanuel. See Airaksinen,Timo and Siitonen, Arto. 'Kant on Hobbes, Peace, and Obedience' in *History of European Ideas*, 30 (3) (September 2004) 315-28.

Kermode, Frank. *The Sense of an Ending: Studies in the Theory of Fiction*. London and Oxford: Oxford University Press (1968).

Ketterer, David. *New Worlds for Old: The Apocalyptic Imagination, Science Fiction and American Literature*. Indiana: Indiana University Press (1974).

Lebow, Richard Ned and Stein, Janice Gross. *We All Lost the Cold War*. Princeton: Princeton University Press (1994).

Lindsey, Hal and Carlson, Carole C. *The Late, Great Planet Earth*. New York: Bantam [1970] (1973).

McGuire, Gregory. 'Salman Rushdie and *The Wizard of Oz*.' BBC Radio 4 (27 December 2008, 10.30 am).

Mill, John Stuart. *Utilitarianism*. London: Parker, Son and Bourne (1863).

Mills, C. Wright. *The Sociological Imagination*. Oxford: Oxford University Press (1959).

Oppenheimer, Robert (1945). Quoting from *Bhagavad Gita*. Viewable on: http://www.sacred-texts.com/hin/sbe08/index.htm

Plato. *The Republic*. Trans. Desmond Lee. London: Penguin Classics (1987).

—. *Symposium*. Trans. Christopher Gill. London: Penguin Classics (2003).

Pope, Alexander. 'An Essay on Criticism' (1711). Viewable on: http://poetry.eserver.org/essay-on-criticism.html

Poundstone, William. *Prisoner's Dilemma*. New York: Anchor Books (1992).

Propp, Vladimir. *Morphology of the Folktale*. Trans. Laurence Scott. 2nd ed. Austin: University of Texas Press [1928] (1968).

Reagan, Ronald in Vidal, Gore. 'Armageddon?' in *Armageddon? Essays 1983-1987*. London: Grafton (1989).

Rees, Martin. *Our Final Century*. London: Arrow Books (2003). Also published under the title *Our Final Hour* outside the UK..

Rotman, Brian. *Signifying Nothing: The Semiotics of Zero*. Stanford University Press [1987] (1993).

Sartre, Jean-Paul Sartre. '"Aminadab" or the fantastic considered as a language' in *Situations*, I (1947).

Seed, David (ed.). *Imagining Apocalypse: Studies in Cultural Crisis*. London: Macmillan Press Ltd. (2000).

Sontag, Susan. 'The Imagination of Disaster' [1966] in her *Against Interpretation and Other Essays*. London: Penguin Classics (1979).

Todorov, Tzevetan, *The Conquest of America: The Question of the Other*. Trans. R. Howarf. New York: Harper and Row (1984).

Vidal, Gore. 'Armageddon?' in *Armageddon? Essays 1983-1987*. London: Grafton (1989).

Warner, Marina. *No Go the Bogeyman: Scaring, Lulling and Making Mock*. London: Vintage (1998).

—. *From the Beast to the Blonde: On Fairy Tales and Their Tellers*. London: Vintage (1995).

Wells, H.G. *A Modern Utopia*. London: Penguin [1905] (2005).

—. *Anticipations of the Reaction of Mechanical and Scientific Progress upon Human Life and Thought*. New York: Dover [1901] (1999).

Wittgenstein, Ludwig. *Tractatus Logicus-Philosophicus*. London: Routledge Classics [1921] (2001).

Worthington, Jay. 'Mein Royalties' in *Cabinet*, Issue 10 (2003).

Zipes, Jack. *Fairy Tale as Myth/Myth as Fairy Tale*. Kentucky: University of Kentucky Press (1994).

Index

9/11 (11 September 2001) 9-11, 15, 22, 93
  See also terrorism, World Trade Center
Adam xvi, xxii, 6 (fig. 6), 8, 14, 19 (fig. 10), 21, 51, 52, 63, 68-69, 71, 82, 103, 113, 119, 147
  See also Eve, Fall, Genesis
Adams, Douglas 42, 110-11, 127-28, 148, 171, 177
  See also
  The Hitchhiker's Guide to the Galaxy
  So Long, and Thanks for All the Fish
adolescence xvi, xviii, xix, xxi, 33, 55, 57, 69, 84
  See also childhood
Adorno, Theodor 56, 61
A.I. Artificial Intelligence 119, 121-24, 126
  See also Spielberg, Steven
Aldiss, Brian 139
  See also 'Dick's Maledictory Web'
Alien 31
Allah 10
  See also God
Alumbrados 66
Ancient Greece xvii, 8, 13, 15, 16, 18, 20, 74, 104, 108
Anderson, Poul 43, 75, 76, 88-89, 91, 98, 160
  See also Tau Zero
androids 42, 118, 120, 122-23
  See also computers, machines, robots
The Andromeda Strain 64, 121
  See also Crichton, Michael
Animal Farm 101
  See also Orwell, George
Apocalypse in Lilac 59 (fig. 13)
  See also Chagall, Marc
apokalupsis/apokalupsus 15
Aristotle 103, 111

Armageddon 8, 15, 22, 24, 56, 68, 112, 150, 159-160
Armageddon xxv, 31, 45, 64
Asbjørnsen, Peter Christen 145
Attack of the Puppet People 127
Atwood, Margaret xxv, 42, 48, 55, 64, 68-70, 73, 75, 76-77, 90, 91, 93, 98, 113, 114, 141, 153, 161
  See also The Handmaid's Tail
  Oryx and Crake
Auschwitz 56
  See also Hitler, Adolf
  The Holocaust
Auster, Paul xxii, xxv, 9, 76, 83-84, 85

Bakhtin, Mikhail 111
Ballard, J.G. 2, 3, 9, 15, 64, 86, 129
  See also The Drowned World
Barnes, Julian xxv, 142-147, 161, 163, 168, 169, 171, 176
The BBC 39, 68, 165
The Bed-Sitting Room 44
Bellamy, Edward 153
Benson, Robert Hugh 64
Berger, James 15, 22, 53, 56, 57, 60-62, 63, 64, 68, 100, 150-51, 160
Bergman, Ingmar 105, 106 (fig. 17), 107 (fig. 18), 108, 145, 175
  See also The Seventh Seal
Bettelheim, Bruno xvi
The Bible xvi, xxii, 8, 133, 164
  See also
  Cities of the Plain
  Genesis, the Book of
  Revelation, the Book of
Big Bang 13, 104
Big Brother 93, 130, 142, 143, 151, 164
  See also Nineteen Eighty-Four
  Orwell, George

Big Brother 112
bildungsroman xvii, 82, 138
Black Death 47, 75
Blade Runner xxv, 120, 121, 122, 123
  See also Ridley Scott
Blake, William xvii (fig. 2) 4 (fig. 4), 5
blindness 31, 45, 94, 99
  See also *Blindness*
  Day of the Triffids
Blindness 31, 94-100
Blish, James 43
The Blob 64, 79-80
The Body Snatchers 32, 33, 93, 178
  See also Finney, Jack
body-snatching xix
Booker, M. Keith 53, 79, 127, 140, 151
Bosch, Hieronymus xvi (fig. 1)
  See also *The Last Judgement*
The Boy in the Striped Pyjamas 57-58
Bradbury, Ray 60, 87, 91, 93, 100, 120, 136, 152, 162, 164, 169
  See also *Fahrenheit 451*
Bradshaw, John 12
Brave New World 69, 80, 87, 101, 120, 128, 133, 135, 136, 140, 143, 147, 149, 152, 153-54, 160, 164
  See also Huxley, Aldous
Brockmeier, Kevin 9, 43, 44
Browning, Robert 147, 168
Buddhism 66
Bulletin of Atomic Sudies 24
Bush, George W. 93
By Dawn's Early Light 27, 28, 30, 58, 118

Caeiro, Alberto 72
Cameron, James 11, 75, 115, 117, 119
  See also *The Terminator*
  Terminator 2: Judgement Day
Camus, Albert 94
cannibalism xix, xxiii
Čapek, Karel 118, 123
Carey, John 146, 162
cataclysm xviii, xix, xx, xxv, 15, 22, 30, 36, 38, 43, 47, 51, 53, 56, 64, 66, 68, 70-71, 75, 77, 86, 89, 91, 100, 101, 113, 119, 137, 151, 158, 176
Caute, David 93
Chagall, Marc 59
  See also *Apocalypse in Lilac*

Chaplin, Charlie 100
childhood/children xv, xvi-xix, xxi, xxii, xxiii, xxiv, 32, 37-38, 39, 41, 45, 51-52, 53, 58, 69-70, 71, 73, 76, 77, 78, 81, 82, 83, 84, 89, 90, 105-06, 115-16, 119, 120, 125-26, 127, 133, 134-38, 150, 156-57, 159-60, 166-67, 169, 173, 175-76
  See also adolescence
The Children of Men 76, 79-91, 100, 102, 138, 153-54
  See also James, P.D.
Chodorow, Nancy 51
Christianity xxiii, 14, 66, 75, 79, 115, 154, 157, 159, 160, 166, 175
The Chrysalids 35, 37, 40, 66, 91, 109, 114, 115, 121-23, 126, 149, 166, 167
  See also John Wyndham
Cities of the Plain xxiv, 62 (fig. 4), 69, 104
  See also Bible
civilization xxi, 2, 3, 5, 7, 11, 21, 22, 39, 57, 70, 79, 82, 83, 87, 98, 107, 115, 116, 118, 126, 129, 135, 165, 166-67
Clarens, Carlos 123
Clarke, Arthur C. 107
Clarkson, Helen 64
Close Encounters of the Third Kind 31, 123
  See also Spielberg, Steven
Cohen, Arthur 56, 57
Cold War 21-23, 28, 92, 100, 127
computers 25, 26, 27, 42, 110, 111, 118, 119, 124, 136, 148, 150, 152
'Conditionally Human' 120, 121-22, 130
  See also Miller, Walter M.
'Consider Her Ways' 73, 74, 75-76, 77
  See also Wyndham, John
Coover, Robert 100
'The Country of the Blind' 95-99
  See also Wells, H.G.
Crichton, Michael 34, 64, 117, 119, 121
  See also *The Andromeda Strain*
  Jurassic Park
  Prey
  State of Fear
crime xviii, 115, 125, 142, 175
Crossley, Robert 31, 106, 137
culture xvi, xx, 11, 12, 20, 30, 56, 74, 80, 87, 103, 104, 107, 115, 132, 140, 152, 153, 155, 171

Dafni, Reuven 57 (fig. 12)
Dahl, Roald 119
'Dark Benediction' 33, 86, 96
　See also Miller, Walter M.
Darwin, Charles 16, 38, 60
Darwinism 35, 38, 161, 165, 168, 169
The Day After 45, 64
The Day After Tomorrow xxiv, 9, 45, 47, 64
The Day of the Triffids 31, 35, 37, 38, 39-41, 81, 91, 94, 95, 96, 97, 99, 101, 149
　See also Wyndham, John
The Day the Earth Stood Still 31, 123, 125, 127
Deep Impact 9, 46
Derrida, Jacques xviii, 65, 167
deterrence 23, 24
　See also Cold War
Dick, Philip K. 5, 9, 15, 66, 79, 80, 91, 93, 94, 100, 111, 120, 122, 123, 128-30, 139, 147, 148, 149, 154, 162, 164
　See also
　Do Androids Dream of Electric Sheep?
　Dr. Bloodmoney
　The Penultimate Truth
　The Simulacra
　Time Out of Joint
　We Can Build You
　The World Jones Made
Dickens, Charles xvii
Dinnerstein, Dorothy 51
dinosaurs 2, 5, 21
Disch, Thomas M. 64
Do Androids Dream of Electric Sheep? 122-23
　See also Dick, Philip K.
Doré, Gustave 19 (fig. 10)
Dr. Bloodmoney 66, 79, 111, 139, 149, 154
　See also Dick, Philip K.
Dream 122, 123, 143, 144, 145, 146
The Drowned World 2, 3, 9, 15, 64, 129
　See also Ballard, J.G.
Dr. Strangelove or: How I Learned to Stop Worrying and Love the Bomb 42, 60, 64, 129
Dunbar, R.I.M. 12
Dürer, Albrecht 29 (fig. 11)
dystopia 91, 100, 132, 133, 135, 138, 139-40, 146-47, 149, 153, 154, 167

Eco, Umberto 111
Edda, Poetic and Prose 54
　See also Ragnarök
Eden xvi, xxiii, 7, 8, 14, 19 (fig. 10), 20, 63, 103-105, 113-15, 119, 138, 147-148
　See also Fall, paradise
Einstein, Albert 22-24
　See also Russell-Einstein Manifesto
El Greco 158 (fig. 22)
Eloi 73, 74, 153, 167-68
　See also *The Time Machine*, Wells, H.G.
environment xv, xxiv, 3, 12, 15, 21, 35, 44, 71, 87, 119, 125, 129, 148
Escape from New York 83, 85
eschaton 15
E.T.: The Extra-Terrestrial 31, 123
　See also Spielberg, Steven
Eurydice 104
evangelism xviii, 56, 66, 160, 166
Evans, Joyce A. 53, 79
Eve xvi, 6 (fig. 6), 7, 14, 19 (fig. 10), 21, 51, 52, 63, 68, 69, 71, 77, 98, 103, 113, 119, 147, 174
　See also Adam, Fall, Genesis
evolution 2-3, 15, 35, 50, 73, 114, 122, 165, 169
　See also Darwinism, recapitulation

Fahrenheit 451 60, 87, 91, 120, 134, 136, 152, 164
　See also Bradbury, Ray
Fail-Safe xxiv, 27-28, 30, 58, 92
fairy tales xvi, xvii, xix, xx, 7
The Fall 8, 19, 20, 53, 118, 138, 139
　See also Adam, Eve, Genesis, Bible
fantastic xix, 46
fantasy 140, 151
Farmer, Philip José 139
fascism 94, 165
Findley, Timothy 147, 157, 173-76
Finney, Jack 32
　See also *The Body Snatchers*
Flammarion, Camille 64
floods/The Flood xxiv, 18, 48, 51, 52, 55, 68, 70, 89, 104, 114, 173 (fig. 24), 174, 175, 176
Forster, E.M. xxv, 119, 120, 128, 130, 136, 141, 153, 164
Foucault, Michel 56, 93, 140, 151

Four Riders 29
Franco, Francisco 165
Frankenstein 120
Frazer, James 145
free will 14, 52, 108, 128, 136, 149, 163, 169
Freud, Sigmund xix, 119, 165
Friedrich, Caspar David 72 (fig. 15), 73
Frost, Robert 25
Fukuyama, Francis 157

Gaia theory 39, 128
Gaiman, Neil 144-145
Gannon, Charles E. 44-45
Genesis, the Book of xvi, 8, 14, 18, 30, 48, 49, 51, 52, 53, 62, 68, 71, 79, 90, 103, 113, 157, 173, 174
   See also Adam, Eve, Fall, flood, paradise
genocide xxiii, 64, 122, 123, 155, 156, 167
   See also The Holocaust
Gershwin, George and Ira 164
God xvi, 1, 5, 8, 10, 20, 21, 22, 31, 41, 42, 47, 49, 51, 52, 53, 62, 65, 66, 69, 70, 77, 78, 90, 103, 104, 105, 107, 108, 110, 111, 113, 115, 116, 117, 119, 121, 132, 137, 139, 143, 154, 159, 161, 162, 167, 169, 173, 174, 175, 176
Golding, William xix
good and evil xvi, 22, 34, 103, 117, 164
Grainville, François-Xavier Cousin de 64
The Great Day of His Wrath 172 (fig. 23)
   See also Martin, John
Greimas, Julien xvi
Groundhog Day 144, 171

Hadron Collider 13, 104, 127
Hamilton, Andy 110
Hammett, Dashiell 100
The Handmaid's Tale 42, 75-77, 90, 91-92
   See also Atwood, Margaret
Harris, Thomas xix, 1
Harry Potter series xv, 55, 144
   See also Rowling, J.K.
   Voldemort
Hegel, Georg Wilhelm Friedrich 16
Hell 63, 172
Hellman, Lillian 100
Herculano, Alexandre xxiv
Herman, Barbara 57, 61
Hiroshima 8, 15, 21, 30, 67, 68, 127
Hirst, Damien 120

The Hitchhiker's Guide to the Galaxy 42, 110, 128, 148, 171
   See also Adams, Douglas
Hitler, Adolf 23, 59, 136, 155, 157, 165, 167
   See also The Holocaust, World War II
Hobbes, Thomas 132-33
The Holocaust 15, 56, 59, 61-62 (fig. 14)
   See also World War II
holocaust xx, 17, 70, 93-94, 159, 175
   See also post-holocaust
homo sapiens 13, 35, 128, 130
Hood, Thomas 64
horror xvi, xvii, xix, 16, 23, 31, 34, 55, 60, 61, 65, 105, 110, 119, 127, 140, 169
   See also fantasy, body-snatching
The Human Condition (La condition humaine) 109 (fig. 19), 110
   See also Magritte, René
humanity xviii, xxiv, 2, 3, 5, 14, 21, 23, 24, 33, 37, 38-40, 45, 50, 52, 56, 62, 63, 64, 70, 71, 74, 79, 81, 82, 86, 87, 93, 98, 100, 101, 103, 106, 108, 109, 112-17, 119, 120, 121, 122-25, 129, 130, 136, 137, 140, 141, 146, 147, 148, 150, 160, 161, 165, 168, 174, 175
Huxley, Aldous xxiv, xxv, 69, 80, 87, 91, 93, 100, 101, 120, 128, 129, 133-35, 136, 140, 143, 147, 149, 152, 153, 154, 160, 161, 162, 164, 169
   See also Brave New World

I Am Legend 33, 50, 86, 96
iconoclasm 21, 111
I Married a Monster from Outer Space 123
incest xviii, 12, 54, 173, 175
The Incredible Shrinking Man 50
Independence Day 9, 31, 45, 64, 117
infinity 20, 176
Invasion of the Body Snatchers 32-33, 91, 123, 168
I, Robot xxv, 117, 119, 121, 123, 124, 126, 127, 128
Irving, Washington 153

Jackson, Rosemary 68, 140
James, P.D. 11, 15, 39, 43, 53, 56, 68, 76, 79, 90, 91, 92, 100, 115, 129, 138, 145, 150, 153, 154, 159
   See also The Children of Men
Jameson, Fredric 139, 151

Jehovah 15, 51
  See also God
Jurassic Park 121
  See also Crichton, Michael

Kant, Immanuel 61, 132
Kennedy, John F. 24, 92
Kermode, Frank 56
Kerr, Judith xviii
Ketterer, David 86, 153, 155
Kiefer, Anselm 62 (fig. 14)
Kilmer, Joyce 104
King Kong 1, 2, 5, 7 (fig. 7), 10 (fig. 8), 9-11, 13, 121
knowledge xvi, xxv, 13, 14, 24, 37, 39, 49, 53, 65, 74, 82, 87, 96, 98, 99, 103, 104, 112, 129, 132, 139, 148, 152, 163
The Kraken Wakes 35, 37, 40, 82, 97, 123, 149
  See also Wyndham, John

Larkin, Philip 12
The Last Judgement xvi (fig. 1)
  See also Bosch, Hieronymus
The Last Man 18 (fig. 9)
  See also Martin, John
Lebow, Richard Ned 24
Lem, Stanislaw 83, 85-86
  See also Solaris
Levin, Ira xxv, 69, 80, 87, 91, 100, 101, 119, 120, 128-30, 135, 136, 141-43, 147-49, 152-54, 161, 162, 164, 169
  See also This Perfect Day
Lindsey, Hal 56, 66, 159
Lot 62 (fig. 14)
  See also Genesis
Loyola, Don Inacio de xv, xxiii
Lucifer 147, 174-76
  See also Satan

Machado de Assis, Joaquim Maria 161, 162
machines xv, 26, 61, 74, 93, 94, 103, 105, 115-23, 125, 128-30, 148, 152, 153
  See also computers, robots
MacNeice, Louis 14, 20
Magritte, René 4 (fig. 3), 5 (fig. 5), 109 (fig. 19), 110
Manhattan Project 21, 105
  See also Cold War
  Einstein, Albert
  Oppenheimer, J. Robert
Manicheans 66, 164

A Map of Utopia 131 (fig. 20)
  See also More, Thomas
Martin, John 18 (fig. 9), 172 (fig. 23)
Marxism 136, 165, 169
Mary 77, 90, 119, 178, 180
  See also Bible, God
Matheson, Richard 33, 50, 86, 96
The Matrix 110, 148, 183
McCarthy, Cormac xxi, xxii, 9, 31, 32, 54, 70, 71, 73, 100
  See also The Road
McCaughrean, Geraldine 157
McGuire, Gregory 138
Merrill, Judith xix, 67, 68, 70, 92
metempsychosis 50
Meyer, Stephenie 33, 34, 45, 64, 96
Michelangelo 156 (fig. 21), 173 (fig. 24)
The Midwich Cuckoos 35, 37, 40, 109, 110, 114, 115, 121, 123, 126, 165, 167
  See also Wyndham, John
Mill, John Stuart 135, 162
millenarian xviii, 15, 56, 66, 158
  See also Armageddon, dystopia, Revelation, utopia
Miller, Walter C. 33, 34, 66, 86, 87, 96, 100, 120-22, 130
  See also 'Dark Benediction'
Mills, C. Wright 139-40
Milton, John 52, 63, 174
modernism xxiv, 56
Moe, Jørgen 177
Moore, Catherine 42
More, Thomas xxv, 22, 91, 109, 131 (fig. 20), 138, 140, 159, 161, 164
Morlocks 73-74, 167
  See also The Time Machine
  Wells, H.G.
Mussolini, Benito 165
mythology 13, 54, 133

Nagasaki 30, 68, 127
  See also Hiroshima
nanotechnology xv, 117, 122
Neanderthal 5
Nebuchadnezzar 4 (fig. 4), 5
  See also Blake, William
neocortex 12
Newcomb, Simon 30
New Jerusalem 63, 66, 132, 138, 154
  See also Revelation, utopia

192   The End of the World

Nineteen Eighty-Four 91, 101, 128, 130, 135, 136, 141, 143, 147, 151, 163, 164
   See also Big Brother
   Orwell, George
Noah 49, 51, 52, 157, 173, 174, 175, 176
   See also floods, Genesis
nothingness xxiv, 20, 43, 63, 108, 169
nuclear war xix, xxi, xxii, 22-27, 33, 41-42, 54, 87, 94, 118, 159, 164

Oakley, Robert xviii, xx
O'Brien, Robert C. xxi, xxiv
The Omen 31, 169
The Opening of the Fifth Seal 158 (fig. 22)
   See also El Greco
Oppenheimer, J. Robert 13, 21, 23, 58, 92, 100, 105
Orpheus 14, 104
Orwell, George xxiv, 91, 93, 100-01, 128-29, 135-36, 141-43, 147, 151-52, 162-64, 169
   See also Animal Farm
   Nineteen Eighty-Four
Oryx and Crake xxv, 48, 55, 64, 68-70, 113, 114, 141, 153
   See also Atwood, Margaret

palaeo-neurology 12
palingenesis 49-50
Pandora 13-14, 104
paradise 24, 63
Pauling, Linus 23, 100
The Penultimate Truth 9, 80, 93, 120, 128, 148, 164
   See also Dick, Philip K.
Peyrouton de Ladebat, Monique xviii, xx
phantasmagoria xix
Pinochet, Augusto 165
Planet of the Apes xxiv, 96
Plato xxv, 69, 149, 154-55, 161, 164
Poe, Edgar Allan 64-65, 144, 172
possession xix, xx, 9, 33, 41, 48, 83, 87, 120, 168
post-holocaust 79, 140, 162
Poundstone, William 21-22
Prey 117, 119
   See also Crichton, Michael
primeval 2-5, 40, 51, 98, 115, 167, 175
Propp, Vladimir xvi
Psyche 14, 104
Pullman, Philip 79, 169

Quatermass and the Pit 110

radiation xxi, xxiii, 3, 38, 43, 45, 50, 60, 68, 92
Ragnarök 51, 54
   See also Edda
Rapture xviii, 66, 106, 154, 159-60
   See also Revelation, the Book of
Reagan, Ronald 22, 93, 133, 159-60
recapitulation 3, 49
Rees, Martin 24, 25, 39, 66, 86-87
Revelation, the Book of xviii, 1, 15, 56, 63, 64, 66, 77, 78 (fig. 16), 104, 106, 132, 139, 154
   See also Bible, Rapture
The Road xxi, xxii, 9, 54, 70, 71, 100, 179, 183
   See also McCarthy, Cormac
Robinson, Marilynne 24
robots 94, 116-28
   See also androids, computers, machines
Rosemary's Baby 31, 169
Rosenberg, Julius and Ethel 31, 100
Roshwald, Mordecai 43, 45, 64, 118
Rosoff, Meg 84-86
routinization 151
Rowling, J.K. xv, xvi, 84, 144-45
   See also Harry Potter, Voldemort
Rubens, Peter Paul 6 (fig. 6), 78 (fig. 16)
Russell, Bertrand 22-24
Russell-Einstein Manifesto 23-24
   See also Cold War

Salazar, António de Oliveira 165
Saramago, José 31, 45-46, 93-100
Sartre, Jean-Paul 140
Satan 52, 63, 110, 117, 144, 161, 174, 175
   See also God, Lucifer
Scarrow, Alex xx
Scott, Ridley xxv, 120-22
   See also Blade Runner
Second Life 112, 128
Seed, David 43, 159
Self, Will 89-91, 98
The Seventh Seal 105-07, 145, 175
   See also Bergman, Ingmar
Shelley, Percy Bysshe 13, 105, 120
Shiel, M.P. 68, 70
Shoah See The Holocaust
Shute, Nevil 9, 43-45, 60-61, 64

Silverberg, Robert 42
Simak, Clifford D. 122
The Simulacra 5, 15, 80, 148
　See also Dick, Philip K.
Socrates 135, 162
Solaris 48, 83, 85-86
　See also Lem, Stanislaw
So Long, and Thanks for All the Fish 42, 111, 171, 177
　See also Adams, Douglas
Sontag, Susan 18, 21-23, 50
Spielberg, Steven 31, 64, 117, 119, 123-24, 126
　See also
　A.I. Artificial Intelligence
　Close Encounters of the Third Kind
　E.T.: The Extra-Terrestrial
Stapledon, Olaf 30
State of Fear 34-35
　See also Crichton, Michael
Stevenson, Robert Louis 120
Stewart, George R. 66, 77, 80, 81-83, 89, 91, 96, 98, 149, 157
Stoicism 66
The Stoics 50
Sturgeon, Theodor 109
Sturluson, Snorri 51, 54-56
survival xv, xx, xxii, xxiii, xxv, 8, 12, 30-32, 37-42, 47, 48, 51, 52, 57, 58, 68, 70, 71, 82, 85, 86, 94, 97, 99, 105, 107, 112-115, 116, 121, 124, 125, 128, 130, 137, 139, 161, 165-67
Survivors 39, 94, 96
Swindells, Robert E. xviii, xxii-xxiv

taboo xix, 12, 103, 165
Tau Zero 43, 88, 89, 160
　See also Anderson, Poul
Telles, Lygia Fagundes 34, 35-36, 37
The Terminator 11, 75, 115-17, 119, 120, 148
　See also James Cameron
Terminator 2: Judgement Day 116
terrorism 25, 44
　See also 9/11
This Perfect Day 69, 80, 87, 91, 101, 119, 120, 128, 135, 136, 141, 142, 143, 147, 148, 149, 152, 153, 154, 161, 164
　See also Levin, Ira
The Time Machine 73, 143, 153, 167
　See also Wells, H.G.

Time out of Joint 147-48
　See also Dick, Philip K.
Tolstoy, Leo xvii
Torga, Miguel 52, 108, 117, 130
To the Devil a Daughter 31, 169
transgression xviii-xix, 136
trauma xxiii, 15, 20, 57, 74, 85
Tree of Knowledge 14, 20
Tree of Life 21
　See also Adam, Eden, Eve, Fall, Genesis
Trouble with Lichen 114, 120, 143-44, 171
　See also Wyndham, John
The Truman Show 111-13, 148-49, 154
Twilight series 33-34
　See also Meyer, Stephenie

utopia xxv, 15, 62, 100, 131-70

vampirism xix, 33-34, 86
Vidal, Gore 133, 159-60
The Virgin as the Woman of the Apocalypse 78 (fig. 16)
　See also Rubens, Peter Paul
Virus 64
Voldemort xvi, 55, 144-45
　See also
　Harry Potter
　Rowling, J.K.
Vonnegut, Kurt 17, 41-42, 86, 113, 114, 134, 148

Wagner, Richard 51, 54, 56
Wanderer above the Sea of Fog 72 (fig. 15)
　See also Friedrich, Caspar David
war, as shortcut to utopia 158
　See also Cold War
　nuclear war
　World War II
The War Game 44
WarGames 25-28, 53, 118
War of the Worlds 31, 64, 117
Waterworld 3, 15, 129
Web 35
　See also Wyndham, John
We Can Build You 123
　See also Dick, Philip K.
Welles, Orson 100
Wells, H.G. xxv, 48, 64, 73-74, 93, 95-100, 117, 153, 155-57, 167
　See also 'The Country of the Blind'
　The Time Machine

Wilhelm, Kate 77, 81, 141, 149
Willis, Connie 74, 75
Wittgenstein, Ludwig 61, 65
The Wizard of Oz 138
Wolfe, Bernard 80, 118
The Wonders of Nature (Les Merveilles de la nature) 5
  See also Magritte, René
The World Jones Made 66, 162
  See also Dick, Philip K.
World Trade Center 9-10
  See also 9/11
World War II 24, 56-58, 67
  See also Auschwitz
  Hitler, Adolf
  The Holocaust
Wyndham, John xxv, 31, 35, 37, 41, 66, 73, 77, 81-82, 91, 94-101, 109-10, 114-15, 118-24, 126-27, 143-44, 149, 165-66, 169, 171
  See also
  The Chrysalids
  'Consider Her Ways'
  The Day of the Triffids
  Kraken Wakes
  The Midwich Cuckoos
  Trouble with Lichen
  Web

Yaweh 173-76
  See also God, floods
Yeats, W.B. 173-74

Zipes, Jack xvi

The End of the World...
...but not of this book

At Open Book Publishers, we are changing the nature of the traditional academic book. The title you have just read will not be left on a library shelf, but will be accessed online by hundreds of readers each month across the globe. We make all our books free to read online so that students, researchers and members of the public who can't afford a printed edition can still have access to the same ideas as you.

Our digital publishing model also allows us to produce online supplementary material, including extra chapters, reviews, links and other digital resources. Find *The End of the World* on our website to access its online extras. Please check this page regularly for ongoing updates, and join the conversation by leaving your own comments:

http://www.openbookpublishers.com/product.php/106

If you enjoyed the book you have just read, and feel that research like this should be available to all readers, regardless of their income, please think about donating to us. Our company is run entirely by academics, and our publishing decisions are based on intellectual merit and public value rather than on commercial viability. We do not operate for profit and all donations, as with all other revenue we generate, will be used to finance new Open Access publications.

For further information about what we do, how to donate to OBP, additional digital material related to our titles or to order our books, please visit our website.

www.ingramcontent.com/pod-product-compliance
Lightning Source LLC
Chambersburg PA
CBHW050557170426
43201CB00011B/1734

9781906924508